Office
of
Literacy

Developing Assessment Literacy: A Guide for Elementary and Middle School Teachers

Developing Assessment Literacy: A Guide for Elementary and Middle School Teachers

John R. Criswell
Edinboro University of Pennslyvania
Edinboro, PA

Christopher-Gordon Publishers, Inc.
Norwood, Massachusetts

Copyright Acknowledgments

Every effort has been made to contact copyright holders for permission to reproduce borrowed material where necessary. We apologize for any oversights and would be happy to rectify them in future printings.

"Performance Profile" from the *Iowa Test of Basic Skills* ® (ITBS®) copyright © 2001 by The Riverside Publishing Company. Reproduced with permission from the publisher. All rights reserved.

"Take-Home Comprehension Rubric" reprinted with permission from Elizabeth Auer and Danielle Proctor.

Anecdotal records used with permission of Susan Cumming, Union City Elementary School.

"Millcreek Township School District Grade Two Report Card" reprinted courtesy of Millcreek Township School District.

"Union City School District Report Card" reprinted courtesy of Union City School District.

Table 2 "Differences in classroom and standardized assessments" from *Balanced assessment: The key to accountability and improved student learning* (2003) pp 10 reprinted with permission of The National Education Association.

Material from "Improving feedback as a means to increase learning in elementary and middle school classrooms" from *Pennsylvania Educational Leadership* 24 (2) used with permission from the Pennsylvania Association of Supervision and Curriculum Development.

Classroom management plan used with permission from Ashley Cottengim.

"Name the Graph" reprinted courtesy of Northwest Regional Laboratory.

Material from Criswell, J.R., & Criswell, S.J., (2004). Asking essay questions: Answering contemporary needs. 124 (3), 510-516 reprinted with permission from Project Innovation.

Material from "Taking a look at grade reporting changes" from Elizabeth Forward Forum reprinted with permission from the Board of Education, Elizabeth Forward School District.

"Stain Continuums" reprinted courtesy of Katy Luce and Melissa Ash.

Copyright © 2006 by Christopher-Gordon Publishers, Inc.

Christopher~Gordon Publishers, Inc.
Bridging Theory and Practice

1502 Providence Highway, Suite 12
Norwood, MA 02062

800-934-8322 • 781-762-5577
www.Christopher-Gordon.com

Printed in Canada
10 9 8 7 6 5 4 3 2 1   09 08 07 06

ISBN: 1-929024-93-2
Library of Congress Catalogue Number: 2006921651

This book is dedicated
to Harry and Nina,
my father and my mother.

Contents

Preface xiii

Acknowledgments xvii

Introduction xix

Part I: Fundamentals of Classroom Assessment 1

Chapter 1: Developing Entry-Level Understandings of Classroom
      Assessment: An Important Beginning 3
    Goals of the Chapter 3
    Developing a Common Language 3
    Three Principles of Sound Assessment 4
    Types of Assessment 12
    Indicators of Quality 14
    Summary 19
    Teaching Activities 19

Chapter 2: Planning for Instruction: The Need for Assessment-Related
      Decision Making 21
    Goals of the Chapter 21
    The Teacher as Decision Maker: Planning Decisions 21
    The Recognized Importance of Instructional Planning 22
    Powerful Elements at Work in Instructional Planning: Constants
      and Context 23
    Time as a Constant in Instructional Planning 24
    Developmental Levels of Children as a Constant in Planning 26
    The Type of Content as a Constant Planning Decision 27
    Checking the Quality of Your Lesson Plans 29
    Summary 31
    Teaching Activities 31

Chapter 3: Questions: The Essence of Teaching and Assessment 33
    Goals of the Chapter 33
    The Importance of Questioning 33
    Oral Questions 33
    Written Questions 38
    True/False Questions 39
    Multiple-Choice Questions 41
    Matching Questions 44
    Completion Questions 47
    Essay Questions 48
    Summary 54
    Teaching Activities 54

Chapter 4: Performance Assessment: A Powerful Tool 57
    Goals of the Chapter 57
    The Use of Performance Assessment 57
    Terminology and Definitions 58
    Implementing Performance Assessment 60
    Planning and Designing Performance Assessments 61
    How to Develop Scoring Rubrics 76
    Ethical Issues in Performance Assessment 80
    Summary 81
    Teaching Activities 82

Chapter 5: Portfolios: Expanding the Assessment of Student Learning 83
    Goals of the Chapter 83
    The Implementation of Portfolios 83
    The Purposes of Portfolios 86
    Recommendations for Teachers Using Portfolios 89
    Developing a Writing Portfolio 90
    Arranging the Portfolio's Contents 95
    Summary 96
    Teaching Activities 96

Chapter 6: Grading and Report Cards: Challenging Decisions 99
    Goals of the Chapter 99
    Grading Guidelines 99
    Grading in American Schools 100
    The Impact of Grading on Learning 101
    Grading as a Comparison 101
    Grading and Its Relationship to Report Cards 105
    Calculating a Student Grade 106
    Grading Students With Exceptionalities 108
    Calculating a Weighted Grade 109

Report Card Formats 112

Summary 116

Teaching Activities 116

Chapter 7: Standardized Testing: Literacy in an Era of Accountability 117

Goals of the Chapter 117

The Purpose of Standardized Tests 117

What Teachers Need to Know About Standardized Tests 120

How to Administer Standardized Tests in Your Classroom 121

How to Interpret the Results of Standardized Tests to Parents,
   Teachers, and Other School Professionals 123

Achievement Tests Versus Intelligence Tests 129

Standard Error of Measurement 130

Who Uses Standardized Assessment Data? 130

Information About Tests That Teachers Should Know 132

Summary 133

Teaching Activities 133

Part II: Assessment in the Context of the Classroom 135

Chapter 8: August: Making Greater Use of Assessment to Begin the New
   School Year 137

Goals of the Chapter 137

Preteaching Activities 137

Preparing Communications to Parents 138

Essential Elements of the First Communication 139

Using Web Pages to Facilitate Communication 142

Developing a Letter Explaining Grading Policies to Parents 143

Organizing a Grade Book Prior to the Start of Classes 146

Developing a Classroom Management Plan Prior to the Arrival
   of the Students 149

Summary 154

Teaching Activities 154

Chapter 9: September: Focusing on Reading and Mathematics 155

Goals of the Chapter 155

The Importance of Reading 155

The Challenge of Developing Literacy in Children 156

Differences in Ages and Grades 156

Phonemic Awareness 157

Phonics Instruction 157

Fluency 158

Vocabulary 162

Text Comprehension 163

Preparing Students for State Reading Tests 166
Teaching and Assessing Mathematics 169
Numbers and Operations 170
Measurement 171
Problem Solving 173
Communication 174
Summary 177
Teaching Activities 177

Chapter 10: October: Building Tests to Gauge Student Success 179
Goals of the Chapter 179
The First Summative Assessments 179
Table of Specifications, or Test Blueprint 180
Test Length 183
Numbering and Weighting Test Items 184
Developing Objective Questions 185
Developing an Answer Key 186
Accommodating and Modifying the Test for Students With
    Exceptionalities 187
Modifying Day-to-Day Assessments for Students in Your
    Classroom 188
Modifying Objective Item Formats 189
Modifying Essay Item Formats 190
Summary 191
Teaching Activities 193

Chapter 11: November: Planning an Effective Parent-Teacher Conference 195
Goals of the Chapter 195
The Importance of Parental Involvement 195
Reasons for Parent-Teacher Conferences 196
Common Logistical Arrangements and Atmosphere 197
Discussing Strengths and Weaknesses 198
Organizing the Data: A Framework for Sharing Student Work
    Samples 199
Areas of Concern or Weakness 201
Areas of Strength 202
Concluding the Meeting With a Summary or a Plan 202
The Role of Students in Parent-Teacher Conferences 203
Frequency of Conferences 204
Summary 205
Teaching Activities 205

Chapter 12: December: Using and Assessing Learning Centers and
    Project-Based Learning 207
    Goals of the Chapter 207
    Enhancing Classroom Instruction 207
    Learning Centers 208
    Learning Centers That Reinforce Material or Skills in Different
        Stages of Mastery 209
    Learning Centers That Provide Students With an Opportunity to
        Explore Different Topics 210
    Learning Centers for Diagnostic Purposes 211
    Assessing Student Dispositions and Behaviors in Using Learning
        Centers 212
    Project-Based Learning 213
    Challenges in Assessment of Project-Based Learning 216
    Summary 220
    Teaching Activity 221

Chapter 13: January: Using Assessment Information to Identify Retention
    Candidates and Design Effective Interventions 223
    Goals of the Chapter 223
    A Fresh Start 223
    The Retention of Elementary School Children 224
    Key Personnel in the Retention Decision-Making Process 226
    Student Histories of Achievement and Other Sources of Important
        Data 227
    Developing a Timetable for the Effective Review of Information 233
    Examples of Curriculum-Based Interventions to Share at a Pupil
        Personnel Meeting 235
    Monitoring Student Progress From January to May 236
    Summer Activities as an Intervention 237
    Summary 237
    Teaching Activities 238

Chapter 14: February and March: Welcoming New Students Into Your
    Classroom—Dealing With the Movement of Families 239
    Goals of the Chapter 239
    Student Mobility 239
    The Effect of Student Mobility on Achievement 240
    Types of Student Movement 241
    Two Major Goals in Welcoming a New Student 245
    Academic Placement Starts With Reading 248
    Making a Suitable Math Placement 249
    Summary 250
    Teaching Activities 250

Chapter 15: April: Preparing for Externally Developed Tests by Focused
     Instruction and Improved Feedback 253
     Goals of the Chapter 253
     The Importance of Sustained Preparation 253
     Examining the Required State Tests 254
     The Importance of Feedback to Increased Achievement 256
     Feedback and Its Presence in Classrooms 256
     Qualities of Effective Feedback.. 257
     Common Forms of Teacher Feedback 259
     Suggestions for Improving Feedback Practices 263
     Summary 264
     Teaching Activities 264

Chapter 16: May: Challenging Assessment Issues and Professional
     Development 265
     Goals of the Chapter 265
     The Need for Assessment Literacy 265
     Addressing Your Own Assessment Literacy.............................. 266
     Becoming a More Complete Professional 272
     Summary 275
     Teaching Activities 275

Appendix A: Essential Components of a Lesson Plan and Their Importance
     to Assessment 277
     Goals of the Appendix.. 277
     Essential Components of a Lesson Plan Format 277

Appendix B: Gaining a Framework of Thinking 281
     Goals of the Appendix.. 281
     Levels of Thinking 281
     Bloom's Taxonomy of the Cognitive Domain 282
     Bloom's Taxonomy of the Affective Domain..................................... 285

References 287

About the Author 293

Index 295

Preface

The title of this book, *Developing Assessment Literacy: A Guide for Elementary and Middle School Teachers,* provides the guiding premise for the content of this book. The development of the text grew from a desire to address the instructional needs of elementary and middle school teachers in a teacher preparation program and from efforts to develop assessment literacy with practicing teachers. The content has been shaped by changes in the way classroom assessment is recognized by educators and the general public.

In the 1990s, classroom assessment began to compete with more formal types of assessment for its place in teacher preparation curricula; however, measurement texts lagged behind, with only several authors offering works that were devoted primarily to classroom assessment. Since that time there has been movement toward a greater emphasis on classroom assessment as part of teacher competency. Nevertheless, the developers of measurement materials, for the most part, continue to resist acknowledging the fundamental instructional differences between the assessment needs of elementary teachers and those of secondary teachers. There also seems to be a lack of recognition that teacher candidates and teachers possess different levels of professional development needs, based on their experiences. First-year teachers as well as teacher candidates do not possess the same assessment understandings and skills that experienced teachers do. This book is designed to address the needs of persons who are interested in gaining entry-level understanding of assessment and applying that knowledge and skill in elementary and middle school classrooms. There is an underlying hope that this resource, used as a first text, will contribute to the development of a teaching profession that has an increased degree of assessment literacy.

The complex process of developing assessment-literate teachers is dependent on a variety of conditions, including dedicated and knowledgeable professors and trainers, rich and diverse clinical experience or inservice, and learning materials that inform and effectively shape practice. An equally important component is the dedication of courses and/or inservice experiences that focus on the development of assessment literacy. Although deans, curriculum directors, and other school personnel might debate the organization and sequence of the content of curricula and professional development activities, the decisions that will most likely improve the assessment literacy of elementary and middle school teachers rest on the interactions with individual professors, trainers, or colleagues. This text is designed with the idea that beginning and experienced teachers can become more assessment literate if specific and understandable material is used in conjunction with sound teaching and/or training. In order to achieve that purpose, the structure of the book is intentionally related to actual classroom issues and activities.

The development of this work differs from others in the organizational presentation of assessment content. Part I resembles typical assessment offerings in a shortened version that focuses on the knowledge and skills that are essential to elementary and middle school teachers. This section includes chapters on basic understandings, planning, questions, performance assessment, portfolios, standardized testing, and grading and report cards. Content decisions were made in alignment with the *Standards for Teacher Competence in Educational Assessment of Students* developed in 1990 by the National Council for Measurement in Education, the American Federation of Teachers, and the National Education Association. This arrangement is based on the need to develop fundamental knowledge and skills of assessment, measurement, and evaluation so that subsequent discussions are not hindered by sloppy and conflicting interpretations. Its brevity is designed to afford time to apply entry-level assessment knowledge to the practical classroom issues presented in Part II.

The contents of Part II are presented in a sequence that approximates the major events and issues that are characteristic of a school year anywhere in the United States. The development of this section assumes that the actions of teaching are ordered less by assessment topics and more by the framework of the classroom's yearly events. Despite the notion that assessment is a daily part of teaching, its presence often goes unnoticed and thus its importance is neglected. The purpose of choosing the activities herein is to identify a significant assessment presence and promote the importance of assessment literacy as a means by which to facilitate informed decisions that affect children. Understanding how assessment fits within the context of classrooms may stimulate elementary and middle school teachers to approach it as an essential aspect of classroom teaching. For example, the retention of students in a grade level is one of the most difficult decisions facing new and experienced teachers each year. Although retention decisions generally rest upon the assessment skills of the teacher, few measurement texts mention it, much less discuss how to plan and design intervention strategies within the scope and sequence of yearly teaching activities. By addressing topics that are central to a teacher's environmental concerns, this book tries to narrow the "gap" that exists between content offerings and classroom issues and practices.

Another example of how this text addresses important classroom assessment topics lies in the area of reading instruction with elementary and middle school students. Much of a teacher's instructional day is spent on the development of print literacy, reading and writing, and the effective integration of those areas. Adequate assessment skills for elementary and middle school teachers should include the ability to measure reading success in children. One could argue that an elementary teacher is hardly assessment literate without a fundamental understanding of how to measure the reading and writing skills of children.

This text is written for elementary teacher candidates and beginning teachers interested in gaining a foothold in assessment literacy. The knowledge, skills, and dispositions associated with levels of teacher development vary greatly, according to an individual's experience with teaching children. Beginning teachers have limited experiences from which to draw; therefore, a text designed for their needs must provide clear explanations, examples, and an organizational framework that facilitates their understanding. This is important because the understanding and application of sound assessment concepts and practices is affected by the level of abstraction teacher candidates must face. For example, without having seen an example of a teacher's anecdotal records, teacher candidates cannot be expected to construct a framework for their use or reflect on their importance. This text provides focused explanations and examples to facilitate the reader's understanding.

Unfortunately, the study of measurement continues to inspire avoidance among teachers, and its reputation for being disconnected from elementary and middle school teaching is persistent. This is partly because the writing style of measurement texts has been complex, theoretical, and often perceived as unfriendly to teacher candidates and teachers. For that reason, the tone of this book is intentionally conversational (written largely in the second person) and sprinkled with attempts at humor. Topics are discussed in a way intended for entry-level understanding. The comprehensive and theoretical coverage of measurement topics is best left to other writers who see that as the purpose of their works.

The specific focus on the needs of elementary and middle school teachers, the conversational tone, and the unique arrangement of content is designed to make this text a valuable entry-level resource for teachers and teacher candidates as they attempt to enhance their knowledge and skills in the area of classroom assessment.

Acknowledgments

Many persons impacted the writing of this book, and I want to take this opportunity to thank all those who contributed in any way to its completion. I am particularly grateful to my wife, Susan J. Criswell, who sacrificed to ensure that I had both the time and energy to write. She is a wonderful professor, administrator, mother, grandmother, wife, and companion.

Colleagues have been instrumental in shaping the direction and emphasis of this book. I have had the good fortune to be in the company of many outstanding teachers and fine educators who possessed the energy, creativity, and ability to inspire students and school professionals. Thanks to Harry Wilson, Bruce Smith, Nick Stupiansky, Gloria Gerbracht, Kathleen Benson, Maureen Walcavich, Bob Zanotti, Jim Flynn, Marilyn Sheerer, and others. My teaching and ultimately the contents of this book were affected by my interactions with these accomplished professionals.

The completion of this book has also been shaped by persons who inspire by their actions. Gene Allegre, Joe Short, Charley Whitehead, and Jim Baumgartner have added to the pages of this text in ways that are difficult to explain. They are spirited individuals who possess an uncanny knack for putting things in a proper perspective.

I also want to thank Dr. Frank G. Pogue, president of Edinboro University of Pennsylvania, for granting the sabbatical that permitted me to devote a semester of my time exclusively to the completion of this book. His administrative support of my efforts has been consistent and much appreciated.

My students have always been a great motivating force in my teaching and writing. Although I have enjoyed teaching at all levels, the opportunity to teach students who are interested in becoming elementary and middle school teachers has been a wonderful opportunity. Their excitement and interest is infectious, renewing, and inspirational. They have made my job easier. A special thanks is extended to students who made contributions to this book.

Thanks to Sue Canavan, who has been a wonderfully encouraging person to work with since the day I contacted Christopher-Gordon Publishers with an idea and several chapters. Ben Raphael was a pleasure to work with; he has been encouraging and pleasant. I would also like to thank the external reviewers for their contributions, suggestions, and recommendations: Kouider Mokhtari, Mary Shoop, Marsha Beard, and Sally Wagner.

Finally, I would like to thank Kate Liston, managing editor, and Judith Antonelli, copy editor, for their expertise and guidance. I would be remiss not to mention how deeply grateful I am to the teachers, students, administrators, and staff at the Union City Elementary School in Union City, Pennsylvania. The Leadership Committee provided essential feedback and secured important student samples that helped to give life to the descriptions offered in this text. Great thanks to Deborah Sturm, Lisa Frisina, Kathryn Thomas, Gwen Horner, Dina Wadding, Marlene Kuzma, Liz Auer, Susan Cumming, and Laura Schaaf.

Finally, thanks to Murphy for being such a good listener.

Introduction

It's difficult to imagine that not long ago, teacher preparation paid little attention to the development of classroom assessment skills in teacher candidates. Courses in assessment, if they existed at all in teacher preparation, were almost exclusively devoted to the understanding and interpretation of standardized tests and their derived scores. As a result, many teachers went on to work in classrooms lacking systematic instruction or experiences in how to effectively assess student success. These same teachers no doubt also lacked some of the fundamental skills essential to gauging the quality of their own instruction. After an awakening in the last two decades to the importance of classroom assessment, both in measurement of student success and evaluation of teaching quality, it is safe to say that there is universal acceptance of the necessity for teachers to be assessment literate.

The presence and influence of assessment in today's schools is unprecedented. With the reauthorization of the Elementary and Secondary Education Act (ESEA, or the No Child Left Behind Act), the focus of accountability for teaching results was placed directly on schools and individual teachers. The Act calls for mandatory testing in grades 3–8 and includes close scrutiny of the disaggregated scores of four subpopulations. One thrust of No Child Left Behind is a greater emphasis on the success of the individual child. This legislation ensures that teachers must be more conscious of and skillful in the measurement of the achievement of all their students on a daily basis.

Virtually every learned society or regulatory body concerned with the quality of the teaching profession includes knowledge of assessment literacy as a requisite for teacher competency. The American Federation of Teachers (AFT), the National Council on Measurement in Education, and the National Education Association (1990) developed standards that ultimately defined the content and skills of assessment literacy. Since their inception, these guidelines have been instrumental in shaping the skills and knowledge reflected in accrediting agencies' standards as well as in state certification guidelines. The Interstate New Teacher Assessment Support Consortium (INTASC) standards (1992) acknowledges classroom assessment as a critical component of effective teacher practice. The Association for Childhood Education International (ACEI), the learned society for undergraduate elementary education, recognizes assessment within its guidelines for high-quality program development. Danielson (1996) is specific in her advocacy for assessment literacy among accomplished teachers.

Although the above references influence undergraduate preparation, the professional development of practicing teachers is also concerned with assessment literacy. The theoretical framework for Part I of this book is closely construction around the standards developed by AFT et al. (1990).

The emphasis on enhanced assessment knowledge and skills is not limited to undergraduate teacher preparation. Advanced professional development frameworks—including, most notably, the National Board for Professional Teaching Standards (NBPTS)—acknowledge assessment as a key element in the development of accomplished practicing teachers. Assessment is currently recognized as a key skill of all teachers who aspire to develop in all aspects of their profession.

The development and use of standards in reference to the assessment literacy of teachers was also a result of influences within the assessment community. Recognition of the importance of classroom assessment triggered the need for teachers in pre-K through 12 classrooms to possess enhanced assessment knowledge and skills. Acknowledging the value of performance assessments in the assessment community resulted in the recognized value of requiring teachers to be knowledgeable in their approach to assessing student processes and products. The acceptance of portfolios as a means by which to assess student success also required deeper levels of understanding of assessment practice and measurement issues.

In the last two decades, there has been an acceptance of performance assessment as part of the accountability and reform efforts in education. As with most educational shifts, multiple conditions emerged that served as a catalyst to push performance assessment into a level of increased acceptance. At least three major conditions helped to encourage the use of performance assessments in elementary schools and middle schools.

First, assessing student performance was part of a larger approach to measuring the effectiveness of curriculum by learner outcome rather than by "seat time." In a learner outcome or standards-driven system, teachers and students work toward identifying what a student knows and, more important, what a student can do. Assessing what a student can do requires the development of classroom measures that support the use of performance assessment in place of written objective tests.

Second, a shift in reading instruction from isolated skill development to integrated instructional practices argued for the need for authentic performances. The lines separating reading and writing instruction became less defined as separate skills, and teaching their application required a greater use of performance assessment. It also became important to assess the reader's ability to interact with the text. These changes resulted in the increased use of anecdotal records, portfolios, and scoring rubrics.

Third, the emergence of content and performance standards from learned groups such as the National Council of Teachers of Mathematics (NCTM) and the American Association for the Advancement of Science (AAAS) promoted the need for performance assessments. It is unlikely that the teaching profession and the general public will ever relinquish the value of assessing what students can do. Being skillful in assessing the knowledge, skills, and dispositions of all students will remain an essential teaching skill.

Acknowledging the importance of assessment literacy is a first step in promoting the development of teachers who can plan, teach, and assess students in their classrooms. The difficulty lies with promoting and facilitating that development so that it results in teachers who are functionally literate in their classrooms. Texts used by teachers in training often provide a knowledge of literate practice that is removed or isolated from the experiences of classroom teachers. Therefore, the recognition of the importance of assessment in typical classroom practices remains obscured. The purpose of this text is to provide for the development of assessment understanding (Part I) and link that understanding to events that occur in the daily lives of teachers (Part II). Part II's devotion to the use of assessment in the yearly practices of elementary and middle school teachers is designed to enhance the functional literacy of teachers and school personnel.

Structure of This Book

Because the scope and sequence of content in this text differs from that of other assessment resources, the following guidelines may help the reader to make decisions about the presentation and use of its material.

Part I contains material that might typically be found in classroom assessment textbooks.

Chapter 1 develops entry-level understandings of classroom assessment. Three fundamental principles frame a discussion of concepts and vocabulary essential to elementary and middle school assessment.

Chapter 2 discusses instructional planning as it relates to effective classroom assessment. Contextual issues that impact planning for assessment are presented.

Chapter 3 focuses on questions. Suggestions for the development and use of oral and written questions are provided. Advantages and disadvantages of each type of question format are also discussed.

Chapter 4 on performance assessment and chapter 5 on portfolios include a discussion of alternative practices that expand the assessment of elementary and middle school children.

Chapter 6 examines grading and report cards. Several grading strategies are presented along with examples of contemporary report cards.

Finally, chapter 7 discusses standardized testing, its use in elementary and middle schools, and the interpretation of derived scores.

Part II contains material that is arranged in a chronological order of classroom events. Because assessment is an essential part of most classroom activities, these chapters weave the content from the first section through key events that take place in elementary and middle school classrooms. Table I-1 shows how the chapters of Part II can be paired with the material in Part I.

Table I-1.   Part II Chapters Related to Part I Content

Chapter 8 August: Making Greater Use of Assessment to Begin the New School Year	Addresses the organization of three elements in the classroom prior to the arrival of students: • Planning a communication to parents (chapter 1) • Setting up a classroom management plan (chapter 6) • Setting up a gradebook (chapter 6)
Chapter 9 September: Focusing on Reading and Math	Discusses important elements of reading, possible teaching strategies, and suggested assessment procedures (chapters 1 and 4); running and anecdotal records, accepted math standards, instructional methods, and assessments that can be used in elementary and middle school classrooms (chapters 1 and 4)
Chapter 10 October: Building Tests to Gauge Student Success	Takes the information concerning written questions and uses it to effectively construct a classroom test (chapter 3). Accommodations and modifications of test questions are provided.
Chapter 11 November: Planning an Effective Parent-Teacher Conference	Takes important information that is assembled from a variety of assessments and effectively prepares it to share at different types of parent conferences. Organizational strategies are offered (chapters 1, 4, 6, and 7).
Chapter 12 December: Using and Assessing Learning Centers and Project-Based Learning	Discusses how learning centers are developed and assessed using rubrics and anecdotal records. Similar assessment instruments are discussed with their use in project-based learning experiences (chapter 4).
Chapter 13 January: Using Assessment Information to Identify Retention Candidates and to Design Effective Interventions	Making decisions about the design of effective intervention strategies requires the identification of critical data and its ethical use. Discusses data sources and multiple sources that can be used to develop intervention strategies (chapters 1, 6, and 7).
Chapter 14 February and March: Welcoming New Students Into Your Classroom— Dealing With the Movement of Families	Assessments are essential to designing specific and needs-directed instructional strategies. Strategies are suggested for collecting information that will assist in the most appropriate placement for new students (chapters 1 and 4).
Chapter 15 April: Preparing for Externally Developed Assessment by Focused Instruction and Improved Feedback	Discusses the preparation for state-mandated testing, with particular emphasis on instructional feedback in a variety of subject areas (chapters 1, 4, and 7). Examples in areas of student writing.
Chapter 16 May: Challenging Assessment Issues and Professional Development	Uses the standards for the assessment of students and discusses the possible areas of increased professional development. Can be used as an exiting instructional area that addresses the completion of all chapters in Part I.

Two appendixes are provided at the end of the book to develop basic understanding in areas that are essential to teacher competency. Appendix A is devoted to entry-level understandings of instructional planning. Appendix B contains detailed discussions of Bloom's taxonomy in the cognitive and affective domains. The purpose of these two appendixes is to provide entry-level understanding of the prerequisite knowledge essential to the understanding of classroom assessment. Because of experiential differences in the readers of this text, these subjects are provided for optional consideration.

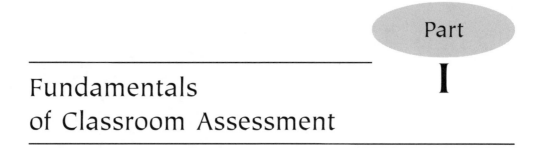

Fundamentals
of Classroom Assessment

Developing Entry-Level Understandings of Classroom Assessment: An Important Beginning

Goals of the Chapter

1. To be able to recall the fundamental principles of effective assessment

2. To be able to define the important terminology associated with assessment literacy

3. To be able to recognize the quality indicators of assessment instruments

Developing a Common Language

Before we can begin to discuss the development of teaching practices that embody sound assessment, there is a need to have a working knowledge of the important principles and supporting terminology. Let's begin with some basic definitions.

Education has long suffered from a severe case of "edu-speak"—that is, poorly defined or overused vocabulary that is often unintelligible to anyone outside the field. Simply ask a group of educators from different areas to define *cooperative learning* and you are likely to be surprised by the variety of definitions. Inaccurate and ambiguous definitions complicate the mastery of any area of study. This is why clear definitions of assessment terms and concepts are a necessary beginning to the study of classroom assessment.

It would make sense for us to begin by clarifying the difference between *assessment* and *evaluation,* since these terms are often used interchangeably by teachers, administrators, parents, and policy makers. Clearly defined terms, you will see, aid the study of and facilitate discussions centering on assessment issues.

Assessment refers to all the processes, techniques, and instruments a teacher might use to collect data concerning students. Examples of assessments include tests, reports, and quizzes, as well as observations, logs, and interviews. Assessment as a term used in a lesson-plan format refers to how you might measure what students learned from your teaching. In fact, I require that students who are developing lesson plans in my classes actually label the section "Assessment of Student Learning." In this way, they avoid any confusion about whether they are assessing their own teaching performance or student achievement of the lesson objective.

Evaluation refers to the judgments that are made from the data generated by the assessments. You can see the close relationship between the two words, but hopefully you can also recognize a distinct difference. An example of an evaluation might be the decision the teacher makes concerning a grade based on assessment data. Other types of evaluations include placement decisions or grouping decisions. In the development of lesson plans, often an "evaluation section" is included; however, in this case the term refers to the teacher making an evaluation about the success or lack of success of the lesson. You can see how a teacher's evaluation of a lesson should be dependent primarily on assessment information, indicating how much students learned. One rule that may help you remember the difference is to consider that an evaluation usually refers to the success of the teacher, and an assessment usually refers to the success of the students.

If you had been an observer of teacher preparation in prior decades, you might have been surprised to find out how little emphasis was placed on the importance of teachers' understanding of assessment practices. Much of the emphasis in teacher training at that time dealt with preparing teachers to teach, and teacher preparation institutions largely ignored the area of assessment. Assessment was viewed as the responsibility of persons working closely with standardized tests and other formal measurements. Currently, assessment is considered an important component of sound instruction that cannot be separated from it. For that reason, it is critical to understand some contemporary principles of sound assessment.

Three Principles of Sound Assessment

The following three principles of assessment are meant to guide our actions as persons who understand assessment as part of instruction. Table 1-1 summarizes these principles.

Table 1-1.   Three Principles of Sound Assessment

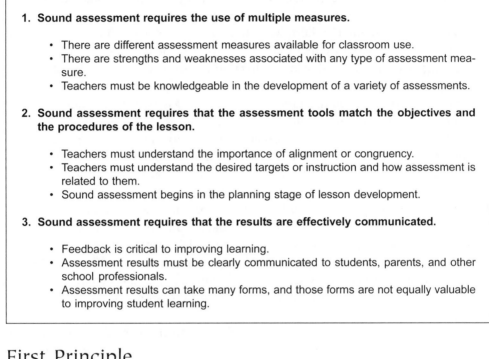

1. **Sound assessment requires the use of multiple measures.**

   - There are different assessment measures available for classroom use.
   - There are strengths and weaknesses associated with any type of assessment measure.
   - Teachers must be knowledgeable in the development of a variety of assessments.

2. **Sound assessment requires that the assessment tools match the objectives and the procedures of the lesson.**

   - Teachers must understand the importance of alignment or congruency.
   - Teachers must understand the desired targets or instruction and how assessment is related to them.
   - Sound assessment begins in the planning stage of lesson development.

3. **Sound assessment requires that the results are effectively communicated.**

   - Feedback is critical to improving learning.
   - Assessment results must be clearly communicated to students, parents, and other school professionals.
   - Assessment results can take many forms, and those forms are not equally valuable to improving student learning.

First Principle

Sound assessment requires the use of multiple measures.

A common emphasis in contemporary assessment is the encouragement of school professionals to use multiple forms of assessments when making important judgments about students. Multiple measures are recommended by the American Educational Research Association, American Psychological Association, and National Council on Measurement in Education (1999). Standard 13.7 states that "in educational settings a decision or characterization that will have major impact on a student should not be made on a simple test score. Other relevant information should be taken into account if it enhances the overall validity of the decision." The use of a single score implies the use of a single assessment.

You might remember from your own school experiences receiving a grade based on a single measure or being placed in a certain instructional group based on a single test score. That was quite acceptable at the time, but its limitations are painfully obvious now and constitute an action that you as a professional teacher must avoid. Much of the support for using multiple measures comes from the idea that students learn differently and are capable of displaying that knowledge in very different ways (Wiggins & McTighe, 1998).

We now also recognize that students do better on some types of exams than others. Expanded definitions of literacy have caused reading and writing assessments to change from multiple-choice tests to performance-based activities. You might remember from your elementary school days that there were no formal measures of your ability to express yourself in written communication. You might have taken a standardized test asking you multiple-choice questions concerning grammar, usage, mechanics, and spelling, but few elementary schools were testing the actual composition skills of the students. Today we recognize that to logically assess students' written expression we must ask them to write instead of answering multiple-choice questions. Written composition is more than the recognition of correct answers in a multiple-choice format. Classroom teachers must understand a wide range of assessment techniques and realize the advantages and disadvantages of each.

When we decide to limit our assessment measures to a few types, we lose the opportunity to gain a broad perspective of what children can do if given the opportunity. Ferrara and McTighe (1992a) suggest that basing high-stakes decisions on one assessment is very much like using a single snapshot to depict one's appearance. (Perhaps if you were to reach into your wallet and reexamine the photo on your driver's license you would get an immediate sense of what it would be like to be characterized by one assessment.) This is the reason Ferrara and McTighe suggest that a photo album characterizes a student more completely than a single snapshot does. To best show what a student knows and can do, we should implement different types of assessments and use the collective data drawn from those assessments to make decisions.

The use of a single measure can also be criticized from the realization that every assessment contains some degree of error. In measurement circles and classrooms this concept is known as the standard error of measurement. We would like to think that any assessment we develop would accurately generate a score that represents what students know and can do, but the reality is that no assessment instrument can generate a true score that precisely and confidently characterizes exactly what a student knows about a content area. This concept will be discussed in more detail in chapter 7. For now, let's examine one classroom example.

Ms. Hamrick has completed three chapters in social studies and is developing a test to administer to her sixth graders. She believes that in order to assess them adequately she should generate two questions per instructional objective. After some thought, she wonders if maybe three questions per objective would provide a truer score. Three questions seem better to her, but the length of her class period might not accommodate this. For the test to adequately fit the time allotment, she must compromise the number of questions she can ask. Do you see how this might affect the precision and interpretive value of the test score? Could Ms. Hamrick use a different type of assessment (other than a test) to assist her inference making about what the students learned?

How can we sum up the use of multiple measures in a classroom? Suppose I want to show how well a student performs in math. Rather than simply focusing on how many problems he or she can answer correctly, I'd like to know how well the student understands math concepts and can solve word problems. I'd also be interested in how well the student understands geometry and standard measure. Before I render a judgment on the capability of this student in math, I will need to assess areas other than calculations. More important, I would need to use a variety of assessments to make that decision.

- Would you agree that assessing the areas of geometry and standard measure in addition to problem solving provides a more appropriate picture of what the child understands about mathematics?

- What types of assessments, other than written tests, could be used to measure student understanding of geometry and measurement?

- Are student dispositions and attitudes important to student success in mathematics? If you answered yes, think about how you might measure them. If you answered no, then rethink your answer!

- Does the combination of scores render a truer picture of student capability than a single score would?

Second Principle

Sound assessment requires that the assessment tools match the objectives and the procedures of the lesson.

This principle focuses the teacher's attention on providing an assessment or assessments that are linked to instruction. The danger in not attending to this results, in part, from the first principle. Suppose that we take the first principle to heart and begin creating a lesson plan that uses a performance assessment to gauge student learning. If we do not adequately plan for the lesson by targeting specifically what we want students to learn and then provide them with opportunities to learn that material, our students' results are likely to be poor. This occurs in classrooms all too often, and teachers comment about students not being able to handle thinking or higher level material. We can improve the chances of students being able to succeed at these types of tasks if we are careful in our planning. *Alignment* and *congruency* are terms used to describe the idea of making sure that the instructional objectives, the procedures for the delivery of instruction, and the assessments are mutually supportive.

An example might help to clarify this. Despite some of the newer approaches to teaching spelling in American schools, most classrooms continue to have students study a word list and practice that list four days a week. The student's mastery of that spelling list is generally assessed on Friday by a test in which the students write the correct spelling of the word that the teacher pronounces. (I have often contended that if a person was dropped from an airplane anywhere in the United States and was in doubt of the day of the week, all he or she would have to do would be to go to the closest elementary school and observe a spelling lesson. If the class was being intro-duced to the word list, there is a fairly good chance it would be Monday. If they are taking their final practice test, it is probably Thursday.)

Let's focus now on the congruency and alignment of the instructional activities generally associated with teaching the correct spelling of the words on the spelling list. What is the objective for my spelling lesson? Our fundamental goal for the students is to provide practice spelling the words so that on Friday they have a chance at spelling all the words correctly. We are likely to accept 80% mastery as an acceptable level of achievement for our students on Friday's spelling exam. Therefore, our objective probably sounds something like this: "Given practice sessions, the students will be able to spell at least 80% of the words on this week's spelling list." Does this objective guide our instruction? Let's plan some sessions or activities that will permit our students to practice the correct spelling of the words on the list so that they might achieve our instructional objective.

In planning for the instructional activities, we should remember that there are two elements that increase the value of practice. First, practice usually requires *repetition*. The more repetition one engages in, the more likely one is to acquire an attainable skill. Many repetitions might improve my golf swing, but I will never improve it enough to be able to play on the Professional Golfers Association tour. The spelling list is certainly an attainable goal for most of our students, so we will need to provide repetition in our instructional activities.

A second element that enhances the value of our practice is *perfection*. Obvious problems are associated with students practicing an incorrect spelling of a word on the word list.

What are the instructional activities for my spelling lesson? Keeping our objective in mind, let's plan some activities that will help our class practice the correct spelling of the word list. Some of the activities that are typically mentioned for spelling exercises include the following:

- A crossword puzzle of the word list
- A spelling bee
- Using each word in a sentence
- Scrambled letters in a word
- A word-find
- Writing the words in shaving cream on the student desks
- Using all the words to construct a story
- Various seasonal or high-interest games
- Relay races requiring the spelling of words

As you can see, there are quite a number of instructional activities that can be used to provide some level of spelling practice for your students. Let's examine the activities based on what we know about two things: the qualities of good practice and the type of exam that the students will take on Friday.

Activity	Practice
Crossword	One repetition
Spelling bee	One repetition, if that!
Using each word in a sentence	One repetition
Scrambled letters in a word	One repetition
A word-find	One repetition
Using all the words in a story	One repetition

You should be seeing a pattern! Now examine how closely the instructional activity matches the type of test that we will be giving to students on Friday. Recall that the spelling test is usually administered by the teacher reading a word and the students recalling the correct spelling and writing it on their paper.

Activity	Same Format as the Test
Crossword puzzle of the word list	No blocks on Friday
A spelling bee	Same format
Using each word in a sentence	Different format
Scrambled letters in a word	Different format
A word-find	Different format
Using all the words in a story	Different format

You can see that Friday's format of reading the word list to the students isn't practiced very often in our suggested teaching activities, and although the spelling bee has the same format, it fails miserably as an activity because the persons who get better from participating in a spelling bee are already the best spellers. The first persons to be eliminated from a spelling bee are often the poorest spellers in your classroom. Instead, the persons who should be getting the most practice are the poorest spellers, not the best ones. (If you are not a good speller, can you name an activity that is more boring to watch than a spelling bee?)

Consider the value of the word-find. How many times on Friday's test—or, more important, at any other time in your life—are you required to identify the spelling of a word that is written backwards or diagonally? What is the value of the scrambled-letter word practice for Friday's test? Think about how children approach the spelling of a word. Do all of the letters pop into their heads and then they unscramble them? Our concern for alignment or congruency suggests that the instructional activities should prepare the student to successfully perform on the assessment we design. Unfortunately, we do not do a good job of aligning our instruction around something as simple as a spelling-word list.

This discussion of congruency and alignment is meant to show the level of disconnect that sometimes accompanies our teaching. As a former classroom teacher, I have not forgotten that the school year can be long and that there is value in novel activities that motivate children. Each of the activities I have described is not harmful in teaching children. In fact, having students work with understanding component parts of words is an important part of gaining word knowledge.

In fact, I believe that some of the activities should be used in the same way we allow our children to eat junk food. Having a candy bar occasionally is delightful, but if junk food constitutes the mainstay of your diet, you are likely to be a very unhealthy person. In the same manner, some of the spelling activities will trigger excitement and delight in your students, but their constant use is not instructionally sound.

Reflection: Why is it so important for teachers to be able to align their classroom assessments with their objectives and teaching activities?

Why is it so important for teachers to be able to align their classroom assessments with their objectives and teaching activities?

Third Principle

Sound assessment requires that the results are effectively communicated.

We have discussed the value of using multiple forms of assessment and how in order to use those measures most effectively we need to align our instruction. Perhaps one of the most formidable assessment tasks that future teachers face is convincing the public and their peers that multiple forms of assessment are important and worthy. The teaching profession is making progress at raising the awareness of the value of alternative assessment practices, but to say that teachers are knowledgeable and embracing of newer forms of assessment would be an exaggeration. Therefore, if new teachers are to make strides as advocates for alternative forms of assessment, they must be able to demonstrate the value to their students, school personnel, and parents. That demonstration hinges on clear communication.

Three separate groups should be targeted for effective communication in elementary and middle schools. First, and most important, we should be concerned with providing feedback to the student. Providing feedback begins before the student is engaged in the assessment process. The student should understand what the target is in order to focus his or her effort and energy. During instructional practices, student learning can be enhanced when formative assessments are used to guide the student. *Formative assessments* provide feedback to the student about his or her progress. They also can be used by teachers to judge the effectiveness of their teaching. You are probably familiar with the practice of testing students after the completion of a unit or a critical skill. This is known as a *summative assessment* because its purpose is to collect information about the student success after instruction. Summative assessment provides information about the deficiency or adequacy of the student's response. We will spend some time later discussing how we can use summative assessment as part of a continual learning process. Chapter 15 suggests practices to develop high-quality feedback with students.

Second, we should focus on communicating with other school personnel. Other teachers, administrators, counselors, and psychologists might request assessment data. This will be difficult for inexperienced teachers, who are not used to communicating assessment data to other school professionals. This text, however, should provide you with the entry-level skills to clearly communicate and discuss assessment results with school personnel. With the present emphasis on accountability, it is important for faculty members to communicate, share, and discuss assessment results. There is enormous value in having an elementary or middle school staff that respects and supports each other.

As the opportunity arises, share your materials or your beliefs about assessment. The important part is the discussion you engage in with your peers. In order to extend the communication of assessment results, it might be helpful to participate in the development of assessment projects or tasks. For example, try developing a performance assessment with persons who teach the same grade as you. These collaborative projects can be rich and valuable assessment experiences for novice teachers. Later we will discuss some steps in the collaborative development of performance assessments.

Finally, but not least, is the need to communicate assessment results with the parents of your students. This is time-consuming and can be frustrating, but in the long run it will probably serve you well. You can increase your success with students by involving parents and others in your communications. "Assessment must provide an effective communication with parents and other partners in the learning enterprise in a way which helps them support learning" (Harlen, Gipps, Broadfoot, & Nuttall, 1992). By sharing and communicating you are enlisting more help for student learning.

What kinds of communications with parents should you develop? Consider the following forms. What are the pros and cons of each?

- Newsletters that tell of upcoming assessments, both in-class and standardized
- Phone messages and individual notes to parents
- E-mail contact
- Conferencing after school
- Report cards

Notice that I left report cards for last. That's because it is the most prevalent and familiar method of communication, and we sometimes become too dependent on it as the sole means of communication. Report cards are typically distributed at 9-week periods. Some situations must be addressed in a shorter time frame and cannot wait for 9 weeks to be communicated to the parent. In chapter 11 you will read about the types of information and data that can and should be shared with parents.

Types of Assessments

If you are familiar with "attribute blocks" and have sorted them with primary-age children, you know that these blocks can be classified in numerous ways. We can sort them by shape, size, and color. Assessment tools and procedures also have many dimensions and we can effectively classify or organize them to facilitate our understanding (Figure 1-1). In schools and other professional settings you will hear assessments referred to in a variety of ways, so it is important for you to be able to understand their definitions and characteristics.

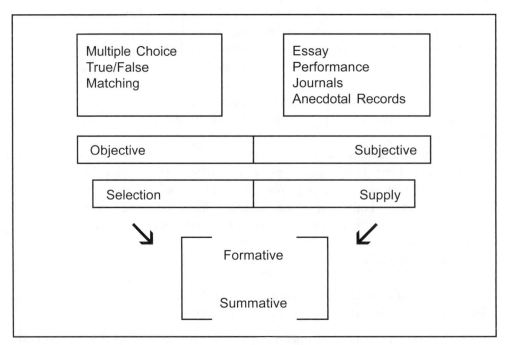

Figure 1-1. Types of Assessments

Objective and Subjective Assessments

All assessments can be grouped by whether they are objective or subjective, which depends on how they are scored. If two scorers can agree on whether the answers to the test are correct or incorrect, then the assessment is considered to be objective. Example of objective assessment formats include true/false, matching, multiple choice, and in some instances completion.

Subjective assessments are those in which the scorers may not agree on the correctness of the student answer. The most familiar example of a subjective measure is an essay question. Your experiences in school should help you to understand how two persons might score an essay response differently even though the student's written response did not change. Other types of subjective assessments include reports, observations, and logs. Unfortunately, subjective assessments are erroneously thought by some school professionals to be too heavily biased to be useful in classrooms. This is not true. Subjectivity in assessments demands a higher degree of interpretation, but that does not automatically mean there is bias on the part of the scorer. If teachers relegate themselves to using only those assessments that are objective in nature in order to avoid bias, they will be missing the opportunity to employ a wide variety of assessments. Narrowing our assessment choices to objective item formats alone violates our first principle of sound assessment.

Selection and Supply Assessments

Assessments can also be described by the type of response students must render to answer the question. In this case, we can differentiate selection from supply formats. Multiple choice, true/false, and matching are *selection* formats because the question actually contains the answer and the student must recognize the correct answer to respond properly. This differs from a *supply* format, in which the student must generate or recall the correct response. In the supply format there are no responses from which to choose. Examples of supply items are essay exams, projects, and reports.

This is important to know as a classroom teacher because in most cases recognition items (the selection format) require an easier mental process and are more susceptible to guessing. Consider this example. You are walking across campus one day and a person who was in your class last semester says, "Hello, how are you doing?" and calls you by your first name. You immediately recognize the face of the individual and you can even remember where he sat in class, but you can not think of his name. So you say, "Hi" and hope that the person's name comes to you as you strike up a conversation. You are not suffering from a premature senior moment; recognizing a face is easier than recalling a name. (Had the person presented you with a list of names from which to choose, your chances of getting his name correct would likely improve.) The reference here to a multiple-choice (selection) format is obvious.

Formative and Summative Assessments

We have already discussed the difference between formative and summative assessments (Table 1-2).

Formative assessments are used to gauge the understanding of students during instruction. For example, if you were teaching a social studies lesson and you administered a quick quiz during instruction or made a keen observation of student participation levels, you might decide to reteach part of the lesson. This is an example of a formative assessment. Formative assessments are designed so that teachers can gauge the learning that is taking place and, if necessary, modify their instruction to address areas of deficiency.

Table 1-2. Formative vs. Summative Assessment

	Purpose	Takes Place	Examples
Formative	To assess student understanding of material and to adjust teaching strategies if necessary.	Usually during instruction. Post-instructional assessments can be used for formative purposes.	• Oral questioning • Observation • Every pupil response techniques • Quick writes
Summative	To assess student understanding or competence to determine student gain or grades.	Usually associated with the completion of a unit of study, course, or performance task.	• End-of-chapter tests • Culminating activities • Standardized testing

Summative assessments are designed to measure the achievement after instruction. For example, most social studies and science textbooks offer end-of-the-chapter tests. Other summative measures that are not tests can provide information about the success of student learning and the effectiveness of teaching. For example, the completion of a three-panel travel brochure in social studies can serve as an effective summative measure to an instructional unit. The primary purpose of these tests or projects is to measure how much of the content and/or skills has been retained or mastered by the students.

Try your skill at recognizing the types of assessment formats that have been discussed using these examples:

- A fourth-grade teacher decides to administer a short true/false pretest on Wednesday prior to Friday's larger end-of-the-chapter exam. Is Wednesday's exam objective or subjective, summative or formative, selection or supply?

- A sixth-grade social studies teacher decides to test the important skills covered in a geography chapter by having students complete a travel brochure. Is the travel brochure objective or subjective, summative or formative, selection or supply?

Indicators of Quality

Validity and reliability are considered by the assessment community, as well as by the teaching profession, as key measures indicating the quality of an assessment. It is easy to understand why you would need to be familiar with these concepts as a beginning or veteran teacher. If you subscribe to the principles of sound assessment, you will be using a variety of assessments, trying to match them to your instructional practices, and communicating the results to different groups. It is extremely important in all of these situations for you to be using assessments of the highest quality.

Let's discuss the two terms, their different types, and some of their more recognized uses in elementary classrooms. It is important to recognize that there is a sense of strain between the definitions of these concepts, which have been developed for large-scale assessments but adapted for classroom assessment. Brookhart (2003) contends that measurement theory needs to address the strain and that more attention should be given to assessments developed around classroom purposes and uses. The examples that follow are intended to ground the concepts in classroom-related situations.

Validity

Validity means that a test or an assessment measures what it claims to measure and leads users to draw accurate and meaningful conclusions about what students know and can do (Kober, 2002; Nitko, 2001). This definition is derived from decades of study based mostly on large-scale standardized measures. Over that period, the measurement community recognized three important types of validity: content, criteria, and construct validity.

Content validity refers to how adequately an assessment samples the content domain. A content domain refers to the entire area designated for assessment. If one were to develop a test on a chapter in science, the content domain to be assessed is the knowledge, skills, and dispositions within that specific chapter. Content validity would be concerned with how comprehensively the assessment sampled the content of the science chapter.

Another example of content validity in elementary and middle schools is provided in the following vignette. To prepare his students to take the written portion of the state-mandated tests, Mr. Gonzales decides to require a writing assignment each week of the school year. To facilitate feedback to his students, he provides a rating scale that indicates the student's mastery of spelling, grammar, mechanics, and usage for each assignment. Students are encouraged to make their corrections based on his editorial comments. He fails because he limits the definition of "good" writing to proficient use of grammar, usage, mechanics, and spelling. The content domain of effective writing has not been adequately developed or sampled. Mr. Gonzales should expand the rating scale to include focus, organization, style, and content if there is to be a greater degree of content validity (Mabry, 1999). It is easy to see how content validity is a measure of assessment quality.

Criteria validity refers to the degree to which an assessment permits the teacher to predict how well students will do on a subsequent measure. This type of validity is more commonly associated with standardized testing and its ability to predict future performances of students. A helpful example common to elementary schools is the use of aptitude or intelligence tests to predict the general degrees of success that students should maintain in an educational setting. It is critical to have a general idea of the student's cognitive abilities when trying to make decisions about referrals for special education placements. In high-stake decisions affecting children, teachers must have confidence that a high degree of criteria validity is present in the aptitude test.

Construct validity refers to the degree to which an assessment is able to measure a theoretical construct. Although elementary teachers are unlikely to develop tests that attempt to measure theoretical constructs such as anxiety and stress in their students, they might attempt to develop tests that measure higher order thinking skills. The development of assessments that measure similar types of constructs requires procedures that go beyond the necessary skill levels of beginning teachers.

It is important for teachers to recognize each of the three forms of validity, but we will postpone developing a greater depth of understanding until we address specific types of assessments, such as rubrics, anecdotal records, and essay test items, in their specific contexts.

You might be wondering how one improves the quality (validity) of an assessment. Any time you construct an assessment you should try to develop it as soundly as possible. That is, avoid anything that interferes with the direct assessment of the student's learning, and also attempt to make sure that the student clearly understands the questions and has an appropriate amount of time in which to complete the assessment.

After you have made sure that the testing or assessments practices promote a high degree of validity, you must be careful with the interpretation that you make with the results. As Popham (2002) indicates, "Tests (assessment in general) themselves do not possess validity. Educational tests are used so that educators can make inferences about a student's status." In short, we have to be extremely careful not to over-interpret the results of the assessment and assume that the student possesses strengths or weaknesses that are not evidenced by the test data.

Here is an example that points out the potential danger of poor inference making. Perhaps, due to inexperience, you use an invalid measure to assess student understanding of a concept. After administering several word problems in mathematics to your third graders, you assume, based on their poor results, that they have not yet mastered their multiplication tables. In reality, the major determiners of their lack of success were the inabilities to read the word problems and the lack of problem-solving skills. The poor inference making has produced a distorted idea of what the student knows. Consequently, you will direct your teaching inappropriately and you will likely communicate false information to your students and their parents.

A more specific example might provide additional clarification. Consider the actions of a kindergarten or first-grade teacher who assesses students' recognition of the alphabet by having them recite it. As you might recall, children can memorize the names of the letters of the alphabet without being able to identify any of the letters appearing in isolation. (This is why some young children think that L-M-N-O-P is one letter.) Thus, by having the students recite the alphabet, the teacher would be assuming that they are also able to identify the letters in isolation. There is a strong likelihood that the teacher would be making an invalid and dangerous assumption.

In sum, beginning teachers need to understand the various types of validity, and they must also recognize the importance of developing sound assessment instruments and avoid misinterpreting their results.

Reliability

The second quality that should be present in all assessments is reliability. *Reliability* refers to consistency in student results—that is, that the scores the assessment yields are consistent and stable across multiple test administrations. To be a reliable assessment, the test, product, or activity should be free from wide swings of student success based on outside influences. For example, suppose we teach a unit on making graphs to third graders, and the culminating assessment asks student to create three bar graphs from data tables the teacher provides. On the first day, students are permitted to use crayons, the next day they are required to use stickers, and on the third day they are told to use stamps and stamp pads to complete the bar graph. After the assignment is completed, we find that the consistency of responses had more to do with the materials the students were permitted to use rather than student understanding. The assessment did not have a high degree of reliability because its consistency was placed at risk by the materials used by the students to complete the activity. The students' fine motor control was a factor that determined their success, and the use of a variety of writing tools caused the results to be inconsistent.

In the measurement community, in the same way that validity exists in multiple forms, three areas of reliability are frequently mentioned: stability, alternate form, and internal consistency reliability. These types of reliability are generally associated with standardized testing and large-scale measures, but they appear in elementary classrooms in different forms.

Stability reliability refers to the idea that if students were to retake an assessment, without any outside influence, they would be likely to score in the same range as they did the first time. It is of fundamental importance that any assessment generates data that will remain stable. Yet, how often does an elementary teacher retest a classroom of children using the exact same test without any intervention? The answer is not very often. However, if we think of the graphing example presented above, we can see how stability can be influenced in an elementary classroom.

Alternative form reliability refers to the application of two forms of a test by a teacher or school district for the purpose of decision making. An example of this can be seen in standardized tests. Many times schools will purchase two forms of the same test. The questions are different but are designed for the same purpose and the same audience. It is important to know that both forms of the test will generate similar results from student efforts.

In another example, if a middle school teacher has several sections of a course, he or she might generate two forms of a test using different questions. Are the tests of equivalent difficulty, or is one class taking a harder exam?

Internal consistency reliability refers to the degree to which multiple scorers agree on the scores of a subjective assessment activity. A high degree of this type of reliability is associated with the scoring of student writing. Many states now impose a state writing exam for students in several grades. Student writing pieces are sent to the state departments of education for scoring. Multiple persons are involved in the scoring, so it is vital that there is a high degree of internal consistency reliability among the scorers. The persons who are scoring the papers are generally trained for several days in order to control the variance in the scores.

If your school administers writing exams as a way of obtaining baseline data on writers at the beginning of the school year, it would be prudent to have multiple readers who are experienced in scoring writing or who have participated in training. This will help to ensure that the score that is given to each student is not determined inappropriately by the person who scores the writing sample.

Can you list several ways in which the absence of validity and reliability might affect your perceptions of students? How might invalid and unreliable assessments affect your relationship with parents?

Validity and Reliability on a Continuum

Let's discuss one final issue concerning validity and reliability. Neither of these qualities appears in assessments as absolutes. In other words, it is not a question of an assessment either having validity or not having validity. Instead, an assessment is usually said to have a high degree of validity or a low degree of validity. Seldom are assessments totally invalid and unreliable. Consider validity and reliability to exist on a continuum, some assessments having higher degrees of validity and reliability than others. For example, suppose I wanted to try to make an inference about your ability to be a good classroom teacher from a set of assessments. Examine Table 1-3.

These measures differ in their ability to support an inference concerning your ability to teach. The measures that closely approximate teaching provide for lower inference making, and the amount of data also assists in the inference making. The examples provided are not absolute indicators of your ability to teach, but they exist on a continuum from high to low in their ability to support the inference. Assessments can have high degrees of validity and reliability, and others can have low degrees of validity and reliability.

Summary
The study of assessment can be ordered by the pursuit of several guiding principles. The assessment community acknowledges the importance of using multiple measures to inform decisions that impact students. Ensuring that assessment measures are effectively aligned with the planned objectives and instruction enriches the use of multiple measures for instructional purposes. Any assessment activity that fails to clearly communicate to students, school professionals, and parents or guardians ranges from unnecessary to dangerous.

Assessment measures can be described and sorted into a number of different categories by their purposes and uses. Clear understanding of terminology such as objective

Table 1-3.   Validity and Inference Making

Which of the following data sources allow me to make the strongest inference concerning the quality of your classroom teaching?

Types of Data	Your grade in this assessment class	Your transcript indicating all the grades you received toward the completion of your degree	Observations of your classroom teaching during your student teaching semester	Observations of your classroom teaching during your first year of employment
Possible Concerns	1. Disconnect between classroom work and actual classroom teaching 2. Number of data sources	1. Disconnect between classroom work and actual classroom teaching 2. Are all grades in areas that affect classroom teaching?	1. Frequency of observations 2. Your role in the actual success of the classroom	1. Frequency of observations

As you can see, there are variables that affect the ability to make inferences. In the case of observation (as an assessment technique), we need to be concerned about frequency and authenticity. Is there a continuum of weak to stronger inference in this example? In which direction does it develop?

and subjective, formative and summative, and selection and supply facilitates the discussion and application of important assessment concepts. Validity and reliability are the two indicators of quality upon which all assessments can be judged.

Teaching Activities

1. To recognize assessment's central purpose in teaching, put yourself in this position. Suppose you are going to an interview for your first teaching position and you are asked by the person interviewing you, "Tell me what you have learned about planning for instruction." Your answer might address a variety of topics, but some aspect of your response should address the contemporary emphasis on the assessment of student learning. Try sketching out a response to the interviewer; it will be good practice for your first interview.

2. To assess your understanding of congruence and alignment, try the following task. Sketch out the format for a lesson sequence (more than one lesson plan) that is designed to develop the skill necessary to write a descriptive paragraph with a group of fifth graders. Try writing one to use with third graders.

3. Using Figure 1-2, discuss the differences between formative and summative assessment and add examples where appropriate.

4. Because communication with parents is important to the sound use of assessment in classrooms, try writing a letter that you can use as the introductory letter in your first teaching position. What kinds of things do you want to share about yourself, what bridges do you want to make between them and you, what tone should you use, and just how important is it to be error free?

5. Validity and reliability are universally recognized as measures of quality in assessment. Their importance in educational settings cannot be disputed. Their observable presence and perceived importance, however, is not equal in all classroom settings. This activity is designed to focus discussion on issues of validity where it is perhaps most important to classroom teachers: in justifying the grades given to students. It is critical for teachers to be knowledgeable about validity so that they have confidence in their measurements and are able to communicate their thinking to parents and other school professionals.

   Following are several statements taken from report cards. For each statement, brainstorm several assessments that might be used to generate evidence of the student's ability to accomplish the performance.

   - Understands and interprets what he or she reads
   - Uses correct sentence form
   - Demonstrates use of addition and subtraction processes
   - Demonstrates understanding of the investigative process
   - Demonstrates ability to use reference materials
   - Demonstrates understanding of interpreting maps, globes, tables, and charts

   Are all assessments equally sound in providing evidence that the student can complete the statement? What is the effect of assigning the tasks as homework? What

Planning for Instruction: The Need for Assessment-Related Decision Making

1. To understand the importance of instructional planning
2. To understand the conflicting forces that impact planning in elementary classrooms
3. To be able to identify the desired targets for instruction
4. To be able to check the assessment quality of a constructed lesson plan

The Teacher as Decision Maker: Planning Decisions

One very practical and widely accepted view of teaching identifies it as a decision-making occupation. Any job that requires an adult to manage and teach 25–30 children for approximately 7 hours a day for 180 school days a year must be grounded in decisions. Many other professions require decision making, and our views of successful persons in those occupations are based largely on the quality of their decisions. For example, the quality of a surgeon can be judged on the basis of her decision making, and if she consistently makes poor decisions, her patient load will be seriously reduced. Similarly, law enforcement officials are typically confronted with critical decisions as part of the daily routine of their job. Although life-and-death decisions are not usually a part of classroom teaching, your performance is likely to be judged by the decisions you make about the management, treatment, and teaching of children.

Classrooms are fast-paced, complex environments that require teachers to make many decisions. Shavelson (1987) considers decision making as the basic teaching skill. Mosston and Ashworth (1990) refer to decision making as "the primary behavior that governs all of the behaviors that follow; how we organize students; how we manage time, space, and equipment; how we create and conduct cognitive connections with learners." In a single day an elementary teacher may engage in several hundred interpersonal exchanges with students (Jackson, 1967). Not all interactions require careful deliberation; nevertheless, teachers make their best decisions (responses) when their judgments are based on multiple data sources. This chapter focuses on a specific area of teacher decision making that has a direct impact on teaching and learning: planning for instruction.

The Recognized Importance of Instructional Planning

Instructional planning is a cornerstone of effective teaching. Danielson (1996) lists planning and preparation as one of the four domains of professional practice. Interstate New Teacher Assessment Support Consortium (INTASC) (1992) includes, among its 10 standards, one that recognizes the importance of planning: "The teacher plans instruction based upon knowledge of subject matter, students, the community, and curriculum goals."

Why Is Daily Lesson Planning Necessary?

Despite all the time, energy, and thought required by diverse classroom responsibilities and urgencies, there is a single purpose that should be your focus: to create an environment that facilitates learning by all students in your classroom. This is what teachers are hired to do, and few other purposes are more central to the effectiveness of a classroom teacher. A fundamental step to achieving that end is making effective decisions that result in sound instructional planning.

Remember, you are planning so that your instruction will maximize the opportunity for all children to learn in your classroom. A misconception persists about instructional planning that would be somewhat humorous if it weren't so dangerously erroneous. When asked why teachers write instructional plans, more than one person has responded, "Teachers write lesson plans so that if a substitute teacher has to come in, he or she will know what to teach!" If that is true, then teachers engage in a tremendous amount of time writing to a person who is seldom present in the classroom. Certainly, having a carefully written lesson plan for a substitute teacher is a professional courtesy that will contribute to your students' learning in your absence. More important, however, the lesson plan is written for *your* use in delivering quality instruction to the students in your class.

You might be asking, "Why does an assessment text begin with lesson planning; isn't assessment something that takes place toward the end of the lesson?" This is not really so. According to Grant Wiggins (1993), for too long we have acted on the premise that assessment is what we design after teaching and learning are over. Effective assessment begins at the moment that teachers begin to plan lessons. The traditional assumption that assessments or tests take place at the end of a lesson or unit is reasonable, because in most cases we have experienced summative tests and questions administered at those times. However, if you aspire to develop lessons that are aligned and congruent (the second principle of sound assessment), it is important to identify your assessment practices and tools in the planning stage of the lesson. The assessments should collect evidence that allows you to determine to what degree your students have mastered the goals specifically stated in the objective of the lesson. In effect, you should be judging your own success on *what the pupils are able to do after* your instruction instead of *what you did during* your instruction.

Powerful Elements at Work in Instructional Planning: Constants and Context

Two conflicting forces impact instructional planning: constants, or elements that stay the same, and contextual issues, elements that are specific to the classroom in which you are teaching. This can be confusing for beginning teachers, who often search for constants from which to develop a personal repertoire of actions and beliefs. The presence of a lesson-plan format suggests a degree of uniformity in teaching. However, teacher candidates become more familiar with the structure of planning through direct interaction with children in classrooms. You come to understand that the specifics of the classroom have a great impact on your planning actions. To be sure, all aspects of teaching can be affected by the context of the setting. For example, we all know that certain classroom management techniques work effectively in some classrooms but are virtually ineffective in others. One of the primary reasons for this is that the children in one classroom come from different backgrounds (part of the context), and so the management techniques affect their behavior in different ways.

It would be impossible to suggest that the contextual factors that impact elementary classrooms can be adequately addressed within the scope of this text. The constants, however, can provide a structure from which novice teachers can construct and develop appropriate planning skills.

Table 2-1 summarizes the constants and the context in planning lessons. The fundamental constants you will be considering are the availability of time, student developmental levels, and the nature of the content. As for the contextual issues in planning for instruction, you must be flexible, reflective, and responsive as they arise.

Table 2-1.   Teacher Decision Making in Planning for Instruction

1. CONSTANTS
   Without fail, teachers will address the following concerns when planning for instruction:

   • TIME
     How much time is there for the lesson?
     How long should each part of the lesson take?
     How long will the students need to adequately reach the objective?

   • DEVELOPMENTAL LEVELS OF THE CHILDREN
     Are the students capable of understanding the major concepts?
     Can the material be presented in ways that make it easier for children to under-
       stand?
     Are there key vocabulary words that make the lesson more understandable?
     What materials would assist the students' ability to understand the material?

   • TYPE OF CONTENT (DESIRED TARGETS)
     How can I best teach and assess this knowledge?
     How can I best teach and assess these skills?
     How can I influence and assess the dispositions in this lesson?

2. CONTEXT
   Each situation that teachers deal with contains a mixture of variables that makes the
   planning for that classroom unique. It should be understood that regardless of the time
   spent planning the constants, teachers who can perceive the needs of the context and
   adjust accordingly will be more effective planners.

Time as a Constant in Instructional Planning

Before you can begin instructional planning for an individual lesson, you must consider the amount of time you believe will be appropriate for students to be able to complete the learning task or activities. Because most elementary schools operate on roughly a 6- to 7-hour day for approximately 180 days a year, you are forced to work within this blueprint of time. Another time concern that might affect your planning is the length of the grading period. Most reporting systems are set up on a fixed amount of time, with every grade level in the school receiving report cards on the same day. Most report cards are issued every 9 weeks, but some districts use a 6-week time frame. Your schedule must allow for the consistent delivery of instruction but also permit the adequate assessment of student progress in many areas. The classroom assessments should lead, with minimal adaptation, to information that can be reported or communicated. Creating a report card that outlines what you will have to report to the child and his or her parents is critical. It might be helpful to plan your daily schedule and weekly schedule for the first grading period (9 weeks) and adjust it according to need.

The following example shows the schedule of one teacher. It helps to show the importance of time and its impact on classroom management, instruction, and grading.

Mon./Wed./Fri.	**Tues./Thurs.**
9:00–9:30 Handwriting	9:00–10:30 Reading
9:30–10:00 English	10:30–10:50 Break
10:00–10:20 Spelling	10:50–12:00 Math
10:20–10:30 Break	12:00–12:50 Lunch
10:30–12:00 Reading	12:50–1:20 Health
12:00–12:50 Lunch	1:20–2:00 Science
12:50–1:30 Social studies	2:00–2:20 Spelling
1:30–2:00 Music	2:20–2:50 Art or library
2:00–2:50 Math	
3:00 Dismissal	

If you adhere to this schedule, there will be more opportunities to teach social studies than science. English will be taught only 3 times a week. Do you notice any other differences? Remember, the idea here is to demonstrate how your weekly schedule determines the time you have to teach and assess. It is important to develop a sense of how much instructional time you will dedicate to certain subjects. Certainly, a good rule is that the more important the subject, the more time spent on it. Instructional time is an extremely important commodity for effective teachers; they guard it and they spend it judiciously. If you want to know what subject is most important to a teacher, you do not have to ask; you simply find out what subject is taught most in his or her classroom.

Consider this second schedule:

Mon./Wed./Fri.	**Tues./Thurs.**
9:00–10:20 Language arts	9:00–10:30 Math
10:20–10:30 Break	10:20–10:30 Break
10:30–12:00 Language arts	10:30–12:00 Language arts
12:00–12:50 Lunch	12:00–12:50 Lunch
12:50–1:30 Social studies	12:50–2:00 Science
1:30–2:00 Creative arts	2:20–2:50 Research on computer
2:00–2:50 Math	3:00 Dismissal
3:00 Dismissal	

Realizing that there are 45 instructional days in a 9-week grading period, you begin to get an idea of how the timetable you establish for instruction will impact your fundamental assessment practices. This gives you an idea of when to schedule testing and/or performance assessments within the grading period. These are the first steps to developing a sense of instructional pacing. If you begin to design lessons without a consideration of the time factors, you will be "driving only as far as your headlights allow you to see." Plan your trip in advance; know your time restrictions as you plan for teaching and assessing. Remember, however, that there are other important factors that impact instructional planning. Teachers must also be concerned with student developmental levels and the nature of the content.

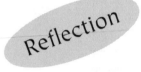

Teachers can be referred to as "prisoners of time." What aspects of teaching make this a reasonable descriptor?

Developmental Levels of Children as a Constant in Planning

The development level of the children is an area where beginning teachers typically have some difficulty. With experience, teachers gain knowledge of the types of activities that are appropriate and challenging for their students. Unfortunately, there is no quick means of gaining experience, so teachers' manuals for the grade levels you teach are an important resource. The manual provides activities and content that closely match what your students should be able to master. Following the teachers' manual is acceptable; however, an undue level of reliance and rigidity based on the manual's contents is not encouraged. Manuals are written for an audience without the knowledge of what the individual needs of that audience might be (i.e., context). Therefore, strict adherence to the teachers' manual will probably deny the higher achievers and the lower achievers the attention and meaningful instruction they require. The teachers' manual is your resource and will usually offer developmentally appropriate content; however, the development of lessons that meet the needs of *all* your students is your ultimate goal.

Figuring out what does or does not constitute developmentally appropriate practice requires more than simply memorizing a particular set of do's and don'ts. It requires thinking about each practice in context and making judgments about each child and the environment in which he or she is functioning. It would be advisable to keep in mind some general criteria concerning developmentally appropriate practice suggested by Danielson (1996).

Teachers who plan and prepare by demonstrating knowledge of students consider the following characteristics:

- Intellectual, social, and emotional characteristics of age groups
- Knowledge of the students' approaches to learning
- Awareness of the students' prior skills and knowledge
- Knowledge of the students' interests or heritage

If you feel uncomfortable with your understanding of child development, this text is not designed to fill that gap, so it would be advisable to seek information from one of the many excellent child development books on the market or log on to the National Association for the Education of Young Children Web site (www.naeyc.org/about/positions.asp) to locate information and resources.

The Type of Content as a Constant Planning Decision

Content simply refers to the types of material children are expected to master. Typically, our teaching can be divided into three distinct areas: knowledge, skills, and attitudes or dispositions. Stiggins (2001) refers to these areas as "desired targets" and also includes products and thinking. As content changes, so too do the effective methods to teach and ultimately assess it. Knowledge acquisition requires different teaching and assessment approaches than does the development of skills or dispositions in students. For that reason, objectives, instructional activities, and assessments must focus on the desired target of your lesson (the second principle of sound assessment).

Knowledge, skills, and dispositions are important to classroom teaching because they are deeply rooted in everyday life. Let's examine some typical contexts in which their presence might illuminate our understanding. Can you think of an occupation, an activity, or an area of study that possesses the combination of knowledge, skills, and dispositions?

What about driving a car? What are the knowledge, skills, and dispositions essential to safely operating a motor vehicle in the United States?

Knowledge (the facts, concepts, and generalizations that inform the safe operation of a motor vehicle): A driver should know the laws of the motor vehicle code. For example, what does a flashing red light indicate to a driver? What does a dotted white line indicate? How far from the curb should a car be parked? A driver should know the function of each of the controls of the car. What does the brake make the car do? What is the turn signal for? How does one activate the windshield wipers?

Skills (the actions that are used in conjunction with the knowledge required to operate the motor vehicle): Hand-eye coordination enables you to operate the car in such a manner that you do not hit things. Do you have the dexterity to turn on the ignition and let up on it when the car's engine starts? Do you have the foot dexterity to manipulate the brake in such a way that your passenger is not pasted on the windshield? Can you parallel-park the vehicle in a parking space? Finally—the ultimate driving skill—can you successfully operate a car with standard transmission (stick shift) from a stopped position on a hill?

Dispositions (attitudes that contribute to the safe operation of the car): Drivers have a wide variety of attitudes and dispositions. Some of these have triggered the use of the term *road rage*. Examples of other attitudes that describe drivers are patient, courteous, cautious, and aggressive.

 Think about the learning that is necessary to develop the knowledge, skills, and dispositions needed to operate a vehicle safely. From your own experiences, how did you acquire (learn) these different targets?

Why spend time examining this real-life situation? If we were to teach drivers according to the desired targets, our lessons and the supporting assessments aimed at achieving each would be very different. Teaching the rules and responsibilities of the motor vehicle code should be designed in a much different manner than a practice session designed to teach parallel parking. The assessment of these two activities also differs significantly. Imagine the degree of faith you would have in other drivers if you knew that they merely passed a true/false test to obtain a driver's license. You can see now why most states require a written test on the laws and an actual performance test to award the driver's license. The assessment practices required by the Department of Motor Vehicles make sense. Perhaps some day an assessment will be generated to gauge the dispositions of the drivers. We can be much more precise in our planning for lessons if we are aware of our targets for instruction and assessment. Table 2-2 gives some examples for various disciplines. What are some examples of knowledge, skills, and attitudes or dispositions associated with, for instance, social studies? What are some facts that are typically associated with it? What are some of the concepts or generalizations? What skills are associated with geography, history, anthropology, and civics? What are the attitudes to be reinforced or developed from the study of social studies?

Table 2-2.   Desired Targets by Discipline

Science	Knowledge Skills Att./Dis.	There are three forms of matter. Classifying Respect for the environment
Reading/Language Arts	Knowledge Skills Att./Dis.	Elements of a story Distinguishing fact from opinion Reading for enjoyment
Social Studies	Knowledge Skills Att./Dis.	John Adams was the 2nd president of the U.S. Map reading Tolerance of cultural differences
Mathematics	Knowledge Skills Att./Dis.	4 + 4 = 8 Estimation Inquisitiveness

The importance of recognizing the difference among the three desired targets is that instruction and assessment methods should be customized to enhance the opportunity for student success in achieving the specific desired target. Planning for that must occur before the lesson is underway, not during or after the instructional process. The nature of the content requires a constant instructional planning decision.

A critical aspect of contemporary planning is the use of assessment data to direct instructional practices. Appendix A of this book lists the components of a lesson plan and their importance to assessment. In the past, the pacing of instruction was based largely on following the scheduled pacing of a textbook. For example, mathematics textbooks typically contained 360 pages because the school years in most states were 180 instructional days. An examination of math texts will show the "two-page spread." The left page discussed and helped to explain the skill, whereas the right page provided additional examples, practice problems, and numerous problems for homework. The pacing was convenient but artificial—two pages a day for all 180 school days! Other elementary and middle school subject textbooks had a similar organization. Today, sound instructional planning focuses on the success of the students and not on an artificial pacing prescribed by a textbook company.

As lessons are taught, the success of the student is measured by assessments that are congruent with the objectives and instructional activities of the lesson. The rate of learning can be uneven, however, especially in the case of student encounters with new or abstract material. Teachers must be able to recognize the instructional needs of different groups of students. Using contemporary standards of quality, lesson planning must do more than plan for the delivery of instruction. Quality lesson plans must consider previous assessment data and include instructional strategies that consider the needs of all students in the classroom. Following is a set of questions that will help you to determine whether your plan fits the instructional needs of contemporary classrooms.

Checking the Quality of Your Lesson Plans

Much emphasis here has been placed on the development of lesson plans, but it is equally important for you to be able to judge the quality of the plans that you prepare. An evaluation of lesson plan quality should address the following: (a) goals and objectives, (b) delivery of instruction, (c) assessments, and (d) reporting success.

Although there are hundreds of specific questions that can be generated under each of these four areas, those shown in Table 2-3 are most common. As you can see, there is a healthy presence of assessment literacy necessary for effective classroom instruction.

Table 2-3.   Judging the Assessment Quality of a Lesson Plan

Objectives	Comments
Am I clear about pinpointing my desired targets?	
What level of student competence am I trying to achieve? Do I know the student's strengths and weaknesses? Is student achievement data available that will guide my intended instruction? Did I use that data to plan this lesson?	
How much time should this lesson take? What materials are necessary to complete this lesson? What accommodations should I make for exceptional learners and those who fail to understand on the first try?	
What assessment tools are necessary to make decisions about the effectiveness of my teaching and successful student learning?	
Delivery of Instruction	
What instructional strategy should I employ?	
What formative assessments will check student understanding?	
How often and in what forms do students get feedback?	
Do I intend to group students based on previous data to facilitate success? How do I provide the necessary feedback to students so I increase the likelihood that students will learn the material?	
Assessment of Student Learning	
Are the assessments valid and reliable?	
Does the assessment tool match the desired targets?	
Did I make appropriate accommodations?	
Reporting Success	
Have I provided sufficient, accurate, and timely feedback to the student that will assist in student success?	
Do the assessments generate data that can be easily communicated?	
Are the grades or marks given to students easily transposed to a 6- or 9-week report (report card)?	

Summary

Precise planning is a fundamental practice that leads to effective teaching and learning. Lesson-plan formats differ but have essential common elements: objectives, procedures, materials, assessment of student learning, and accommodations. These components serve as an adequate structure for the design of lessons that can promote learning for all students. Teachers must constantly react to the contingencies of time, developmental levels of children, and nature of content when planning to teach.

In an environment that is focused on the assessment of student learning, planning for learning is increasingly necessary. It is virtually impossible to determine the success of a lesson regardless of the quality of the assessment if the planning for the lesson is sloppy. Skillful planning is a necessary step in providing for the instructional needs of all children. Teachers should be concerned that the quality of their instructional plans will lead directly to sound assessment practices.

Teaching Activities

1. Using Table 2-2, develop another real-life example indicating the presence of knowledge, skills, and disposition in an authentic non-instructional scenario. Example: What are the desirable characteristics of a perfect waiter or waitress?

2. Obtain current state standards for student achievement. Review several of the standards and decide whether they support the development of knowledge, skills, and disposition, or a combination of them. Design a lesson plan that is aligned with the purpose of a standard.

3. Examine the schedules of the two teachers in chapter 2.
    * Which subjects are taught more often?
    * What are some of the problems inherent in teaching something every other day?
    * What might be done to address these problems?
    * Can you propose changes to the schedules that would better fit your teaching style?

4. Locate a teacher's manual from a primary grade level (K–3) and one from an intermediate level (4–6). Examine a lesson plan that is designed for teaching the same knowledge or skill but at a different grade level. Discuss how the lesson plan differs because of the developmental differences in the children at each of the grade levels.

5. Using Table 2-3, assess a lesson plan that has already been created. Lesson plans to be evaluated may be obtained from textbooks, Web sites, and teacher candidates or practicing teachers. It might be helpful to start by examining a scant lesson plan on a Web site; this provides the teachers with a common, easy target. The ability to recognize areas of weakness in that plan can be transferred to the critique of their own lesson plans.

Chapter

3

Questions: The Essence of Teaching and Assessment

Goals of the Chapter

1. To be able to list several procedures that promote effective oral questioning

2. To be able to construct well-written objective test items

3. To be able to construct and plan for the effective scoring of essay questions

4. To recognize the advantages and disadvantages of different test item formats

---

The Importance of Questioning

Few areas of teacher activity and behavior are more important to effective instruction and assessment than questioning is. Questions require thinking, and the answers they generate verify levels of student understanding for both the teacher and the student. Questions might be thought of as a bridge between the assumptions about our teaching and the reality of what students have learned. Learning about questions and the art of questioning can help teachers to be more effective in assessing what their students know. Questions that assess what students have learned can help us to make decisions about the success of our teaching and student learning.

Oral Questions

Some assessment textbooks treat written questions as higher on the educational hierarchy than oral questions. However, this book is devoted to elementary and middle school classrooms, so oral questions are treated with the same regard as written questions. If you spend enough time in primary-age classrooms, it soon becomes obvious that oral questioning is more prevalent than written questioning (perhaps because the children's reading skills are emerging at this point). Thus, oral questions are an important assessment tool with elementary children.

Effective questioning can be enhanced by adherence to some procedural guidelines. Following are some strategies to get you off to a good start when posing questions to your class. Table 3-1 summarizes these strategies.

Table 3-1. The Effective Use of Oral Questions

Ask, Pause, and Call (APC)	Refer to this sequence in asking oral questions. Its use requires the entire class to consider the question. Calling a student's name and then asking the question might prevent other students from thinking about the answer.
Adequate Wait Time	Allowing students sufficient time (2–4 seconds) to think about the questions increases the frequency and quality of responses. This also encourages students to think through an answer rather than offering a guess in order to meet the short wait time.
Distribution of Questions	All students should have an equal opportunity to answer questions. Exercise care in treatment of gender balance in questioning. In science and math instruction, be especially careful to exercise equal treatment.
Higher Level Questions	Attention is given to the use of higher level questions (refer to Bloom's taxonomy). Higher level questions can be cued for use at certain points in the lesson development. They frequently make excellent introduction and closure questions.
Every Pupil Response Technique (EPRT)	Formative measures designed to quickly assess students require oral or signal responses to questions by all students. If only one student responds, it might not represent the understanding of the entire class.

Ask, Pause, and Call

The ask, pause, and call (APC) format reminds us to first ask the question, then pause, and finally call upon someone to answer the question after the students have had sufficient time to think through the answer. You might ask, "Why is that so important?" If we call on someone first—for example, "Scott, name a famous rock group in which all four members are deceased"—this immediately lets all the other students know that this question is Scott's and that they will probably not be called on to answer the question, so they do not have to think about the answer. By using APC, you keep the level of concern high for all students, allowing them to believe that they might be called upon to answer—then you designate someone to answer.

Reflection   Are there times when you might want to use a student's name before asking a question?

Wait Time

Wait time refers to the time in which a teacher waits after asking a question and calling on someone to answer. Research suggests (and you have probably already heard this from your mother) that there are benefits for those who wait. The research suggests that teachers should wait approximately 1–2 seconds after calling on a student for his or her response. This amount of wait time might be appropriate for students who already know the answer, but it fails to provide enough time for other students to be able to think about it if they don't. On the other hand, teachers who wait approximately 2–3 seconds after questioning tend to get fewer incorrect responses, more complete answers, and a higher degree of participation from students (Rowe, 1972).

The effective use of wait time is an acquired skill that comes from practice. Getting correct responses from students provides a lively pace to your classroom, which is usually desirable from a management standpoint. As you gain confidence in being able to manage your classroom, try to remember that pace and classroom control are not the primary reasons for questioning. Try not to limit your questioning to only those students who you suspect will provide the correct answers.

Calling on students who do not have their hands raised might slow the pace of the lesson, but there are benefits for you and the students, if you can be patient for a few more seconds. In your first attempts, you might feel awkward periods of silence, but remember, you are not going to wait 45 seconds, so try not to fill the vacuum. The students will feel the pressure of the vacuum, too. Resist giving the answer; let *them* fill the void. Other options for extending wait time include redirecting the question and/or restating the question.

Distribution of the Questions

Keeping APC and wait time in mind, you should also be concerned about the distribution of your questions. By distribution we mean a balance in whom you ask. One of the best personal guidelines is the "democratic classroom." Explain to your students that each of them has an equal opportunity to respond. We have all been in classrooms where one student seems to think that it is his or her right (or mission in life) to answer every one of the teacher's questions. This kind of behavior, though difficult to squelch, can be harmful to your teaching. First, if one person is dominating in responding, you will have difficulty gauging the understanding of the others. Because the same person is answering most of the questions, you do not know what the other students know, and, more important, you do not know what the other students have failed to understand. Second, students begin to believe that this person has all the answers and that they do not need to answer. They also might begin to believe that you favor that student, which has a whole realm of negative consequences! Strategies that engage all students in answering questions include the every pupil response technique described below and the practice of requiring every student to answer one question each before any student can answer a second question. This can be accomplished by giving students cards that they return to the teacher after answering a question or by drawing names from a hat.

Another aspect that you should consider is gender balance. A personal experience will illustrate a situation that you should avoid. As an elementary principal, I had the responsibility to observe teachers in many classrooms. During my observation of a fifth-grade science class with 12 girls and 11 boys, the teacher was conducting a review before a test to be given the following day. I noticed that the pace of the questioning was rapid, and the students were being whipped into a frenzy of participation. I drew a line down the middle of a piece of paper; on the top right I wrote *girls* and on the top left I wrote *boys*. As the teacher called on a student to respond, I placed a tally mark in the column indicating the gender of the responder. At the end of the lesson, 60–65 questions had been asked, yet the results indicated that girls had answered fewer than 10 questions! One can easily see the downside of teacher questioning if there is no awareness of gender balance. The democratic classroom philosophy will help to clarify things for you here. It makes good assessment sense to balance the oral questioning if we want to make accurate judgments about student understanding.

Every Pupil Response Technique (EPRT)

A means by which we can question students in a democratic way and also provide some formative data to our instruction is to employ the every pupil response technique (EPRT). EPRT allows all students to respond collectively, and it is especially useful in primary grades. For example, suppose you are teaching the concept of "island" to primary-age children. As you point to the pictures on the board that are examples and nonexamples of islands, the students use a "thumbs up" if the picture represents an island and a "thumbs down" if the picture represents a land form other than an island. Another example is yes and no cards. After the teacher reads a statement, students indicate their agreement (yes) or disagreement (no) by holding up a card.

In the upper grades, suppose you are teaching the concept of electrical circuits. Given several drawings of circuits, students might hold up a tongue depressor with a paper light glued to the end indicating that the circuit is closed.

The advantages of this technique are that it maximizes the number of respondents, it permits formative judgments to be easily drawn, and it does not encumber the teacher with papers to be graded. Every assessment method has some disadvantage, however. In this case, students might rely on others to respond and then "declare" their answer only after having reviewed the field for the majority view. Expect that to happen, especially in the primary grades. Remember, however, that you are not using this to generate information that has some high-stakes consequence. Instead you are gauging the responses of your students so that you can make adjustments to your teaching and address student misunderstandings (formative assessment). Should you be faced with the majority of students either missing the question or delaying a response in order to be safe, you can infer that this lesson was not as successful as you might have hoped. If that is the case, it is time to design another lesson that either reinforces your original teaching or presents the material using a different approach. As a follow-up to your reteaching, try the EPRT again.

Levels of Questioning and the Relationship to Student Thought

If you recall our discussion of desired targets, you will remember that instruction can be organized into facilitating student learning by the acquisition of knowledge, skills, and dispositions. We want students to know more things, be more skilled, and gain or improve dispositions after spending 180 days in our classrooms. In order to reach those targets, students engage in cognitive activity—in other words, they must think. Cognition, or thinking, is a desirable behavior to encourage and develop in your classroom. Without question it is always present. What has been lacking in American schools is the presence of the direct teaching of *higher level* thinking. Higher level thinking skills seem to be more in demand these days because our country has shifted from a production economy to an electronic information age. Yet, even if the economic atmosphere had not changed, what could be more important than developing the ability to think in our students?

Getting students to use higher level thinking skills is not easy. Some authors suggest that the human mind has an insatiable quest for knowledge and that if one simply offers challenging material, students will joyfully embark on independent thinking. That, unfortunately, has not been the norm in my teaching experience. Most of the students I have had greet higher level thinking with the same disposition that is reserved for a trip to the dentist. Faced with such a motivational task, teachers cannot teach students to think if they do not understand how to differentiate higher level thinking from lower level thinking. Ironically, students can understand the difference. A group of my fifth graders used an organizational framework consisting of easy questions, hard questions, and really hard questions. Other students might refer to "fat" and "thin" questions. As teachers, we need to be a bit more sophisticated about our levels of questioning and use the work of experts such as Benjamin Bloom (1956). We have the best chance of teaching thinking when both the teacher and the students understand the levels of cognition.

Bloom's taxonomy of the cognitive domain arranges thinking (cognitive) processes in ascending order, from lower level thinking to higher level thinking. The purpose of the taxonomy is to provide a primitive but substantial structure by which teachers can understand the different mental processes that humans employ in thought. Bloom's taxonomy presents an organization of cognition that permits us to examine the questions we ask, in order to ask ourselves (in a formative way) if we are asking higher order thinking questions in our daily routine and during our assessments. See Appendix B of this book.

Written Questions

Written questions have historically been the most acceptable mechanism for assessment. Each written question is usually referred to by measurement persons as an *item*. Thus, if we use the term *item format*, we are talking about the type of test question. Traditional assessment practice involves the use of three written test item formats. Your experiences probably tell you that the three most commonly used item formats in American schools are multiple choice, true/false, and matching. There are several reasons that these are so commonplace. For one thing, they are objective item formats, which means that if two people are correcting them, they can agree on whether a given answer is correct or incorrect. There are advantages to objective item formats:

- They are easily correctable, compared to writing samples or essay tests.

- They are easily carried over from one year to the next.

- They provide the opportunity to ask many questions. Essays take so long that they cannot be used with the same degree of ease and comprehensiveness.

There are also disadvantages to objective item formats:

- They require reading skills on the part of the student.

- They limit the scope of the question and suggest that there is a single correct answer to everything.

- They are susceptible to guessing by the student.

- They usually fail to expose how the student arrived at the correct answer (by what thinking process).

Constructing Technically Sound Written Questions

The goal of the remainder of this chapter is to make you aware of how to construct test items that are structurally sound. This is not to suggest that the development of good test questions will make learning easier for students or teaching easier for teachers. Nevertheless, inasmuch as assessment is a key component of teaching and learning, it is the teacher's responsibility to create questions that make the inferences of assessment more valid. We do not want to create questions that by their very design create confusion about what students really know and can do. Children can suffer from test fatigue, especially in the upper grades, if items are constructed that make the test frustrating to use and the correct answers difficult to locate. (A five-page, front-and-back, matching test I once took comes to mind.)

The following sections describe different written-question formats, the advantages and disadvantages of each, and examples of practices to avoid when trying to construct items of each question type.

True/False Questions

In primary grades we can often generate assessments of our students' understanding and the success of our teaching by using yes or no cards that function in the very same manner as a true/false item format. After the teacher has asked a question or presented a statement, the students respond by using the cards to indicate the correct response. You might remember this as the every pupil response technique (EPRT) discussed earlier. Sometimes small individual (and inexpensive) white boards are used so that students can write their individual answers and display them. The students can quickly erase the dry marker print and be ready to respond to the next question.

In the upper elementary grades, true/false (t-f) formats are more commonly found in pencil-and-paper tests. Upper elementary and middle school teachers may require students to change an underlined word to make a statement true if the student believes that the original premise is false. This decreases the student's ability to answer the question by guessing. In this case, the teacher assigns one value to answering the question correctly and another value to changing the false item to the desired response. The t-f format, like every other assessment, has its advantages and disadvantages. The advantages are as follows:

- Test questions can be developed quickly and checked easily because of their objective nature.

- Students can answer many questions in a relatively short period of time (approximately 20 seconds per question).

- The format can be altered to limit the chances of guessing the right answer.

The disadvantages are as follows:

- Good t-f items can be relatively difficult to construct.
- The questions tend to focus on facts and are not useful in assessing higher level thinking.
- This format is susceptible to guessing.

Avoid Unclear or Tricky Items

Try to make an item clearly true or clearly false, calling attention to what you think is important to assess. Making an item unclear only heightens the chance for controversy with your students over whether it was intentionally tricky. In short, nothing good comes from writing fuzzy t-f items.

The following is a poor example: "Dwight E. Eisenhower was president of the United States." (False and tricky, because the middle initial is incorrect, but this is not what you should be interested in assessing.)

A better example is this: "The person who became president of the United States after the death of Franklin D. Roosevelt was Harry Truman." (True, and there are no tricks.)

Avoid designing tests that employ trick questions. The answer that is generated suggests that the student only uncovered the "trick"; the answer has little to do with mastery of any content or skill. Our tests should not be designed for the purpose of tricking students.

Avoid Specific Determiners

It is your responsibility as a teacher to make sure that your students answer the questions based on what they know about the material. If you use certain key words while developing a true/false question, you might be providing a clue to the correct answer. Words that signal to the student that the question is true or false are called *specific determiners*. The danger with them is that students can answer the questions correctly and appear to know the material when they are actually just making reliable educated guesses. Students are unlikely to come up to the teacher after the exam and say, "Actually, I just guessed this item and got it correct, so I do not deserve credit for it!" Ridiculous, right? We must therefore understand that t-f tests are very susceptible to guessing and do everything we can to ensure that we are not making them any easier.

Here are some examples of the use of specific determiners in a t-f question format:

All trees lose their leaves.

Every planet has a moon.

Never attempt to write a report without using an outline.

The words *all, every,* and *never* serve as specific determiners because it is very unlikely that anything will occur or be true 100% of the time. Once the student realizes the exclusionary nature of these words, he or she will notice the word in any t-f test item. In most cases, test-wise students will recognize these words as clues to answer the question "false."

Similarly, there are key words that signal to students that a t-f question is likely to be true. These words include *generally, usually, almost always,* and *seldom.* You should avoid the use of these words in a true/false testing format.

True/false question formats are part of classroom assessment practices. Why is it a good idea not to depend too much on this type of question? What problems might teachers encounter after hastily preparing a few true/false questions?

Multiple-Choice Questions

Teachers and teacher candidates often have a difficult time remembering their own elementary and middle school experiences or any type of testing that existed before the multiple-choice test. This format becomes commonplace in elementary schools as children learn to read. Emerging in grades 3 or 4, it quickly becomes the prominent questioning format in schools. Its acceptance has been so commonplace that until recently, standardized test batteries of more than 450 questions were entirely multiple choice in format.

A multiple-choice format requires the person taking the test to be able to read an item and recognize the correct option among several choices. As we have discussed earlier, recognition differs greatly from recall and provides the student with a greater chance of answering the item correctly.

Let's make sure we understand some important terminology. The long portion of the item that comes before the list of possible answers is referred to as the *stem* of the multiple-choice question. The possible answers that appear beneath the stem are referred to as *response alternatives*. In primary grades it is often acceptable to have only three response alternatives. In higher grades, four response alternatives are more typical.

Here is an example of the stem in a multiple-choice question followed by a set of response alternatives:

> Which one of the following colonies was first to ratify the Constitution?
> A. Pennsylvania
> B. Delaware
> C. North Carolina
> D. New York

Here are some suggestions for constructing multiple-choice items. Limit your questions to three response alternatives at first. Children who are just beginning to use the format might have problems with reading and need time to adjust to the format. Avoid using confusing alternatives like "all of the above" or "none of the above" until the student has gained the ability to reason beyond the concrete.

In the upper elementary and middle school grades, the number of response alternatives can be expanded to four or, in some limited cases, five. Teachers should be straightforward in their questioning and avoid the use of responses such as "A, if B and C are true." This confuses the students, and we should remember that we are giving a test to see *what they have learned*, not to gauge their cognitive ability to unlock abstract and confusing tasks. Your school district is likely to have given students an IQ test already, and we will most likely find a strong correlation between correctly answering the complex questions and a high IQ score. Our purpose is to measure what the students know and can do without intentionally trying to trick them.

Note: If you have strong beliefs about using complex multiple-choice items with your upper elementary and middle school students, do so, but also prepare the students beforehand with classroom activities that employ group work, provide modeling of the required thinking, and ask the questions in a nonthreatening (nontest) environment. You will find that students are much more responsive to these types of questions when they have had practice answering similar questions in class.

Multiple-choice questions have the following advantages:

- They can be answered quickly, compared to essay and other written assignments.
- They are easy to correct, compared to more subjective measures.
- They can test a range of difficulty levels and subject areas.
- Students gradually become or are already familiar with this format.

Multiple-choice questions have the following disadvantages:

- They can be susceptible to guessing.
- Students must be able to read to use the format.
- Constructing good items can be time-consuming.

The ability to adjust the degree of difficulty of a multiple-choice question is important. The degree of difficulty of a question is related to how closely the response alternatives approximate the correct answer to the question. That's why some multiple-choice exercises often say, "Choose the best answer." If all the response alternatives are close to the right answer, you will hear students say that the question was hard. Consider the following example:

What is the capital city of Ohio?

A. London

B. Tokyo

C. Columbus

D. Cairo

The question is not very difficult because only one of the cities listed is even *in* Ohio. Students can eliminate options by even vaguely knowing the locations of the other cities. This question does not necessarily determine that the student knows the capital of Ohio; in fact, there is a strong possibility that we are merely assessing that the student knows which cities are *not* the capital of Ohio. This was not why we asked the question; it makes little sense to test children on how many things they know that are not the correct answer. A better question would be the following:

What is the capital city of Ohio?

A. Cleveland

B. Akron

C. Columbus

D. Toledo

All of the cities here are in Ohio, so the question poses a higher degree of difficulty. Because students cannot as readily eliminate response alternatives, we can make a stronger inference that a correct response by the student indicates that he or she really does know the capital of Ohio.

Another suggestion for making good multiple-choice questions is to have as much material in the stem as possible and avoid repeating parts of the question in the response alternatives. Here is an example:

On April 15, 1865, the

A. army of northern Virginia attacked Washington, DC

B. army of northern Virginia defeated the Union army at the Battle of Bull Run

C. army of northern Virginia surrendered at Appomattox, VA

D. army of northern Virginia fought in the Battle of Sharpsburg

In this question there is a repeated amount of text in each response alternative. Not only is this tiresome reading for the student, it also requires you to type the words "army of northern Virginia" four separate times rather than once. A good rule is to try to make the stem into a question. Although this is not essential to constructing a good test item, it does help students to "get the hang of" multiple-choice questions. More important, it also helps to eliminate repeated text in the response alternatives, thereby conserving time for the students and you.

Avoiding Clues to the Correct Answer

In the multiple-choice format, as with true/false items, it is possible to provide clues to the correct answer. Obviously, you want to avoid having your student scores altered this way. Remember that your questions are designed to measure whether the students can recognize the correct answer, and from that you are inferring their knowledge of the information. If they answer questions correctly because you unintentionally provide clues to the correct answers, then your inference about their knowledge of the subject matter is flawed. They are fooling you, and you are fooling yourself.

One way in which you might provide a clue is by making the correct answer the longest of the response alternatives. Here is an example:

> What was the primary reason the United States entered World War II?
> A. To secure its place in the world
> B. Economic independence
> C. To respond to the sneak attack of the Japanese on Pearl Harbor, Hawaii
> D. To provide help to England

Students who are test-wise have an advantage in this case because if they do not know the right answer, they will default to the longest response. This happens because, in an effort to make the correct answer indisputable, teachers tend to make it more detailed. Teachers do not have a lot of time to develop detailed response alternatives that are good foils, so what is the solution to this problem? Attempt to make all the response alternatives of similar length, and do not be overly concerned with having your answers be irrefutable.

Reflection   How do multiple-choice items differ from true/false questions? Why do you think standardized measures of student achievement lean so heavily on the use of multiple-choice questions?

Matching Questions

The third type of objective written test is matching. This format can be very useful for assessing student knowledge about a group or a collection. Its correct structure is more formal than that of the two previously discussed formats. Matching, like the others, has strengths and weaknesses.

The advantages of matching are as follows:

- It can be used to efficiently assess student knowledge of specific differences between groups that are generally similar.

- It can be efficiently administered and scored.
- It can be constructed easily.

The disadvantages of matching are as follows:

- It is susceptible to guessing.
- It is often ill-constructed or misused.
- It is difficult to apply to all content, compared to true/false and multiple choice formats.

Matching Tests

A key concept in the development of a sound matching exercise is homogeneity. *Homogeneity* refers to the existence of a relationship between the items that are going to be tested. A matching test that includes people's names, wars, terms, and dates will compromise the difficulty of the exam. Instead, we should develop matching tests that have items with a high degree of sameness. For example, a good test might match persons with their important contributions, artists with their memorable works, or elements with some distinguishing characteristic. In this way, the test will provide more possible answers to each premise and will limit the number of items that can be isolated and guessed correctly.

Another consideration for matching tests is the position of the term and its description. A term (the single-word portion) is referred to as the *response*. The longer part, which offers the defining description to the response, is called the *premise*. Practicing teachers often reverse the correct position of these elements. Typically, teachers will put the response on the left side of the page and the premise on the right side of the page. That is incorrect. To facilitate the student's reading of the test, the premise should appear on the left side of the page and the response should appear on the right side of the page. Thus, the student can read the premise and search among the responses to find the appropriate one. This helps to eliminate test fatigue.

There are some other considerations as well. In a matching exercise for elementary or middle school students, we should limit the number of questions to 6–12. Finding more than 10 terms or concepts that possess homogeneity is rare. The idea of having a matching exercise that uses all 26 letters to label the responses is simply out of the question. Keep the number of items reasonable and try to put the entire exercise on one page. This helps students to locate the answers and makes the test a bit easier.

Finally, make sure to provide a space for students to place the correct letter of the answer. Avoid requiring students to draw a line to connect the premise to the appropriate response; this is a nightmare to correct.

Here is an example of a poorly written matching exercise:

Match the phrase on the left with the correct letter:

_____ 1. This is a ceasefire agreement   A. General Matthew Ridgeway

_____ 2. To move against or to attack   B. Truce

_____ 3. The capital city of South Korea   C. Aggression

_____ 4. The 1st commander of all the
       U.N. troops   D. General Douglas MacArthur

    E. Harry S Truman

_____ 5. The president of the United
       States from 1945–1952   F. Seoul

_____ 6. The 2nd commanding officer of
       the U.N. Forces

Although this matching exercise might appear to have homogeneity because the premises come from the same period, it does not, because it requires students to recognize terms, people, and a capital city. This lack of homogeneity results in students being able to rule out possible answers and thus aids student guessing. The same number of responses as premises also offers students a process of elimination. The responses lack any order that would facilitate finding the correct answer.

Here is an example of an improved matching exercise:

Match the phrase on the left with the correct description:

_____ 1. Asked Congress to declare war
       on the Central Powers   A. Adolf Hitler

    B. Amelia Earhart

_____ 2. Completed the first solo nonstop
       flight across the Atlantic Ocean   C. Booker T. Washington

    D. Charles Lindbergh

_____ 3. Developed a plan called the New
       Deal to end the Great Depression   E. Eleanor Roosevelt

_____ 4. Led the Nazi Party in Germany   F. Franklin D. Roosevelt

_____ 5. Disappeared on a flight across
       the Pacific Ocean   G. Harry S Truman

    H. Woodrow Wilson

_____ 6. The 2nd commanding officer of
       the U.N. Forces

This has several different features that make it a well-constructed matching exercise. Notice that the directions indicate that the students must match persons with their actions. This helps to ensure that the exercise has homogeneity among the group of possible responses. The premises appear on the left, which assists the reader in completing the exercise. Other positive features include the use of more responses than premises and the arrangement of responses in alphabetical order. It's also important that students see both genders represented as important historical figures.

Reflection Why do you suppose that matching questions are used less frequently than multiple-choice items on standardized tests? If you review several teacher-constructed matching tests, you will find that the premises and the responses are not consistently placed; why do you think this occurs?

Completion Questions

The fourth type of question is completion, commonly referred to as "fill in the blank." These questions are usually written at the knowledge or comprehension level of Bloom's taxonomy.

The advantages of completion items are as follows:

- They can be easily and quickly constructed.
- They are easily scored.
- They are not as vulnerable to guessing as t-f, multiple-choice, and matching questions.
- They can be used with a word bank in a modified matching exercise.

The disadvantages of completion items are as follows:

- They do not test higher level thinking.
- They can be confusing if not well constructed.

There are three things to keep in mind about constructing completion items. First, do not put too many blanks in a sentence. The following example shows how this can be confusing to the students:

_____ became _____ of the United States on

_____ when _____ was assassinated.

The purpose of this sentence is unintelligible because there are too many blanks. My suggestion for primary classrooms is one blank per question; for middle school, use multiple blanks only when the question asks for items that are related. For example:

The first three months of the calendar year are _____ ,

_____ , and _____ .

Second, word the sentence so that the blank (what you are asking the student) is at the end of the sentence. If you begin the sentence with a blank, the student might become confused about what the sentence means. Notice how confusing the example might be:

_____ is the most famous Civil War battlefield in Pennsylvania.

It is more easily understood in the following format:

The most famous Civil War battlefield in Pennsylvania is_____.

Finally, make sure that the blank is an important part of the content. We do not want to ask questions about something trivial. Let's use the same question as an example:

The most _____ Civil War battlefield in Pennsylvania is Gettysburg.

In this case the answer is *famous*, but that certainly is not what we want to emphasize in the question. Instead, we should be concerned with quizzing the student on the name of the battlefield or the state in which the battlefield is located.

Explain why it is important to use a variety of question types when you assemble a test. Do you have a favorite question type? Do you think that students sometimes have more confidence in their ability to answer one format over another?

Essay Questions

Essay questions have been a stable fixture in teacher assessment activity for decades. The format's universal popularity derives from the essay question's ability to elicit richer information about student achievement than objective item formats do, while also remaining easier to construct and employ than performance assessments.

Based on your classroom experience, you probably have developed some feeling about answering essay questions. Students seem to have dispositions ranging from acceptance to intense dislike about responding to essay questions. Although we cannot control student dispositions toward test items, we should make every effort to ensure that the questions are clearly written and effectively scored and that our feedback contributes to continued learning.

The advantages of essay questions are as follows:

- They are more easily constructed than multiple-choice or matching items.
- They assess the ability of students to communicate their thinking through written expression.
- They can be used to assess higher level thinking.

The disadvantages of essay questions are as follows:

- They require time and effort to score and evaluate.
- They are dependent on the student's writing ability.
- They are restrictive in the amount of content they sample.

Constructing Essay Questions

Using essay tests in elementary grades is particularly tricky and complex for two reasons: the differences in children and the essay questions themselves. Because of the tremendous potential of well-developed essay questions, however, we must learn to remove this complexity.

First, let's examine some obvious differences inherent in children's abilities that make the use of essay questions challenging. If we intend to use essay questions, it is important to make sure that all children can read and understand the question. This can require modifications of time, the use of readers, and other testing adaptations frequently suggested for students with special needs. We should also be concerned that all students can write their answers. Again, it is important to employ adaptations if necessary. A seldom-considered difference is the processing speed of students; not all of your students will work at or complete a task at the same speed. Therefore, as you construct the essay question, it will be necessary to consider whether each student can complete the item in 10 minutes or less. You want to compose an essay question that the "average" student in your classroom can answer within the given time limit. One of the most difficult decisions for a teacher is what to do when a number of students indicate, "I did not have enough time to answer both essays," and you suspect that they knew the material.

Second, let's consider the essay question itself. As with all the other item formats, questions that are generated easily and quickly usually lack high quality. The construction of essay questions appears rather easy, but it must be well thought out.

Essay questions can be effectively organized into two types: a short-answer essay; or *restricted response,* and a longer essay, or *extended responses.* In each case the student is provided with a question and must supply the response with a written essay. A comparison of these two essay formats is found in Table 3-2.

Restricted-Response Items

Popham (2002) succinctly indicates that a restricted-response essay decisively limits the form and content of students' responses. Kubiszyn and Borich (2003) add that these essay formats are most likely to be used to assess knowledge, comprehension, and application types of learning outcomes. Both descriptions shed light on the use of restricted-response essays.

In the restricted-response item we are attempting to check the student's recall of important information. We are not so concerned with the student's use of higher

Table 3-2.   Comparing Two Types of Essay Formats and Objective Item Formats

	Objective Item Formats	Restricted-Response Items	Extended-Response Items
Examples	The town of Bunola is located in what county of Pennsylvania?	Name the three major cultural groups found in Bunola's population and discuss their contributions.	Compare and contrast your lifestyle with the life a child growing up in the 1950s in Bunola, Pennsylvania.
What is assessed?	Knowledge/facts	Knowledge and written expression	Knowledge, written expression, and thinking skills.
Time requirements	20–30 seconds	5–10 minutes	10–15 minutes
Advantages	Speed and convenience in scoring	Limits student ability to guess the correct answer. Requires written expression.	Limits student ability to guess the correct answer and can more easily assess higher order thinking skills.
Content sampling	Large numbers of questions can be asked, so content sampling is high.	Smaller numbers of questions can be asked, so there is a decrease in content sampling.	Limited numbers of questions can be asked, thereby decreasing the content sampling even more.

level thinking here; rather, we gain perspective on the student's recall and ability to translate that through written communication. A typical short-answer essay might ask the student, "Describe the different stages of insect development." Notice the verb; it indicates that the student will employ a lower level cognitive action. Even though it is lower level, there is still value in assessing it.

You might wonder, why use restricted-response questions when you can gauge a student's knowledge by using objective item formats (which are more easily scored)? There are three reasons:

1.   Students get a chance to use written expression to explain their answers. Making students respond in complete sentences can provide additional evidence of their depth of understanding. Unlike objective item formats, in which the teacher sees only the student answer, the essay format reveals more of the student's logic and understanding.

2.   The possibility of guessing the correct answer is removed. Objective item formats (multiple choice, true/false, and matching) have a built-in vulnerability to guessing that is unavailable to students in an essay format. The opportunity to guess the correct answer is especially prevalent in the true/false format.

3. You believe that students should know and be able to recall the information being tested without the benefit of an objective item format. All content that students are required to learn in a classroom is not of equal usefulness or importance. The information that is most important should be recalled rather than recognized. The content of an essay question should always be based on the material that is most important for students to learn (Criswell & Criswell, 2004).

Extended-Response Items

The need to develop higher level thinking in students has become a collective call to action among reformers, policy makers, and teachers. There is a need, especially in upper elementary and middle school classrooms, to have students respond to questions that use signal words such as *explain, defend, compare,* and *create.* If we opt to assess higher order thinking, then we must provide the student with an opportunity to respond in an extended format—one that, according to Bloom, requires analysis, synthesis, and evaluation.

This requires practice and experience on your part. Consider a suitable match between the desired mental activity and the content you intend to assess. Attention to the verb describing the student behavior becomes very important here. If your decision is to begin with "Compare and contrast," you are reasonably assured of requiring the student to analyze some information. (Caution: If your teaching has failed to provide any analysis activities, then testing through analysis is impractical and unethical. Students should not be tested on material or asked to employ skills if they have no prior exposure to or practice with it). It is necessary to prepare elementary and middle school students to answer these types of questions. Developing the ability in students to answer questions efficiently and completely requires intentional and focused teaching. Weak answers might be a signal of an inability to respond to essay questions and not simply a lack of content knowledge.

A means that is often helpful to developing questions at higher levels is to place the student "into" the question. In other words, have the student perform an authentic type of task in which he or she is the decision maker. Here is an example,

> You are a newspaper critic who has been asked to respond to the current fluoride debate in your city. After reviewing the data, write a column for the newspaper that defends your argument either for or against the addition of fluoride to the city's water supply.

After deciding on a reasonably framed question that requires higher mental processes, place yourself in the position of an average student in your classroom. Is it possible for this student to successfully understand and respond to this question?

Scoring Essay Questions

In objective item formats, students select the correct responses; for that reason, the responses are limited and controlled by the teacher. Essays, however, are supply formats; that is, the student must recall information and construct (supply) the answer. The construction of the answer will be different for each student, and that results in difficulty of scoring for the teacher. The student responses are uncontrolled and so may vary in quality and length. Your responsibility lies in scoring each of the different responses fairly. Students will increase the scoring difficulty by attempting to appear to know more than they actually do. Bluffing is a common occurrence in essay responses.

Here are some suggestions to help you make the scoring of essay questions consistent and efficient. First, construct a model answer. Actually compose the answer you are expecting students to generate. It is not important to complete it in a narrative format; an outline of the content will be enough to focus your scoring. Key terms, concepts, and explanations are all possible elements of a model answer. As you read the students' papers you will have to decide the degree to which their response convinces you that they understand the material. For first-year teachers this is often difficult because of their limited experience with scoring items and unfamiliarity with student competency norms for the grade level. Do not be surprised if you read through several essays and decide to go back and change the scores of the first ones. It is also a good idea to keep several student samples depicting different levels of student achievement for your own future reference.

Second, assign point values to each component of the essay that can be added together to generate a score. This should be done with care and thought. Many times teachers assign a point value of 25 to an essay and then only use scores that range from 20–25, essentially inflating everyone's score by 20 points. Examine your model answer and assign points to the question based on the components you can account for—no more, no less. It's possible to construct a test that includes an essay question that is worth 7 points. Resist rounding the value of the question to 10 unless you can account for how the students will legitimately earn the extra 3 points.

Be mindful of how much impact you want the essay to have in respect to the other questions. For example, if you ask 25 objective items in the first part of the test, you should not make one essay question worth 25 points. This creates a situation in which doing poorly on an essay question ensures a poor grade despite the possibility that the student answered all 25 objective items correctly. Assign points judiciously, making sure that you account for them, and balance the weight of the essay with the entire test.

Some measurement texts suggest that you should read each essay a second time to ensure that you have assigned the correct score. Although this is desirable and well intended, in terms of time it is usually out of the question for most middle school teachers. They simply do not have the luxury to reread each essay response and recalculate a grade. This is why having a strong model answer and clearly delineated point values are of great importance.

Another suggestion for scoring essay items fairly is to read all the students' responses to one question before moving on to the next question. That is, if you have two essay questions on your test, read all the student responses to question 1 before reading all the student responses to question 2. This helps to give you a sense of how the class responded and, more important, it keeps you focused on the same student response. Maintaining your focus usually results in increased efficiency and consistency in scoring. Increased efficiency means that you are saving precious time.

Along with scoring each student response to one question at the same time, it is also a good idea to check all the tests in the same sitting. This can be impossible sometimes, based on the class size or the length of the test, but it should always be a goal. If you cannot score the entire set of tests in the same time period, at least attempt to score each individual essay in the same sitting. This helps you to be efficient and consistent. Often I will ask my students, "What time would you prefer that I score your essay questions?" Without fail, I get this question in return: "At what time are you usually in the most generous and lenient mood?" These students understand the importance of mood in scoring essays. We should certainly try to score the essays while maintaining the same mood and fairness for all students.

Another simple procedure for trying to make the scoring fair for all students is to shuffle the order of student papers after scoring all of one of the essay items. Otherwise you might be vulnerable to comparison as a means of evaluation. For example, the scoring of paper B should not be influenced by the quality of paper A. If paper A is very good, paper B might suffer by comparison with paper A, and if paper A is particularly poor, the opposite result can occur. The comparison of student papers should always be based on the model answer, not on each other. It is difficult not to be overly impressed by a quality answer that follows a very incomplete or grossly inaccurate one. For that reason, shuffling the student papers changes the comparisons we might inadvertently be making. Ask yourself this question: If you could place your essay response in a pile with other student responses to be graded by your teacher, would you place it directly following the best paper or the worst?

Feedback as an Important Element in Scoring

The third principle of sound assessment indicates that assessment results should be communicated to students. However, we have a responsibility to do more than communicate the results. Each test we administer to children presents a teaching opportunity. In fact, some children take a deeper interest in testing than in regular classroom activities because they view anything that is graded as having more importance. If the question was important enough to ask as a summative assessment, then it seems entirely appropriate to reinforce student success or address shortcomings in a meaningful way.

For this reason, consider the scores that the students receive to be an incomplete piece of feedback. A score merely tells them how well they did; it does not directly encourage them or inform them how they could improve. There are several ways to improve the feedback given to students who have taken an exam. For the objective items, review the test and explain the answers to the questions that were most frequently missed. If you have time, write a brief explanation of how the student might change his or her study habits or supply an encouraging line about improvement or effort. For the essay items, make sure that the students understand your comments and how you arrived at the score. Supply corrective feedback and suggestions for how the student might improve on the next exam.

Summary

Questions are an essential part of teaching. The effective use of questioning is crucial to enhancing the quality of instruction. In classrooms, questions appear in oral and written forms and are used as formative and summative measures. Each of the question formats that constitute written exams possesses advantages and disadvantages for the teacher. Teachers who vary the types of effective questioning formats will have a clearer understanding of the student's strengths and weaknesses over a broad range of content areas and skills. Uncovering what students understand is central to facilitating their learning and influencing your teaching. Questions are the means by which to do that.

Teaching Activities

1. Observe an elementary or middle school teacher and collect data on the teacher's questioning patterns and processes. Observations can have more than one purpose, and different types of questioning data can be collected in a single setting. However, one must be careful not to assign too many purposes to a single observational setting. Focus the observation on collecting data concerning the teacher's wait time, use of APC, adherence to gender-balanced questioning, and use of higher order questioning.

2. Brainstorm several different ways in which an EPRT could be adapted for use. Make two lists: one for an elementary classroom and one for middle school. Do you think that technology can assist in asking each student for a response?

3. Participate in a jigsaw cooperative learning strategy to create an activity in which you have a chance to teach others some of the fundamental elements of writing sound objective item formats. In a group of four, decide each individual's choice as expert in one of four formats: multiple choice, true/false, matching, and completion. Each group then decides what information will be taught and what type of material will be created to facilitate teaching the members of the group. In the next class meeting, take responsibility for using your expert knowledge to teach other group members.

4. Locate an off-the-shelf exam from a commercial science, health, or social studies textbook series. Apply the suggestions for sound item construction

to an analysis of the located tests or assessments. Share what you have discovered about these types of tests. What are the major lessons to be learned?

5. Distribute an essay question that is worth 10 points. Have a model answer available. Direct half of your class to assign points to the model answer, but do not allow the other half of your class to do so. Provide several student samples for the teacher candidates to score. Examine the scores from the two groups and note the range of scores in each. Discuss with the students some of the implications that can be generated from this exercise.

Performance Assessment: A Powerful Tool

1. To be able to make decisions about the appropriate use of performance assessments in elementary classrooms

2. To recognize and be able to employ the terminology associated with performance assessments

3. To be able to construct rubrics, checklists, and anecdotal record forms for use in elementary classrooms

4. To be able to develop a performance assessment and accompanying instrumentation that is aligned with a designated standard

The Use of Performance Assessment

Performance assessment is a powerful tool that teachers must understand and employ in order to measure what students know, and more important, what they can do. Almost every state has adopted academic standards as curricular targets for students. These standards usually include content statements and observable verbs that ensure that the standard serves as a statement of expectations about what students can do. Teaching that accommodates the acquisition and application of knowledge must employ opportunities for students to demonstrate their achievement. Performance assessments are demonstrations of that mastery.

The following assigned classroom tasks are examples of performance assessments:

- First graders are presented with a calendar of the month of March showing the weather that occurred for each school day. They are asked to make a graph indicating the number of cloudy, sunny, rainy, and snowy days from the data on the calendar.

- Fourth graders must plan a series of nutritional meals costing less than a fixed-dollar value. The 3-day plan should include an explanation of the nutritional value of each meal and the cost of preparing the meal.

- Three sixth-grade students are required to pack a suitcase for a modern-day trip on the *Mayflower*. They are required to research the *Mayflower's* trip to gain an idea of what their needs will be. They may take contemporary items, but the contents of the one suitcase for the three students cannot weigh more than 60 pounds.

An examination of these tasks shows the difficulty of assessing student success if we limit ourselves to using only selection type, objective item formats (multiple choice, true/false, or matching). Selection is an excellent means of assessing knowledge, but the weather in March, for instance, is not the only area we want to assess in students. Our interest is also in assessing the first graders' ability to construct a graph. Similarly, in the other tasks we are trying to assess the student's demonstration of what they have learned and what they are able to do with the information through the development of a product.

 Can you think of performance assessments that you completed? List the knowledge and skills that you needed to employ to be able to successfully complete the performance assessment.

Terminology and Definitions

Along with the increased amount of attention focused on assessment reform, there has been a resultant growth in the vocabulary surrounding performance assessment. Unfortunately, that growth has resulted in misuse and inaccuracies in the terminology. The danger associated with the misuse of terms is that it sometimes causes confusion among educators and, most certainly, the public. Determining how a performance assessment is different from an alternative assessment or an authentic assessment can be tedious and difficult.

The following definitions are offered not to create an argument about terminology but to guide our discussion later in the chapter. They help to clarify and establish boundaries that facilitate your understanding as a practicing professional.

Alternative assessments are any assessments that are not written multiple-choice, matching, or true/false tests. Under this definition, a written essay exam is considered an alternative assessment. Another example might be an oral presentation or a project.

Performance assessments are assessments that require students to use knowledge and skills in the completion of some project or task. Performance assessments are not limited to, but are commonly recognized in elementary schools as, the three Ps:

portfolios, projects, and performance tasks. Portfolios are relatively common, but the difference between performance projects and performance tasks requires clarification. The main difference lies in the amount of student effort and time that is spent completing them. Tasks are usually completed in one or two class periods; projects require multiple class sessions that may encumber weeks of student effort.

Authentic assessments are assessments that require students to complete tasks closely resembling activities that are completed in real life. An example of an authentic assessment might be primary-age children buying items from the school store using class money and computing the correct monetary transaction. For teacher candidates, field experiences and student teaching are exemplary models of performance assessments that involve the application of knowledge and skills in a real-life activity.

Figure 4-1 illustrates the relationship of these three types of assessment.

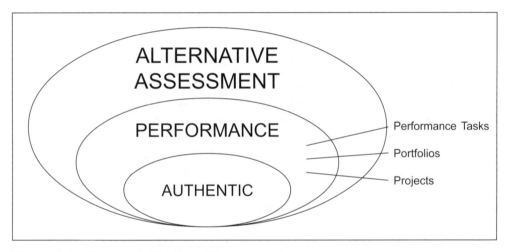

Figure 4-1. Frequently Mentioned Assessments

Performance assessments can be thought of as supply formats rather than selection formats. Supply formats require the student to generate a product, an answer, or a performance rather than choose one from a list of possible answers. Selection formats, on the other hand, include choosing from several options: multiple choice, true/false, or matching. The main drawback of the exclusive use of selection formats is that the teacher is never privy to the student's thinking in selecting the responses. This denies the teacher any opportunity to provide corrective feedback unless the teacher deliberately addresses the questions with each student. Classroom teachers are too busy to permit such close scrutiny of each person's answers.

Performance assessments are therefore beneficial for teachers who want to monitor and provide feedback to students' processes and the development of responses. If we think back to the first principle of sound assessment, the employment of multiple measures, it becomes clear that performance assessments provide a different sort of evidence than might be available from true/false, multiple-choice, and matching tests.

Implementing Performance Assessment

Like every type of classroom assessment, performance assessment begins at the planning stage of the instructional process. Let's approach the planning by looking at the words *performance* and *assessment*. A performance is a well-thought-out opportunity for a student to demonstrate competency in an area of study. An assessment is an instrument that facilitates the collection of information, permitting the teacher to make judgments about the student's competency based on that performance. With this in mind, we must concern ourselves with providing congruence. According to McTighe and Ferrara (1996), we must be careful to make sure that the assessments we construct measure what the student has been prepared to do. Holding students to performance measures for which they have received an inadequate opportunity to learn is insensitive and unethical. In short, effective planning for performance assessments is a thoughtful process.

The Need for Instructional Alignment

All lessons should be designed around clear targets, instructional activities that provide students with opportunities to approximate those target levels, and assessments that collect data concerning student mastery of those targets. The concept of instructional alignment in performance assessment is critical. If we intend to use a particular performance assessment, we have a responsibility to prepare instructional activities that encourage, support, and provide feedback so that students can successfully respond to the performance assessment. If you are unclear about this, reread the second principle of sound assessment in chapter 1.

Unfortunately, instructional alignment has not always been present in the development of alternative assessments. As performance assessments have gained increased acceptance, some teachers have begun to respond to this shift by implementing scoring mechanisms (rubrics, checklists, and portfolios), without clearly thinking about the nature of their instructional goals or activities. Unfortunately, this has amounted to simply changing the assessment form used to generate a score for students. Instead of a student receiving a score of 89% on a writing sample, for instance, he or she would be awarded a 4 on a 5-point holistic rubric. Using a rubric as a scoring instrument does not necessarily make an activity a performance assessment. Any scoring mechanism that is unsupported by meaningful instruction makes little change in what and how students learn.

The term *performance assessment* might itself be part of the problem. The word *assessment* might suggest that the shift to performance-based instruction is primarily concerned with the assessment aspect of teaching. Nothing could be further from the truth. For performance assessment to be part of effective instruction, there must be performance planning and performance instructional activities as well as performance assessment. This is the direct application of the second principle of sound assessment.

Think back to our discussion of reliability and validity in chapter 1. How would these qualities assessments be affected if we failed to prepare students before asking them to complete a performance assessment?

Planning and Designing Performance Assessments

Understanding how to plan and design performance assessments for classroom use is a critical skill for teachers. Unfortunately, there is a not a single best method that will result in valid and reliable performance assessments. Table 4-1 provides four steps that can be used to develop effective performance assessments in elementary and middle schools. In most cases the quality of the assessment is determined by clear thinking and hard work on the part of the developer. The four steps are described below.

Table 4-1. Steps in the Completion of a Performance Assessment that Addresses a Standard

Step 1	Have a clear purpose that identifies the decisions to be made from the performance assessment.
Step 2	Designate a standard and develop a performance task or activity that generates evidence of student mastery of that standard. Redefine the standard. Develop a performance task or project.
Step 3	Choose and develop an appropriate scoring instrument. Checklists Rubrics Anecdotal records
Step 4	Utilize, test, and redesign the assessment and the instrument as necessary.

Clear Purpose

A fundamental understanding in the area of measurement is that every test should have a clear purpose. We should not test or assess children without a clear understanding of the reason we are evaluating them. Performance assessments are no different from any other assessment in this way. The purposes of performance assessments that can be used by classroom teachers are reasonably standard. If one assumes that the performance assessment fits within the instructional design of the school district and/or classroom, then several purposes are typical:

- Performance assessments can be used for diagnostic purposes—to determine student strengths and weaknesses prior to instruction.

- Performance assessments can be used to determine mastery of important knowledge and skills—what children know and are able to do. These are generally administered formatively or summatively and result in classroom grading decisions and/or other rankings.

- Performance assessments can be used for the administrative ranking of students. Many states rely on performance measures as an accountability tool for judging the quality of schools.

If the performance assessment is externally developed and administered to all classrooms, then its purpose is quite different from that of a teacher-constructed performance assessment. For example, most states now require a writing examination that is developed and scored by outside evaluators for state departments of education. The data generated from the assessment is usually pooled in order for school officials to make generalized statements about student success. Frequently, in these types of assessments, individual student results are not returned to the student or the classroom teacher. The purpose of this type of performance assessment is not diagnostic or instructional, but to establish accountability and make comparative judgments about the quality of instruction in schools. Other than such state examinations, there are few justifications for students not to receive feedback concerning their results on a performance assessment. Thus, determining the purpose is the first step of designing performance assessments.

Designated Standards

Because most states now employ standards to develop curriculum and focus teaching effort toward specific areas, it seems practical to design the classroom performance assessments to assess the skills and knowledge delineated in the standards. There are advantages to engaging in the development of these activities with groups of teachers. First, inexperienced teachers might have difficulty relating to appropriate expectations for the achievement of students in a particular grade. Second, teamwork is necessary for the design of sequential and developmental activities that meet district and state curriculum standards.

First, redefine the standard so that everyone in the group has an idea of what is asked of students. Despite the notion that current standards are clearly stated goals and easily understood, one can never be too sure that everyone in the group defines the standard in the same way. There is value in rereading and discussing the standard as a group. Discussion helps to bring clarity and consensus to the group. It is important to discuss how students will be able to show that they have mastered this standard. Most standards are written as content standards and do not have performance levels associated with them. Thus, the group will have to decide not only what the student must be able to do, but also how well must he or she should be able to do it.

Based on a need to be more specific in the use of standards, some states have moved to focusing teacher and student efforts toward parts of the standards. These are referred to as *anchors* or *benchmarks* depending on the state or region. Their purpose is to narrow the range of material that must be emphasized to complete the standard, as well as to identify the content that is likely to be tested by the state assessment.

Here is an example of a state standard for grade 3 math: "Organize and display data using pictures, tallies, tables, bar graphs, and pictographs."

The group would begin by making sure that everyone has the same definition of what it means for third graders to organize and display data. The group also needs to discuss which of the listed options will be the focus of the performance assessment. It is tempting to give students the option of using any of the methods mentioned for displaying the data. If that is the case, the data has to be of the type that can easily and correctly be displayed by any of the suggested means. Since that is rare, it is probably better to select one of the methods. Finally, there should be agreement on the level of sophistication of the table or bar graph. Discussions of this nature must be part of redefining the standards.

Choose a standard or an anchor that applies in the subject and grade you teach or would like to teach. Examine the standard for the knowledge and skills required for students to complete it. Ask another person to examine the same standard and compare your thoughts. If they are different, what are the implications for instruction and assessment?

Second, construct the assessment task that provides evidence of student achievement of the standard. This can be complicated, frustrating, and time-consuming. The time spent brainstorming and discussing tasks might seem fruitless to some members of the group. Despite the appearance of wasted time, however, this is a necessary part of creating a meaningful task. Creating a task that requires children to think also requires teachers to think. With experience and practice you will become more efficient, and the time spent will become more productive.

The creation of the performance task must be based on the developmental abilities of the students. Grade-level groups are usually helpful to inexperienced teachers because the group can come to a consensus on the general developmental needs and expectations of children in that grade. When possible, it is important to pool teacher resource materials and alternate textbooks as a springboard for ideas. Samples of existing performance assessments can be retrieved online, and these can help to activate teacher thinking and creativity. Shepard (1995) says the following:

> Professional, autonomous teachers do not need canned curriculum pack-
> ages or scripted lessons. If you want teachers to try significantly different
> content and modes of instruction . . . they have neither the time nor the
> know-how (initially) to invent their own materials. What worked best was for
> us to supply good examples in response to teacher identified topics. Teach-
> ers then extended the examples and invented entire instructional units. (p.
> 42)

After agreeing on a task, make sure that the task will permit you to make a valid inference about the student's ability to meet the standard. Does the student response or product generate convincing evidence that the student can meet the standard? Would an impartial person outside your classroom be equally convinced? If you can answer these questions affirmatively, you are on the way to developing a useful performance task.

Does the task have different levels of mastery, or does it result in complete mastery or complete failure? If the latter, then you have probably chosen a task that is too narrow. A performance assessment should provide students with an opportunity to display multiple skill levels. Since meaningful skills can be adequately displayed across a continuum of mastery, it's important to design a task that will allow for differences.

Appropriate Scoring Instruments

So far, we have established the purpose and developed the performance task that matches a standard. Now the group must decide what instrument will be used to score students' efforts. The need to assess the skills and knowledge associated with a given performance assessment eliminates or reduces the desirability of written objective testing instruments. McTighe and Ferrara (1996) created a framework of assessment types that provides possible instruments from which to choose. The following instruments are closely associated with performance assessment:

- Checklists
- Rubrics
- Anecdotal records

Let's review some characteristics of each of these instruments, or measurement tools, and discuss why the group might use one versus another to judge and provide feedback to a student in a performance assessment. The choice of the most appropriate instrument is based on the factors of the classroom, the pupils, and the instruction.

Checklists

A checklist is a list of important constructs to be observed or recorded in response to a student's performance or product. For example, suppose that the performance assessment is designed for students to be able to create a PowerPoint presentation. The group has decided that the performance (product) should generate evidence that the student included at least 10 slides, the slides were sequenced and ran effectively, buttons were used to create branching alternatives, multiple fonts and backgrounds were used appropriately, and there were no spelling or grammar errors in the text. As the student demonstrated the PowerPoint presentation, the evaluator would be looking for the presence of these items and checking them off.

Using a checklist to observe a student performance requires some skill and practice. Although a checklist clearly delineates the areas of your focus, the student performance sometimes requires that all of the key areas be performed simultaneously. If so, it is advisable to limit the number of items on the checklist and provide a reasonable amount of time in which to conduct the observation of the student or the product. For instance, you would not want to develop a 20-item checklist to assess a one-minute impromptu speech. Table 4-2 shows two sample checklists.

Table 4-2. Examples of Checklists

Checklist for a PowerPoint Presentation

	Yes	No
Presentation contains at least 10 slides.		
The slides are correctly sequenced and run effectively.		
Buttons offer branching opportunities.		
Multiple fonts and backgrounds are used appropriately.		
There are limited errors in grammar and spelling.		

Checklist for 2-Minute Oral Presentation

Construct	Yes	No
The speaker maintains eye contact throughout the speech.		
The speaker's delivery is clear and well articulated.		
The speech was approximately 2 minutes—not too long and not too short.		
The volume of the speaker's voice is adequate for all persons to hear.		

Checklists have some very definite advantages. They can usually be developed quickly and do not require the same degree of preparation that you will encounter in creating and using other instruments. Since time is so important to teachers, checklists are often a convenient assessment tool. Another advantage is that the checklist helps to focus the student efforts toward what is important. Placing an item on the checklist verifies its importance to the students. It's entirely reasonable to include students' input in the design of the checklist so that they gain a sense of ownership in deciding what is important in the performance. The checklist can be compared to a grocery list. Although there are many items in the grocery store (as there are many observable behaviors in a performance assessment), we choose only the important ones to place in our shopping cart.

A final advantage is the ease with which a checklist can be used. Because of its design, we are merely observing for the presence of a quality or an action. We are not rendering judgment about the degree of the quality or action, and that makes the use of the checklist much easier than some other evaluative instruments.

There are also disadvantages to the use of a checklist. Checklists are yes or no instruments. They provide information about the presence of a quality but do little to explain the adequacy, intensity, or depth of the quality. In a sense, the very nature of what makes a checklist so easy to develop also cripples its ability to generate quality feedback to the student. Here is an example. Suppose that your grade-level group decides to use a checklist to judge the quality of an oral presentation with third graders. They develop the checklist with the students and prepare the students to give their oral presentations. One of the areas each teacher is looking for in this oral presentation is eye contact. A child starts his presentation by focusing on his shoelaces; in the second half, however, he remembers that eye contact is an important part of public speaking and begins to make effective visual contact with the classroom audience. Does the teacher check yes or no for "maintains eye contact"? Clearly the student did, eventually, but this is not the degree of eye contact that all observers might view as acceptable. Thus, a checklist is easily developed and used, but it creates scoring problems because of the limitation of its choices.

 In the above example, could a comments section be used to improve the checklist and indicate how the student might improve his performance?

Rubrics

Another assessment tool is rubrics. There are several definitions for rubrics, so it is important to define them clearly. Rubrics are a combination of scales indicating a continuum of student performance, constructs, or other things that matter, and criteria statements that describe the presence of a quality (Andrade, 2000). Rubrics answer the question: What do various degrees of mastery of a performance task look like? For example, many states utilize *4, 3, 2,* and *1* to describe the degrees of quality of student writing in different areas: focus, ideas, organization, details, content, conventions, and style. Included with these numbers are descriptions of what each of the numbers represents with respect to student writing. Figures 4-2a–e are an example of a math performance task, "Name the Graph," that can be used for the purpose of determining (perhaps as a pretest) what students understand about graphing. This example includes the task (*a*), two student completed samples (*b* and *c*) and an accompanying scoring rubric (*d* and *e*).

Reflection   Examine the two student samples. What differences do you note in them that might influence your instructional decision making? Do the students possess the same instructional needs? Do we need more information?

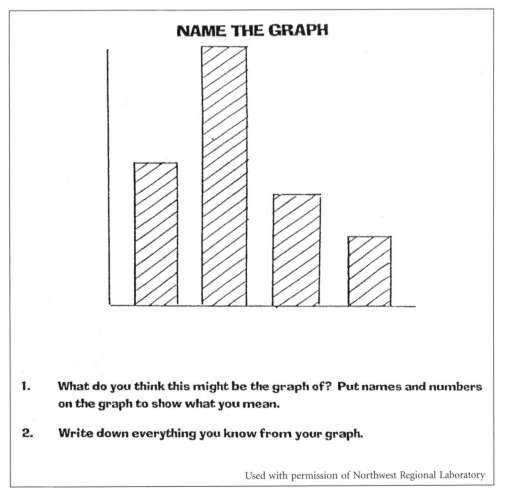

NAME THE GRAPH

1.   **What do you think this might be the graph of? Put names and numbers on the graph to show what you mean.**

2.   **Write down everything you know from your graph.**

Used with permission of Northwest Regional Laboratory

Figure 4-2a. Name the Graph Performance Task

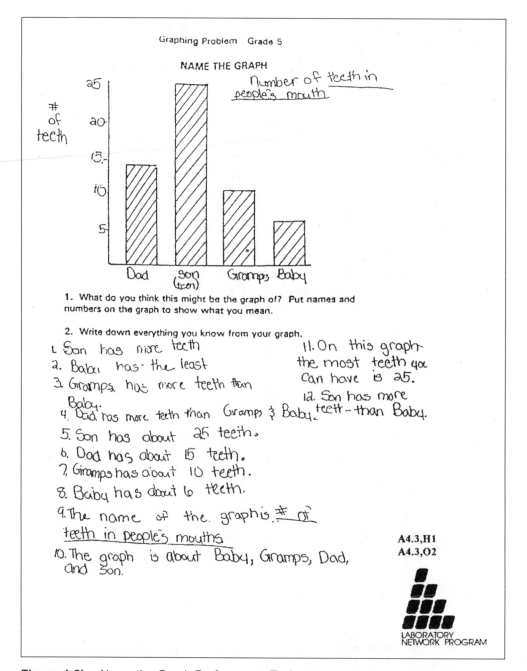

Graphing Problem   Grade 5

NAME THE GRAPH

number of teeth in people's mouth

# of teeth

1. What do you think this might be the graph of? Put names and numbers on the graph to show what you mean.

2. Write down everything you know from your graph.

1. Son has more teeth
2. Baby has the least
3. Gramps has more teeth than Baby.
4. Dad has more teeth than Gramps & Baby.
5. Son has about 25 teeth.
6. Dad has about 15 teeth.
7. Gramps has about 10 teeth.
8. Baby has about 6 teeth.
9. The name of the graph is # of teeth in people's mouths
10. The graph is about Baby, Gramps, Dad, and Son.

11. On this graph the most teeth you can have is 25.
12. Son has more teeth than Baby.

A4.3,H1
A4.3,O2

LABORATORY
NETWORK PROGRAM

Figure 4-2b. Name the Graph Performance Task

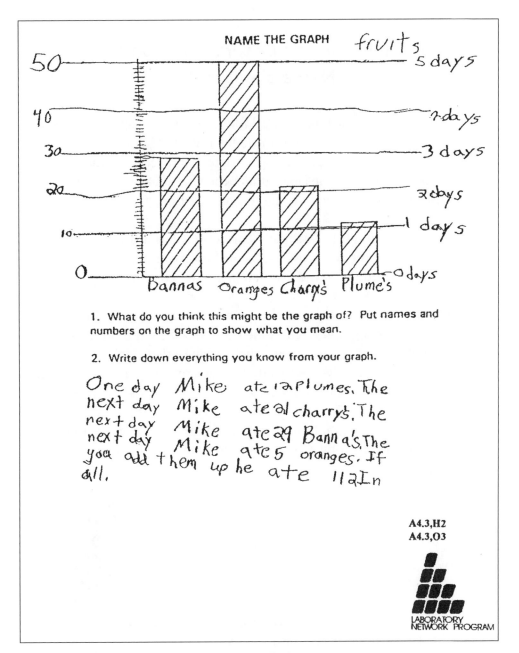

NAME THE GRAPH   fruits

50 ————————————————————— 5 days

40 —————————————————————— 2-days

30 ————————————————————— 3 days

2a ———————————————————— 2 days

10 ————————————————————— 1 days

0 ————————————————————— 0 days

Bannas   Oranges Charry's Plume's

1. What do you think this might be the graph of? Put names and
numbers on the graph to show what you mean.

2. Write down everything you know from your graph.

One day Mike ate 12 Plumes. The
next day Mike ate 21 charry's. The
next day Mike ate 29 Banna's. The
next day Mike ate 5 oranges. If
you add them up he ate 112 In
all.

A4.3,H2
A4.3,O3

LABORATORY
NETWORK PROGRAM

Figure 4-2c. Name the Graph Performance Task

Task-Specific Criteria, Version 1: Name the Graph

4: Has a title under each bar, a label for each axis, and appropriate values listed on the y-axis. Has a title for the whole graph. The values along the y-axis are spaced appropriately and relate to the relative heights of the bars. The labels under each bar make sense. There are at least five things listed for the second question.

3: The student graph is essentially correct but has at least one major thing wrong. For the most part, conclusions in part 2 are reasonable—at least three of the five statements are correct.

2: The student shows some understanding of the sorts of things that might go into a graph, such as the need for labels and numbers, but the response has serious errors, such as labels that don't make sense and numbers on the y-axis that don't bear a relationship to the height of the graphs. Conclusions are sketchy.

1: Most parts of the graph display lack of understanding, are missing, or are just plain wrong. Conclusions do not logically follow from the graph.

A4.3,H2
A4.3,O3

LABORATORY
NETWORK PROGRAM

Figure 4-2d. Name the Graph Performance Task

Task-Specific Criteria, Version 2:
Name the Graph

Number of Points	Feature
1	Graph titled
1	x-axis labeled
1	y-axis labeled
1	Bars labeled
2	Values on y-axis spaced appropriately and related correctly to bars
3	1 point for up to two correct conclusions 2 points for three to four correct conclusions 3 points for five or more correct conclusions

A4.3,H2
A4.3,O3

LABORATORY
NETWORK PROGRAM

Figure 4-2e. Name the Graph Performance Task

An advantage of rubrics is that they contain expanded definitions of performance. This provides the teachers and students with an opportunity to judge a performance according to its relative position on a continuum of mastery. This differs greatly from the checklist's yes or no option. These expanded definitions are helpful in providing feedback to the students and assist in controlling the reliability in scoring. However, reporting to a student that he or she received a 3 on a 5-point rubric does little to improve the student's next performance. We should not substitute a score for direct and precise feedback that will improve the student's skills. The future performances of students are more likely to be impacted by precise and detailed feedback rather than by a single score.

Another advantage is that rubrics can be reused with small amounts of alteration for other performance tasks. The advantage of reusing the rubric is to show the development of the child's skills after repeated practice. This is most likely to occur in middle school. In K–3, however, the rubric will often have to be adjusted because the students frequently master the criteria expressed in the rubric. The degree of difficulty has to be increased in order to challenge the students. In short, the students' achievement outraces the rubric's utility.

A disadvantage is that rubric development takes time. The continuum of performance needs to be clearly thought out. Inexperienced teachers might not be aware of the range of possible student performances in the grade they are assigned to teach. Therefore, it is reasonable to consult an experienced teacher about typical levels of student performance in the grade you're teaching. If you are not able to seek the advice of others, another method you can use to gauge the relative quality of your student performances is to collect all the products and sort them into distinct piles. Designate one pile for below-average performances, one for average, and one for above-average work to get a sense of the range of student achievement. If you can further subdivide the lower and the upper piles, it becomes easy to see how you could have student samples for five different levels of achievement.

Another time-consuming part of rubric development involves the wording of the criteria. Precise wording of the criteria statements helps to ensure understanding between the teacher and the student. Achieving this understanding often requires the examination of anchor papers. Finally, few teacher-developed rubrics succeed in their original form. Often, once you have used a rubric, you will want to alter it to more effectively fit your classroom needs. It is rare that a rubric used for the first time with students is found to work perfectly. These disadvantages are not meant to discourage the use of rubrics but merely to point out realistic problem areas.

Table 4-3 compares the advantages and disadvantages of rubrics and checklists.

Anecdotal Records

Teachers can also judge student performances through the use of anecdotal records. This collection of information is usually achieved through the observation of students. Although teachers constantly make observations of students, these are not to be confused with this instrument. Anecdotal records require the formal transcribing of the teacher's observation of specifically targeted student behaviors.

Anecdotal records are focused on a student behavior and document its frequency or quality. Here is an example. Suppose you are interested in collecting information about a student's independent reading behavior. One means would be to require the student to create a list of all the books that he or she read in a given period. Another

Table 4-3.   Advantages and Disadvantages of Checklists and Rubrics Compared

	Rubric	**Checklist**
Development	Provides for a more detailed description of the student's performance, but is more time consuming to create. Criteria statements for the middle levels are the most difficult to determine.	Easier to construct than rubrics. Criteria statements are not necessary. Few disadvantages.
Inference Making	Because of the multiple levels of performance, the inference making is lower than that of the checklist, but it requires training and practice.	Focuses student effort. Inferences are higher because they are based on limited criteria.
Feedback	Analytical rubrics offer feedback about each specific area, but feedback is static and does not provide information about how the student might reach the next level of the rubric.	Easily generated, but not specific or corrective because of limited criteria statements.
Redoing	If the rubric is well constructed, few major changes are necessary. Poor rubrics require additional levels and criteria statements and can be time-consuming to improve.	Easily completed or changed to align with the purpose of the assessment, but changing may not significantly improve the value of the feedback generated.

way would be to observe the student during sustained silent reading and note, using an anecdotal record, the student's independent reading behavior. In the first example, the list of books is based on student memory and truthfulness. Observing the student's behavior during reading is a more accurate indicator of the student's independent reading activity. In this case the records would be kept on a form that includes a description of the student behavior, the date or time, and the frequency of the behavior (when necessary). In order to complete useful anecdotal records, you should focus on a small number of children at a time. It is equally important to limit the observation to a specific set of student behaviors. Practical suggestions for the completion of anecdotal records include the following:

1. Keep a clipboard that is solely for the purpose of record keeping.

2. Keep a supply of 1-inch mailing labels with the clipboard. Write the names of the students you intend to observe and the date of the observation on the label prior to using them.

3. Write information on the labels that is specific and observable. Keep in mind that you will have to interpret this information in a meaningful way in a conference or for the completion of a report card.

4. Transfer the labels to a portfolio or a binder that keeps student data for a conference with parents or students.

The most important advantage of anecdotal records is that they capture evidence of students in the act of completing a task. Instead of judging the student's actions by examining a product that is completed, anecdotal records document the action of the student in the process, when the teacher can observe the behaviors. Boyd-Batstone (2004) suggests that in a standards-driven environment, it is important for teachers to consider qualitative types of assessments. He states that anecdotal records "provide measures that fill in the gaps to give teachers immediate information to plan for instruction."

Examples of anecdotal records used for classroom management and to document reading progress will be given in chapters 8 and 9.

The most obvious disadvantage associated with anecdotal records is their subjectivity. Observations of students are always subject to a certain level of bias on the part of the teacher. Because of this danger, teachers and the public sometimes look upon observation of students with less credibility than they do other formal (objective) measures of assessment. In short, anecdotal records have not been as respected as other forms of assessment. The acceptance of anecdotal records as an important assessment tool in the developing of reading skills in elementary schools, however, is well documented (Clay, 1993; Goodman, 1978).

Furthermore, to be useful and valid, anecdotal records must indicate frequency. It is difficult and dangerous to develop an accurate inference concerning a student based on a single observation. A general rule is to refrain from any judgment concerning students until after observing the behavior 3 times. Thus, you can understand the difficulty in making observations of all students in a classroom with enough frequency to support inferences. Classrooms are busy places that typically do not lend themselves to the deliberate observation of all students for extended amounts of time. It is therefore sometimes helpful to use anecdotal records as additional support for an inference based on other, more objective measures. Remember the first principle of sound assessment: the use of multiple forms of assessment for effective decision making. Table 4-4 lists the uses of anecdotal records.

Can you see why teachers might select different types of assessment instruments in order to assess different types of performances? Also, a checklist that is used in a formative manner might be developed into a more specific rubric after continued use and development with students. Why might it be a good idea to begin with a checklist?

Table 4-4.   The Uses of Anecdotal Records According to Targeted Behaviors

Target Behaviors	Components	Data
Student Behavior Management	Should include date, frequency, and nature of behavior.	Can be used to inform placement decisions, parent or student conferences, and general classroom management decisions.
Academic Success	Should include data that indicates success or difficulties. For example, in literacy instruction, fluency, miscues, and comprehension comments can be noted.	Informs instructional decisions about individual student needs. Applies directly to the student's instructional needs.
Social Interaction	Should include date, frequency, and nature of behavior.	Can be collected about students' interaction in cooperative learning situations. Can also reveal social relationships among students.

Assessment Testing and Redesign

This brings us to the fourth and final step in the development of a performance assessment. So far, you have established a purpose, developed a performance task, and selected and constructed an appropriate scoring instrument. The main thrust of the fourth step is to encourage the evaluation and redesign of the task as well as the appropriate modification of the instrument. Few checklists or scoring rubrics are ever entirely effective in their first use.

The revision of the task is a necessary give-and-take process that results in wholesale changes, slight modifications, or, in unfortunate situations, the complete scrapping of it. For example, one reason for modifying the task might be that the task requires more or less structure. If there is too little structure, the students will not understand what they are supposed to do. If there is too much structure, the students will not be challenged, and many of the students' products will be identical or closely resemble each other.

Rubrics in particular always seem to require modification. After scoring student products, you might find that the language that seemed so clear in the development part of the process doesn't fit the scoring of students' efforts. In this case, modifying the rubric language will make it more usable for the future. Tierney and Simon (2004) suggest reviewing the criterion statement to make sure that constructs are not mixed and language in consistent.

Another problem with a rubric is that you might have created an incorrect number of levels for the student product or process. For example, suppose your group anticipated that a 3-point rubric would be capable of assessing the students' work, then after scoring, realizes that there are severe quality differences in students who have received the same score. To solve the problem, the group must modify the rubric, making it a 4-point rubric to allow the students' work to be more accurately sorted. Can you imagine a rubric containing too many levels (e.g., 6 points)? What problems might occur from this?

Now that we have concluded the process of planning and designing a performance assessment, let's discuss how to design rubrics, perhaps the most familiar instrument associated with performance assessments.

How to Develop Scoring Rubrics

There are three "C terms" that must be considered when developing scoring rubrics to be used with performance assessments: constructs, continuum, and criteria statements. Each of these terms describes an aspect of rubrics that is critical to their development. Commercially developed rubrics are readily available from publishers and easily retrievable from the Internet. Web sites designed for the development of rubrics include, but are not limited to, the following: www.teach-nology.com and www.rubistar.com.

The information that follows is designed to help you develop rubrics for performances in your classroom. Finding rubrics and checklists that ideally fit your creative instructional goals might be somewhat difficult. After reading this part of the chapter, you should be able to modify existing or commercially developed scoring instruments to your own instructional needs.

Constructs

Constructs are the aspects of student performance that ultimately contribute to the student's successful completion of the performance assessment. The observable aspects of a pupil's performance or product are the means by which teachers judge the rate or depth of a student's achievement. For example, if the purpose of the performance assessment is to observe the quality of a student's oral presentation skills, we must first identify the important elements of a good oral presentation. The following features come to mind: eye contact, posture, rate of speaking, gestures, and organization. Each time we decide to develop a performance assessment, we will need to carefully identify the constructs of student performance.

There are plenty of constructs that could be emphasized in every performance assessment. Part of your job is to sort out the most important constructs that you will emphasize in your teaching. The teacher has a responsibility not only to select the appropriate constructs for students but also to decide what constructs will not be emphasized.

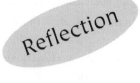

Using a noninstructional example, let's try to clarify what constructs might be used in the assessment of an individual's performance. What constructs might we identify to rate the performance of a server at a restaurant?

You may allow student input when selecting the important constructs. This develops ownership and helps students to recognize the elements of quality that can be applied in their own future work. Students should always be aware of and clearly understand the criteria for which they are being held responsible. Grant Wiggins (1993) coined the simple but powerful phase associated with sharing performance targets with students: "No surprises. No excuses."

There are some necessary cautions in the development of constructs. Inexperienced or beginning teachers might be inclined to include too many constructs in the development of the scoring rubric. This creates an overload for the student and makes the use of the rubric by the teacher nearly impossible. It is not necessary to employ every construct of desirable performance in a scoring rubric. As student skill development increases with time and practice, additional constructs may be included. For example, think about the first lesson in which you were observed teaching students. If you had been expected to perform as an experienced teacher in all aspects of teaching, you probably would have failed miserably. The observer most likely pinpointed several areas of strength and discussed several areas for your improvement. We cannot initially expect students to demonstrate expert performance, nor should we expect them to be accomplished in all aspects of the task. After effective teaching and corrective feedback, however, we will maintain high expectations for their performance.

The key to identifying performance constructs is to examine the task or product and determine the important elements. In the case of a process, you might want to perform a task analysis, in which you trace the development of the task from its first to its last step and keep in mind the important subskills that contribute to the overall completion of the project. For example, if the performance assessment requires that students use the scientific method, then the important constructs are creating a reasonable hypothesis, doing sound testing, making accurate interpretations, and drawing appropriate conclusions. We would also analyze the subtasks in each of these activities. Our job is to determine what we are looking for in the student performance by imagining the logical development of an acceptable product.

Another means of identifying performance constructs is to consider aspects of quality. This is especially true when the result of the performance is a product rather than a process. In the case of a student's handwriting performance, we observe for elements of quality such as slant, letter formation, and letter separation. In a more cognitively related product, we might look for the qualities of written expression, such as organization, content, style, conventions, and focus. This is not to suggest that process and product are easily separated or that that is even desirable. It is merely meant to help you sort out your intended targets.

Let's develop a set of performance constructs for a noninstructional product. Although you might not see its immediate value, this activity will provide you with an opportunity to see how gauging the quality of a product tells you something about the process. Try to come up with the constructs you believe are critical for rating a "well-tied tie." *No bow ties, please!* Remember, you're looking for the components of a product: a tie that is tied correctly and whose appearance is pleasing. If you're arguing about stripes and matching the pattern of the shirt, you're getting off the track. Focus on the tie being tied correctly.

I have identified three constructs (and there may be more). First, the knot should be well tied. Second, the length of the tie should be appropriate. Third (and this one you probably didn't get!) the drape of the tie, or how it lies on the shirt, should be straight and flat.

Continuum

The *continuum* is the range of the construct's intensity, frequency, or quality. In essence, after you have identified a construct you must consider the distance that separates poor student performance from excellent student performance. It has become commonplace for most continuums to be based on a four-point range of student achievement. Typical descriptors on the continuum are *accomplished, proficient, basic,* and *below basic.* This does not rule out using more or fewer descriptors, depending on the specific construct in question.

Rubrics that are available online and from other sources might designate a continuum that exceeds a reasonable display of student performance. For example, in a noninstructional situation, let's say that a scale at a local hospital indicates 10 gradations of pain. It seems difficult to imagine that any person could clearly differentiate among all those levels of pain. At best, something might be extremely painful, moderately painful, or not painful at all. Another example of a continuum is displayed in Figure 4-3. Here one can clearly see that the degree of stain is heaviest in the top example and fades after repeated applications of carpet remover. Notice how the darkness of the stain diminishes from top to bottom.

To use a classroom example, consider the continuums from 1 to 10 for the presence of focus, content, and conventions in a writing sample. Can 10 clearly identifiable differences exist in the quality of any of those three constructs in a student-generated writing piece? A rule for developing a continuum is to use a range of descriptors that possesses clearly identifiable levels of student achievement—no more and no fewer.

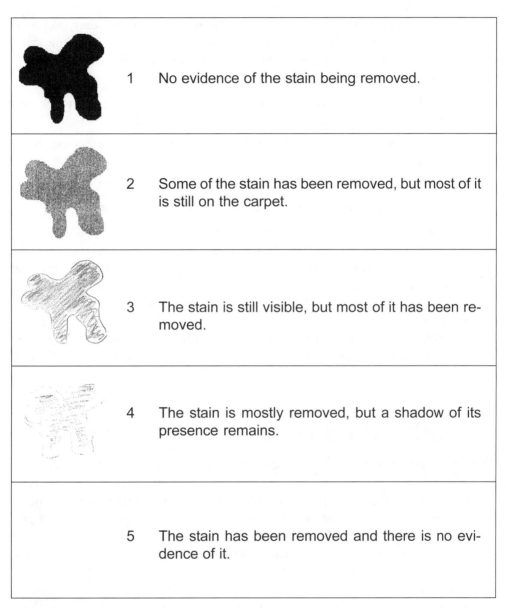

	1	No evidence of the stain being removed.
	2	Some of the stain has been removed, but most of it is still on the carpet.
	3	The stain is still visible, but most of it has been removed.
	4	The stain is mostly removed, but a shadow of its presence remains.
	5	The stain has been removed and there is no evidence of it.

Figure 4-3. Carpet Stain Continuum   *(Used with permission of Melissa Ash and Katy Luce.)*

Criteria Statements

Criteria statements are closely related to the continuum. As we develop the continuum by considering the range of possible student achievement, the *criteria statements* describe key points along the continuum that can be differentiated by both students and teachers. For example, if we are assessing the frequency or intensity of a construct, then criteria statements will include *always, frequently, sometimes,* and *never.*

Others might be more specific; for example, *four or more, two to three, once,* and *none*. Criteria statements can also describe the quality of a construct. Here are some criteria statements that describe a performance task that requires students to choose from among several apparently equal alternatives:

4   Makes a selection that adequately meets the decision criteria and answers the initial decision question

3   Accurately identifies the extent to which each alternative possesses each criterion

2   Identifies important and appropriate criteria for assessing the alternatives

1   Identifies important and appropriate alternatives to be considered

Let's go back to the noninstructional task that we described earlier, the well-tied tie. Each of the constructs (knot, length, and drape) possesses degrees of quality that can generate specific criteria statements. For example, the criteria for a well-tied knot might include its shape, size, and tightness. These criteria were developed by examining the product and identifying the key elements that would provide evidence to a teacher (or in this case, a tie critic) of successful completion of the process. It might be fun to develop a scoring instrument to use in your future encounters with persons who wear ties. (Just be diplomatic about sharing your data with the person wearing the tie.)

Ethical Issues in Performance Assessment

Students should have ample opportunities to practice or complete similar kinds of activities prior to receiving a grade for performance. This is especially true if the performance results in a high-stakes decision for the student. For example, if students are required to make a presentation that determines entrance into a gifted program, then students should have an opportunity to complete similar activities through the course of the year. In some cases, individuals who suggest that you are "teaching the test" will challenge your actions. It is important to understand the nature of what is suggested here in order to defend your judgment and to convince your critics that your intentions are ethical and desirable. Part of providing an appropriate setting for a performance assessment is to provide practice in the assessment itself. There is no value to "ambushing" students by assessing them for a grade or some other high-stakes decision without providing some practice in the performance.

Suppose you would like to assess a student's ability to write a persuasive piece to place in a writing portfolio that is kept by the school district for the purpose of showcasing the student's written expression. If you fail to provide this student with the opportunity to learn how to develop persuasive written arguments, then the school and the teacher have failed along with the student. Nevertheless, your critic might argue, the opportunity to learn is different from being assessed with a similar performance assessment. As long as you use a different writing prompt that requires the student to generate an original piece, you need not worry. The students should be permitted to practice (and ultimately learn) the skills in question. Writing a persuasive piece convincing their parents or guardians to purchase an item is completely different from a piece convincing members of their class to vote for them in the upcoming class election. In this case, you are not teaching the test, you are teaching them to use persuasive writing skills.

The following is a list of important points concerning the scoring of performance assessments:

- Carefully choose the means of communicating the results to students.

- Focus on a small number of areas to judge.

- Share and reinforce the important points with students prior to the assessment.

- Prepare the instrument with language the students and others can understand.

The judgment of student performance begins in the instructional planning stage. Effective performance assessment instruments should not be created after the students have completed the performance project. There is an ethical responsibility on the part of the teacher to share and make transparent the aspects of the performance that are most desirable.

Anchor Papers

Anchor papers are previously generated student samples of performances that are used to assist a teacher's scoring efforts. These can also be provided to students prior to the completion of a performance as a model or as examples of different levels of achievement. If you are attempting to explain to students the quality differences between a paper that has a "distinct" focus and one that has an "adequate" focus, students samples from the past are very helpful.

Collecting student products from year to year helps you to establish your expectations of students for a particular performance. Remember to keep samples of the entire range of student performance. By seeing a range of performances, students will be better able to anticipate the effort and focus they will need to complete the upcoming task.

Summary
Performance assessment provides teachers with the opportunity to determine what students know and what they are able to do. Planning is central to the success of performance assessments. Well-developed performances—whether they are tasks, projects, or portfolios—benefit from the use of systematic processes that identify purposes, alignment with standards, and proper

revisions. Efforts that provide students with opportunities to learn are crucial to both teacher and student success and contribute to the validity and reliability of teacher inferences. Appropriate instruments that support the use of performance assessment include checklists, anecdotal records, and scoring rubrics. The development of performance assessments is time-consuming and might take several efforts, but its importance justifies the necessary time and commitment.

Teaching Activities

1. Choose a state standard from reading, mathematics, or another discipline. Develop a performance assessment that will address the content and skills that are listed in the standard. Follow a step-by-step process that includes clarifying the standard, developing the prerequisite skill and knowledge, designing effective instructional activities, and developing a scoring rubric and/or checklist for the activity. If possible, field-test the performance assessment and score the student samples with others as a group activity. What did you learn from developing, administering, and scoring the performance?

2. Develop a scoring rubric for a writing task that is suitable to a specific grade. Discuss the domains of writing so that everyone in class understands the meaning of words such as *focus, content, organization, conventions,* and *style.* Score several pieces of student writing from the same grade. At a later date, critique your own feedback based on two elements of effective feedback: correctiveness and specificity. Decide if the feedback statements you wrote on students' papers would assist in making them better writers.

3. One of the most important steps in developing a rubric is to recognize the constructs (desirable qualities) of a process or product. An activity that is fun and helps people to identify desirable qualities is to have someone describe three qualities of a perfect mate. If that sounds as if it might invite a loss of control of your audience, ask them instead to identify the desirable qualities of a perfect potato chip.

4. Download a scoring rubric from a Web site and critique the criteria statements. Look for two qualities in the rubric's criteria statements. First, notice if the criteria statements include more than one construct on the continuum. Second, determine if the continuum is consistent. Do the statements develop without shifting from positive to negative within the continuum? How could it be changed in order to make it a better rubric?

Portfolios: Expanding the Assessment of Student Learning

Goals of the Chapter

1. To recognize the need for a clear purpose in the development of a portfolio
2. To be able to describe different purposes for using portfolios
3. To be able to develop an organizational framework for a portfolio
4. To understand the need for teaching that optimizes the use of a portfolio

The Implementation of Portfolios

One area of performance assessment that has gained much attention among elementary educators in the last decade is the use of portfolios. Portfolios have long been part of the assessment of personal work in the arts and other areas that are performance driven. In the early 1990s, riding the wave of assessment attention and expanded definitions of literacy, portfolios were heralded as an assessment process with the power to reform education. Arter and Spandel's (1992) definition of a student portfolio indicates that reformers saw the implementation of portfolios as an opportunity to restructure classroom teaching and learning. Student portfolios were defined as

> purposeful collections of student work that tells the story of the student's efforts, progress, or achievement in (a) given area(s). These collections must include student participation in selection of portfolio content; the guidelines for selection; the criteria for judging merit; and evidence of student reflection. (p. 36)

For classroom teachers who had never experienced portfolio use during their schooling or in their teacher preparation, this was quite a departure from traditional forms of assessment practice. Like most educational innovations, however, portfolios eventually became a reality in school organizations and classroom practices. The shift to using portfolios was not smooth.

One obstacle to the implementation of portfolios was the number of students that teachers meet each day. Middle school teachers questioned whether they could actually shift their daily instructional practices to accommodate the use of portfolios when they were meeting 120 to 140 students every other day. They quickly realized the overwhelming clerical reality of their well-meant instructional intentions.

Another set of challenges arose when teachers struggled with trying to grade the portfolios. Reliability issues in scoring and grading portfolios were raised locally and nationally. Should the portfolio receive a single grade, or should the grade be the average of the portfolio's contents? Completing report cards became more stressful because the basic structure of the report card did not readily accommodate portfolio assessments. Were portfolios to be included as part of the report card grade, or should they remain separate and not be included in the calculation of the student's grade? As with most educational innovations, adoption soon changed to adaptation. What has happened is a wonderful realization that portfolios are like all other assessment measures in that they have strengths and weaknesses. Most school systems have created boundaries or guidelines for the use of portfolios and view them as a useful assessment tool rather than as an instrument to reform teaching and learning. The recognition that portfolios have strengths and weaknesses was an important beginning to their realistic use in elementary and middle school classrooms.

Without question, portfolios expand the range of assessment that is provided by standardized testing practices. The major differences lie in the portfolio's ability to represent growth in many areas that cannot be assessed using standardized testing instruments. These include complex skill areas such as reading and writing and visible evidence of improvement and effort. The differences in the two assessments are illustrated in Table 5-1.

Portfolios can be used with all students. In the case of students with special needs, accommodations can be made to assist the student in the generation of quality written expression. The entire range of possible exception is beyond the scope of this textbook, but Table 5-2 lists some accommodations that might be used to assist the written expression of students with special needs.

Table 5-1. Differences in Assessment Outcomes Between Portfolios and Standardized Testing Practices

Portfolio	Testing
• Represents the range of reading and writing students are engaged in	• Assesses students across a limited range of reading and writing assignments that might not match what students do
• Engages students in assessing their progress and/or accomplishments and establishing ongoing learning goals	• Is scored mechanically or by teachers who have little input
• Measures each student's achievement while allowing for individual differences between students	• Assesses all students on the same dimensions
• Represents a collaborative approach to assessment	• Is not collaborative
• Has a goal of student self-assessment	• Does not have student assessment as a goal
• Addresses improvement, effort, and achievement	• Addresses achievement only
• Links assessment and teaching to learning	• Separates learning, testing, and teaching

From Tierney, Carter, & Desai (1991).

As with all other types of assessment, having a clear purpose for the assessment is of primary importance. The hard lessons learned with the early use of portfolios in classrooms were, in part, based on the reality that teachers and administrators failed to establish a clear purpose for the portfolios. As you will come to find out, if you fail to have a clear purpose for the portfolio, the process for the selection of items to place in the portfolio remains undefined. What frequently results from this lack of definition is a disconnected collection of papers or products that provide evidence of student efforts. Deriving clear inferences and drawing meaningful conclusions from these collections is difficult. Teachers who develop portfolios without clear purposes sacrifice much of the portfolio's effectiveness.

The Purposes of Portfolios

The list of possible purposes for portfolios in schools is extensive, and comprehensive coverage of those purposes exceeds the scope of this text. However, some purposes are more frequent in elementary and middle school classrooms. Teachers may decide to develop portfolios with students for the following reasons:

- To create collections of important work in an area of the curriculum

- To show growth or change over time

- To fulfill a requirement for your school or school district

Although the first two involve the most thought on your part, the third is a real-life possibility. In the case of a district-required portfolio you will need to consult other school personnel or a policy handbook to determine the required components. An example of this is a district wide writing portfolio that requires teachers of each grade to prepare a selected number of entries per school year. The entries are designated for each grade, so much of the selection process has already been done. We will discuss the other two purposes and how they shape the development and use of portfolios in classrooms.

Your experiences can be helpful to gaining an understanding of the purpose. You might have begun a portfolio as a teacher candidate during your undergraduate preparation, or you might be experiencing the development of a professional portfolio as a certification requirement. Wilkerson and Lang (2003) report that about 90% of schools, colleges, and departments of education use some type of portfolio for certification or licensure. Such a portfolio is designed with perhaps a few purposes in mind. One purpose might be to indicate your professional and personal growth from your first education class to your student teaching experience. You have probably been able to observe your growth and development as a teacher candidate from evidence indicating increased competency, richer reflections, or increased student learning. Other stakeholders are interested in your growth as well. Teacher educators might be monitoring how your development matched their expectations for the growth of all teacher candidates within your specific degree program; this portfolio's purpose is to *show growth.* In response to accountability issues, an increasing number of education schools are requiring portfolios and attempting to measure the growth of their graduates in areas of essential teaching skills.

Another purpose, and an important one for you personally as a teacher or a teacher candidate, is to *showcase your best work.* Portfolios developed with this purpose often end up being wonderful resources to use when candidates are seeking their first teaching jobs. These portfolios are collections of work that indicate your successes in teaching and contain rich evidence demonstrating a wide variety of competencies. You might be able to see how the purpose of this portfolio helps to define its contents. Teacher candidates who are attempting to impress hiring committees seldom include a personal philosophy of education that was written when they were first-year teacher candidates. Rather than indicating growth, these portfolios focus on providing evidence of high levels of competency as demonstrated through artifacts (i.e., pictures, plans, units, student samples, and/or credentials). For interview purposes, there might be a danger in including that personal philosophy of education you wrote in your first education class. It might be a noteworthy indication of how much you have grown, but it will probably do little to show your current knowledge, skills, and dispositions toward teaching and learning.

Portfolios are being used as professional development tools and for certification requirements in many states. If you are currently teaching and are required by the state or school district to develop a portfolio, its purpose is usually to evidence your credibility and success as a classroom teacher. These portfolios may require the components of the establishment of professional goals, the plans for achieving those goals, and the evidence that supports the achievement of those goals. The purpose of the portfolio is clearly to serve as an accountability measure that indicates teaching competency to an external evaluator.

Is it possible to have two purposes for the same portfolio? Do you think that would be helpful or harmful to classroom assessment?

These purposes are just two of many that can also be used in elementary and middle school classrooms. Growth portfolios can be used by teachers and students to indicate long-term development, especially in skill areas, to parents and teachers. Showcase portfolios can also be used to share best work with parents and teachers who are interested in samples of a student's work. Nevertheless, always keep in mind that having a clear purpose for your portfolio will make the development of the portfolio easier.

Benefits of a Clearly Articulated Purpose

1. It allows you to focus your attention on the kinds of teaching activities that best generate evidence for possible use in the portfolio.

Since evidence (student samples) is the very core of a portfolio, making sound decisions about the kinds and number of samples is important. In order to generate samples in a responsible way, teachers must plan activities that are aligned with the development of student evidence. For example, if a teacher wants to assess a student's reading comprehension, he or she should provide instruction that develops story maps, directed reading and thinking activities, and cloze activities in addition to what might be called traditional questioning techniques. Teachers who employ portfolios usually indicate that these instrument came to reflect their instructional practice in one of two ways. Either they were using multiple instructional strategies and the use of portfolios seemed logical as a means to document student growth and effort, or they decided to employ portfolios and found it necessary to develop a wider range of instructional strategies in order to generate richer types of evidence. The bottom line is that teachers should recognize that the use of portfolios will impact their instructional practice. This goes back to our second principle of sound assessment: making the goals, instructional activities, and assessment support one another.

2. It helps students to understand why they are completing tasks and reflecting on the products of those activities.

We know that students usually perform best when they have clear expectations and understand the purpose, relevance, or value of the required assignment. By establishing a strong purpose for the portfolio and sharing that purpose with students, you help them to develop a sense of "the big picture." This allows them to recognize the importance of their work. For example, you might develop a portfolio with the intention of having students participate and present at a parent conference. Specifically, you want students to present selections of their important work and discuss their written reflections on the process that went into developing their final product. There is motivational value to having students understand the purpose of the portfolio.

3. It helps the teacher and the student in the selection of evidence to place in the portfolio.

Suppose the purpose of the portfolio is to indicate to parents the growth of their child in the area of literacy (reading and writing). Keeping this purpose in mind, we can now understand what types of student samples will be important to keep as evidence of learning. As we progress through the instructional activities, we can ask ourselves, "Does this piece of student work illustrate the development of one's ability to read and/or express oneself in written communication?" If the answer to that question is "no," then we probably ought not to keep the item for the portfolio. Not long ago, I reviewed a third grader's portfolio and discovered an assignment that required him to conjugate 12 verbs in three columns—present, past, and future tenses. Would this fit the above purpose of a portfolio? Does this show the development of literacy skills? On one level it does, but wouldn't an assignment that requires the student to respond to writing prompts that use past or future tenses be a more valid assessment? For example, suppose a student is given the following assignment: "Using the verbs from the word bank at the bottom of the page, write a short paragraph that explains some of the things you did this morning before you came to school." It is more likely (i.e., authentic) that the student will need to use the correct form of the verb in writing or speaking than in the (inauthentic) conjugation of a list of verbs. By the way, the student's reflection indicated that he kept this piece because "it was fun." From this example you can see how the purpose allows you to make more precise selections about the contents of the portfolio.

Recommendations for Teachers Using Portfolios

Start small. Find an area of the curriculum in which you feel most comfortable with the development of products that support a clear purpose. As mentioned earlier, your district or county may mandate portfolios, thereby making your decision to use portfolios much easier. Should this be the case, focus on learning to use portfolios with children in the required subject area, thereby addressing two teaching functions at the same time. Following is an example.

Some school districts require that a writing portfolio accompany each student from elementary school through high school. Teachers of each grade provide several writing pieces every year to show evidence of the student's growth in writing over time. The examples chosen from each grade may also be required to illustrate one of the recognized styles of writing: narrative, technical, informational, or persuasive. In fact, a select group of teachers, curriculum specialists, or administrators may already have chosen the writing prompts for the portfolio entries for various grade. If you are working in a school system or district that has a curriculum requirement to develop writing portfolios in your classroom, then you already have two major questions answered for you.

Question 1: What is the purpose of writing portfolios in elementary and middle school classrooms? *Answer:* To show growth in the student's written communication skills as a result of the instructional experiences in your classroom.

Question 2: What are the types of writing (purposes) students must understand after leaving my classroom? *Answer:* According to the district guidelines you will probably have to develop student samples that address the writing styles recognized by your state: narrative, informational, technical, or persuasive. School districts might require that students develop technical and creative writing skills, but those skills are generally developed and sharpened later, after the students have developed essential written communication skills.

Questions that might not be answered by the district-mandated writing curriculum are more numerous and specific to your classroom. Answering these questions directly impacts the development and use of portfolios in your classroom. Although you will not be able to anticipate all the challenges of using portfolios as a tool to develop writing skills in students, planning to have portfolios support your instruction is necessary. Here are some important planning questions.

- What instructional practices am I going to use to enhance students' ability to communicate using written expression?
- How often should students be writing?
- How will I offer important feedback that will help students to grow as writers?
- How much involvement will students have in the selection, development, and presentation of portfolio materials?

Let's discuss each of these so that you might be able to more effectively develop your portfolio.

Developing a Writing Portfolio

What instructional practices am I going to use to enhance students' ability to communicate using written expression?

The instructional practices that you will use in your classroom should promote process writing. This approach to writing distances itself from the instructional practice of giving students a dictionary, several blank sheets of paper, and telling them to draft a 500-word essay on "What a Daisy Thinks of Spring." The writing process treats written composition as a set of skills that are best taught when the writer implements systematic procedures. Although these steps differ slightly from state to state, most educators would accept brainstorming, drafting, revising, editing, and rewriting as common practices essential to the development of good writing products. Should you be unfamiliar with how to implement the writing process in your classroom, you can acquire knowledge of its application by looking at language arts textbooks, journals, or Web sites.

Portfolios directly support the use of process writing. Teachers employing process writing understand that children need different amounts of time to work their way through the process to the final product. Portfolios with sample student products can capture the development of a paper from its early rough stages through revision stages to completion. You will also be able to show through student samples how you were able to design instruction that led to the development of a child's skills in brainstorming, drafting, rewriting, or editing. The portfolio makes most sense if you intend to collect samples of the development of the student's writing skills. If you are concerned only with the final product, then a letter grade placed in a grade book will satisfy your needs. The writing process, however, is too messy, too complicated, too rich, and too important to relegate it to a single letter grade assigned to a final product.

How often should students be writing?

How often your students are writing is an important decision based on the numbers of students you meet and the emphasis you want to place on the development of sound writing skills. Because writing skills are so important to students, it is critical to have regularly scheduled opportunities and assignments for writing. I believe that students should write every day, but not always to develop a piece for the portfolio. In the upper elementary grades they can respond to a question using a "quick write" of two or more sentences as a formative assessment measure. They might be required to write out the procedures they used in solving a math problem containing multiple steps. When you decide how much children should write, be careful to remember formal versus informal writing assignments. A daily dose of formal writing might result in motivational problems that extinguish the very interest we want to inspire.

For portfolio (formal) writing assignments it is important to use a schedule that will permit the students and teacher to maintain the momentum of writing. As writers develop pieces for different purposes, there may be occasions to write more frequently. If, however, we establish a schedule of writing that is too infrequent, students find themselves trying to remember what they wrote and so lose valuable time. In the case of major editing, it might be best not to examine the writing for several days in order to bring "fresh eyes" to the editing process. Although developing a sense of timing and pace for formal writing assignments can be messy and time-consuming, the rewards for teachers and students are significant.

Portfolios can be helpful in establishing a schedule for writing. If you engage in process writing, you will immediately discover that students require different amounts of time to develop high-quality written products. Portfolio time should be a regularly scheduled event in your classroom that takes place daily, every other day, or weekly. Obviously, the portfolio doesn't dictate the frequency of your writing instruction, but it does offer you an opportunity to bring organization to a process that requires a high degree of individualization and flexibility. That individualization and flexibility can be noted in Table 5-2, Possible Accommodations for Students with Exceptionalities. Portfolios also offer a means to record accommodations made for student's needs.

Table 5-2. Possible Accommodations for Student With Exceptionalities

Method Accommodations
> Extra time for completion
> Shorter assignments
> Content outlines
> Webbing strategies
> Process-writing strategies
> Story starters
> Positive approaches
> Nonwritten forms (e.g., projects, displays) for written reports
> Study carrel for individual work
> Formulation of sentences aloud
> "Finger-for-spacing" strategy
> Color-coding strategies
> Peer support
> Cross-age tutoring

Material Accommodations
> Note cards
> Word cards
> Sentence cards
> Clipboards
> Pocket dictionary
> Pocket thesaurus
> Peer support
> Highlighter

Table 5-2. **Possible Accommodations for Student With Exceptionalities** *(Cont.)*

Technology Accommodations
    Tape-recorded thoughts before writing
    Tape-recorded story to proofread
    Headphones
    Electronic dictionary
    Electronic thesaurus
    Word Master
    Speaking Dictionary Companion
    Electronic eraser
    Word processor, computer

Have you ever kept a writing portfolio? As a classroom teacher, do you think students might be interested in a writing portfolio you keep and share with them?

How will I offer important feedback that will help students to grow as writers?

Providing corrective, specific, and timely feedback is perhaps the most important but ignored aspect of writing improvement. Several principles ought to guide your beliefs about providing feedback to student writing, and portfolios can be helpful in attaining your goals. There are established qualities of good writing that should be utilized to structure feedback to students. With the emergence of expanded concepts of literacy, there has been a parallel emphasis on improving student written expression that has resulted in a nationwide acceptance of common elements of good writing.

For example, a review of national writing requirements identifies the presence of voice, details, sentence fluency, ideas, content, focus, organization, word choice, conventions, and style as qualities central to good writing. Most states are looking for the same elements but might use a different term to describe the quality. For example, style might include word choice or voice, and content might be derived from the presence of detail and ideas.

If you are not familiar with the standards for good writing, investigate them and become knowledgeable about what they mean and how they can be developed in elementary and middle school children.

Recognizing and teaching the accepted qualities of good writing has some important advantages. First, it provides a common language and vocabulary, thus avoiding the confusion of each teacher defining good writing in his or her own way. In the absence of recognized elements of good writing, some teachers might define good writing with an emphasis on correct grammar and spelling, whereas others might require students to focus on creativity or content. Before states and districts identified specific writing qualities, students frequently spent months figuring out how their teachers defined quality writing. Each student portfolio should definitely include a copy of the district or state standards for good writing. For primary and intermediate grades, achieving general agreement on this might require extra steps. For example, it is important to rewrite the elements of good writing in "kid language—that is, definitions that are understandable at the student's developmental level.

The second advantage is that entire elementary school faculties can focus their collective energy and efforts on a set of clearly defined elements of good writing. With a set of common elements in place, teachers can begin to design ways to get students to improve in those areas. At a time when state test scores are being emphasized for accountability reasons, it is essential to have all teachers working toward a common set of instructional goals. School districts have a better chance of raising the writing scores of students if the faculty focus their instruction over several years rather than one teacher attempting to cram the development of writing skills into the framework of the testing year.

Portfolios can assist in the development of effective feedback for students in several ways. For one thing, portfolios can effectively house the history of feedback given to the student for one writing assignment or for the entire academic year. Despite feedback, students often make the very same errors in subsequent writing pieces. Using the portfolio, teachers can have the students review the corrective feedback so that they will avoid the errors of previous writing assignments.

Children do not become good writers simply by writing often. They become better writers in the same way that people become better at most skills: practice, feedback, practice, feedback, and more practice, feedback. Children also get better at writing if they understand the feedback that is provided to them. It might help to recall some of the writing feedback we received during our own experiences as students. Much feedback, though well intended by the provider (the teacher), was utterly useless to us. Think about the time you got a writing sample back and your teacher had written "Good" in the margin. "Good" what? Or perhaps there was a large question mark placed in the margin of your paper. Many students undoubtedly did not understand the meaning of the question mark, but in order not to look stupid in front of their peers, they chose not to ask the teacher the meaning of the question mark. Thus, even though students' writing skills can be improved by practice and precise feedback, the feedback must be clearly understood by the writer if it is to be meaningful. For more on the importance of instructional feedback, see chapter 15.

Here is an example of how elementary teachers must adapt state or district definitions into "kid language" in order to make the feedback meaningful. Focus is one of the desirable qualities of good writing, according to the standards of several states, and can be defined as the single controlling point made with task awareness about a specific topic (Pennsylvania Department of Education, 2006).

Given the various ages and developmental levels of students, the understanding of focus will require heavy doses of modeling and inspection, followed by discussion and practice. In order to improve the student's understanding, we must use a language that facilitates his or her understanding. Commenting on a student's effort to achieve good focus might include statements like the following:

- I see that you really hit your target audience.

- Your topic sentence really sets the table for the rest of the meal.

- You talked about one thing in this paragraph—great work.

- I can tell you like this topic; you really discussed it.

These comments, and others like them, are helpful to improving student writing because they are specific and understandable. Keeping drafts with corrective comments in a portfolio will help the student to see that good writing evolves and usually isn't a one-time effort that is either good or bad. The idea of using a portfolio to manage this process makes instructional sense because it fits your teaching and the dispositions you want to develop in elementary and middle school writers. This instructional alignment refers to the second principle of sound assessment that was introduced in chapter 1, that assessments should be congruent with the objectives and the instructional activities that are used with students.

The focus of this section has been on the development of student writing as a way to demonstrate the instructional processes that enhance the value of portfolio assessment. The decision to use a portfolio should be based on the need to align the assessment method with desirable instructional activities. If the teacher's instructional activities are limited to an endless supply of completion work sheets and skill and drill exercises, there is little need to employ a portfolio as an assessment tool to indicate growth. A grade book housing the students' scores on each of the work sheets will report their achievement, but the evidence of their growth would be more difficult to infer.

How much involvement will students have in the selection, development, and presentation of portfolio materials?

Care has to be given to the student's role in the process of developing portfolios because ownership is a key element in the involvement of students. Without student input regarding contents, the portfolio becomes the property of the teacher and, in the eyes of students, just another assignment that the teacher thought was necessary. This is not to say that we should turn over the entire responsibility for communicating student achievement and growth to students. Determining the right amount of involvement of students in the development of the portfolio will come with experience and, unfortunately, trial and error. Most teachers who have employed portfolios in their classrooms can testify to a number of false starts and adjustments that were necessary in developing the effective use of portfolios with students. There is too much to be gained from having students be a part of the development to ignore their place in the process. Advantages to the involvement of students include the following:

- The development of reflective skills in the examination of their own products
- A deeper understanding of the process of writing
- The development of internal criteria for quality; being able to assess one's own work
- Taking pride in one's own work

Arranging the Portfolio's Contents

Because the clerical nature of keeping student work at various stages of completion is challenging, it is important that you have a plan for a high degree of organization. You might be fortunate enough to have several students who possess the organizational skills to arrange their portfolios in ways that make the interpretation of the materials easier. If your experiences resemble that of many teachers, however, you will most likely have to develop organizational strategies to assist the students in the maintenance of their portfolios. Their organization starts with you.

Providing an organizational framework is not only helpful to the student, it also assists you, as the classroom teacher, and anyone else who will be reviewing the portfolio's contents. There is no single framework that is vastly superior to others, but it should be related to the purpose. Here is an example of how the organization of two portfolios might be different.

Suppose I wanted to indicate how a student's writing skills have improved during the school year. I would probably want to organize the portfolio around evidence in the main areas—for example, informational pieces as well as samples of persuasive writing. Keeping dated samples that show an increased skill level by the student helps to provide a baseline of student ability, in the same way that weight-loss programs require an initial weigh-in to document and measure later success. The portfolio may also be helpful in reminding the writer of errors committed in earlier pieces. Teachers often indicate that young writers persistently repeat their errors; as a result, you will be writing the same comments on successive writing assignments. Encouraging brief student self-reviews of errors prior to a writing assignment helps to diminish that pattern.

The organization of portfolios to show a student's command of the writing process might be organized differently. In this case, the organization might include brainstorming, works in progress, classroom work, and completed products. Students would be required to keep dated samples, but the most powerful aspect of the portfolio would be its ability to show how the student is managing the writing process and the emergence of quality through the progression of completed products. Concept maps or other prewriting material, outlines, rough drafts with editing comments, and the final draft are some types of samples that indicate student understanding and participation in the writing process. This organization provides a means to draw conclusions about filing skills, underrepresented areas, and the ability to meet deadlines. Both of these frameworks organize the portfolio to assist the student, the teacher, and the reviewer. Figure 5-1 can be used with students as a guide to the development of a portfolio. It would make sense to place this on the outside of the portfolio so that the contents of the portfolio can be easily seen. Teachers who use portfolios regularly recognize how time-consuming portfolio management can be and work to limit the clerical time spent with accounting for the contents and filing student samples. You might also notice that this chart generates a profile of instructional activities in the classroom. This is an additional communication feature of using portfolios.

Summary

Portfolios have developed into a recognizable and essential component of classroom assessment. They are most effectively used when teachers determine a clear purpose for their use and develop sound instructional practices that are aligned with that purpose. Additional elements that can contribute to their overall worth and effectiveness are organizational strategies and involvement of the students. Portfolios provide a window on classroom teaching and student learning that is impossible to generate by any other assessment means. Their effective use can promote desirable skill development in students and successful communication with parents and other school professionals. They are an important component of contemporary classroom assessment.

Teaching Activities

1. After deciding that the purpose of a portfolio is "to showcase the mathematical understanding of a fifth grader for a parent conference," use Figure 5-1 to make decisions about a variety of different student samples. For instance, do you keep the student sample? Another question might be, what does it tell us about the student's writing?

2. Portfolios are used by teachers in many of today's classrooms. If you know of a teacher who is using portfolios, ask to see a sample portfolio. Make sure that the confidentiality of the student is maintained and permission is given to examine the portfolio. Ask the teacher about the process of establishing the portfolio, the role of students in selection and maintenance of the portfolio, and how often entries are included in the portfolio.

Subject Area:_____

Process Area   Date/s: Comments:

_____

_____

_____

_____

Product Area   Date/s: Comments:

_____

_____

_____

Classroom Assignments   Date/s: Comments:

_____

_____

_____

_____

Conferences   Dates: Comments:

_____

_____

_____

_____

Figure 5-1. Portfolio Contents

3. If you are lucky enough to be able to obtain several portfolios that have the same purpose and are designed for the same grade, experiment with trying to grade them. Using the report card of the same school, try to determine how easy or difficult grading portfolios might be. Ask yourself questions about why is this so difficult. Don't give up too easily.

Grading
and Report Cards:
Challenging Decisions

1. To understand that the fundamental purpose of grading is to communicate student success, progress, and achievement to students, parents, and other school professionals

2. To be able to calculate a weighted grade from multiple scores

3. To recognize the fundamental comparisons that are used to generate grades

4. To be able to apply sound grading practices to the calculation of grades

5. To be able to note differences in the ways report cards are constructed and understand how marking systems may differ

Grading Guidelines

Grading and report cards are considered one area of study because to most classroom teachers, grading student progress and/or achievement is an activity directly linked to the report card. To split the activity of grading and completing report cards implies that one activity is unrelated to the other. Because of changes in the formats, as well as the skills, abilities, and subject areas that are reported, the need to coordinate daily grading with reporting progress on a report card is greater now than ever. In fact, any teacher who accepts a position in a new school district or county should review the report card prior to setting up a grading program.

You have probably experienced a variety of grading and reporting practices. As you will see, "no one method of grading and reporting serves all purposes well" (Guskey, 1994). As a teacher decides to develop a grading plan, there are key decisions that ultimately impact students and the grades they receive. Teachers should keep in mind the following guidelines when developing a grading plan:

- Make sure that the grading scheme can be logically communicated—that is, it can be explained to students, parents, and others.

- Be certain that there is fairness in the development of the grading system so that students have a reasonable chance to succeed.

- The grading scheme should have balance, sampling the range of instructional targets in a marking period.

- It should be technically sound; the development of the grading scale should avoid the common errors of uninformed grading schemes.

Grading in American Schools

Grades are part of the social organization called school. As students complete assessments, whether they are tests, reports, or performance assessments, teachers have a responsibility to comment on the quality of student achievement. The judgments that teachers make about the students' work are usually converted to grades or marks. Grades are the traditional means of communication about a child's success in our society. Despite periodic criticism, grades and grading have existed for years because the public considers them to be an essential part of the American school experience and maintains a level of comfort with their general interpretation.

Because of the universal acceptance afforded to grades, their aggregation and interpretation often serve other important sorting functions for school-related awards and ceremonies. For example, grades are often the cornerstone of valedictory awards, grouping or placement decisions, and National Honor Society placement. So concerned are schools with the calculation of grades that by graduation we can often report the precise ranking of each student in a class of hundreds. Because grades are so widely used in schools and respected by the public, one would assume that they are keen indicators of student learning. You will most likely be surprised to realize that despite the presence of grading in elementary and middle school classrooms, it is not an essential component of learning.

Take a few seconds to answer this question. Is grading an important part of student learning? At first you might say, "Of course." How can it not be critical to student learning when its use is so widespread in schools across the country? It's probably difficult to recall a time when you learned something in school that was not graded in some way. Consider a situation outside school in which learning took place without a grade. For example, recall how you learned to whistle or ride a bicycle. Would you have learned how to ride that bicycle faster if you received a grade on your first riding attempts?

We have to be careful not to confuse grading with feedback. Using the bicycling example, if I noticed that you failed to place your feet correctly on the pedals, I would alert you to this problem. That's feedback. On the contrary, it would not make sense to call out to you that your cycling is generally an A but your pedaling is a B. Feedback is essential to instruction, but grading and reporting are not (Guskey, 1994). According to Frisbie and Waltman (1992), grades would not be necessary if there were no need to communicate achievement to parents or others outside the school setting. Grades can motivate students, but learning can occur in the absence of formal grades.

The Impact of Grading on Learning

The process of evaluating student work and assigning a grade is a fundamental teacher responsibility. Grades provide a general idea of how a student performed, answered questions, or completed assignments. Seldom does a grade, in and of itself, satisfy the student's desire to understand how to improve or the specific strengths and weaknesses of his or her efforts (Brookhart, 2004). Thus, grading has a slight impact on learning but is not generally a suitable means by which to improve student achievement. You will see why grades fail to have an impact on student achievement when you realize the many subjective decisions that teachers must make in order to arrive at a grade. These decisions often result in grading being "personalized"—that is, one teacher using a particular set of practices while another teacher employs a different set. Such a variance exists in the primary comparisons that are the fundamental grounding for all grading. After reading about these comparisons you will begin to understand the impact of grades on student achievement.

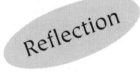

Think about your experiences with grades in regular education settings. Did you perceive grades in a different way as a student than you do as a teacher? How are those perceptions different?

Grading as a Comparison

Teachers often encounter difficulty in grading because they have been exposed to a number of different grading practices and schemes that unfortunately have not been well thought out. Understanding fundamental grading practices facilitates sound decision making. All grades are arrived at by a comparison. In order for teachers to evaluate student work, the work must be compared to a designated goal or a comparable piece of student work. Teachers have options in the types of comparisons they can make of student work. The teacher can compare the student work to:

- a predetermined set of standards (standards)
- the work of other students (other students)
- some of that student's earlier efforts (himself or herself)

Which comparison is the most valid for classroom purposes? Each comparison has advantages and disadvantages, and one can quickly see how the teacher's choice of comparison has the ability to affect the student's score.

Comparing the Student's Work to a Set of Standards

Grading according to standards has been well accepted as a means of comparing students in American schools. Traditionally, the comparisons have been drawn concerning the amount of information students were able to master. Students took an exam and received a score that was converted to the percentage of items correctly answered. Additional student scores were averaged, and a percent score used to indicate the overall achievement of the students. How well a student did was then determined by comparing the student's score to a teacher-developed or districtwide scale such as the following:

100–90	A	Excellent
89–80	B	Good
79–70	C	Average
69–60	D	Below Average
59–0	F	Failure

Comparison of student work to standards with minor variations in the percentage scale continues to be one of the most commonly used grading frameworks in today's schools. This scale is especially common in the middle school years. Most teachers have experienced this type of grading comparison in regular education and may currently be experiencing it with slight modification if they are taking professional development courses.

The advantages to this grading method include the following:

- Flexibility. The teacher is able to assign all As if the students perform above the established score for an A, and, conversely, fail every student if they all score lower than the minimum passing grade.

- Ease of calculation. This grade can easily be averaged and interpreted as what a student knows about a certain subject area.

The disadvantages of this grading method are as follows:

- Understanding the meaning of percentage scores. Percent scores fit a knowledge-driven assessment much more easily than a performance-driven assessment. It is difficult to imagine that there is any real difference between the abilities of two persons who score a 79% and an 80%, respectively, but nonetheless receive different grades. Translating a student's writing ability into a percentage can become quite confusing as one questions exactly how one writer could receive a 79% and the other writer a 46%. Are there actually 99 different levels of writing?

- Outlying scores. Percentages and their averages can be influenced by extremely high or low scores. Thus the average can be distorted, and the true score of the person lost, because of a single score (Canady, 1989).

Comparing the Student's Work to the Work of Other Students

Another grading comparison that teachers might be familiar with from their experiences in regular education classrooms is normative grading. In this method of judging student work, the teacher compares a student test score with all the other test scores in the class and renders a decision based on the score's standing. Comparing the student's work with the work of other students is commonly referred to as "grading on the curve." The idea behind this comparison is that student performance will generally be distributed along a continuum resembling the normal bell curve. With that in mind, elementary teachers might choose to assign percentages of grades as follows:

10%	A	The top 10% of the scores in the class get an A.
20%	B	The next 20% of the scores get a B.
40%	C	The middle 40% of the scores will get a C.
20%	D	The next 20% of the scores will get a D.
10%	F	The remaining scores receive an F.

The advantages of this method include the following:

- Forgiveness. The basic advantage to using the curve is that if test scores are not high, students can be graded relative to their standing in class rather than being compared to a fixed level of performance.

- Familiarity. Despite being criticized for its shortcomings, it continues to be used in classrooms.

The disadvantages of this method include the following:

- Miscommunication. It fails to communicate what a student understands or can do in a subject area. Suppose the scores of the entire class are low—a 60% score is the top score—so you must make the 60% score an A. The student or the parent of the students usually believes that a grade of A indicates a superior degree of mastery in a subject area. In this case, that would not be true.

- Punishment. A teacher using this grading plan will have to fail 10% of the students. Failing a portion of the class, regardless of what students know or can do, is part of the belief system of the normal curve. Sometimes teachers will modify the grading plan to avoid giving failing grades.

- Competition. Normative grading sets up a competition within your classroom that is usually counterproductive. Because one student's grade is enhanced each time another student misses an item on the test, the students are less likely to cooperate.

The number of disadvantages associated with the use of this method should convince you that this is not a grading scheme that is considered "best practice." These shortcomings are presented to discourage the use of grading on the curve as the grounding theory for establishing a grading plan. Let's take a look at what might happen to the grades of students who are evaluated by teachers using two different comparisons to establish a grade. What follows is a frequency distribution derived from a quiz given to 25 students. Calculate the grades that each teacher would give to the very same performance (the raw scores) by students.

TEACHER A	vs.	TEACHER B
Grading on the curve		Grading according to standards
10		No scores
9		II
8		II
7		III
6		JHT
5		JHT
4		IIII
3		IIII
2		No scores
1		No scores
0		No scores

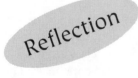

Why do you think students might want to pressure their teacher into grading on the curve? As a teacher, what are your thoughts?

Comparing the Student's Work to His or Her Earlier Efforts

In the third type of comparison, the student's work is compared with previous efforts for evidence of progress and improvement. In the other comparisons, a score is generated that indicates achievement by comparison to either a preestablished standard or the achievement of others. Although growth may be factored into the calculation of the final grade, seldom does it serve as the most important variable in determining the grade. There are several reasons that teachers typically report achievement over growth. First, achievement (especially when measured by objective test items) is a much easier construct to measure than growth. For example, if one uses growth (or gain, in this example) as the main determinant of a grade, then the student who improves the most should receive the highest grade. Given the following two students' scores, what communication problems do you foresee?

Student A:	Test 1 30%	Test 2 65%	Gain 35%	Grade A
Student B:	Test 1 85%	Test 2 93%	Gain 8%	Grade D

How do you explain to a student that, despite his or her knowing 93% of the content, a D grade is assigned based on limited improvement? If you are working with upper-grade elementary students, how long do think it will take before they realize that doing poorly on the first test gives them an advantage on the final grade? Thinking through what your grade is communicating to students and parents is essential to the targets for sound grading, logic, and fairness.

One final note on the discussion of progress and growth seems appropriate. These are constructs that should be reported to students and parents, and they are best communicated through the use of individual student work samples. The ability to show student growth can be facilitated by the use of well-organized portfolios because an individual's growth can be easily shown. The difficulty with reporting growth is putting it into a numerical scale and comparing one student's growth to the growth of a large number of students. Reporting student growth or progress is addressed in greater detail in chapter 5.

Grading and Its Relationship to Report Cards

The immediate purpose of grading student work is to provide communication of student achievement to at least three different groups. Without question, the most important person to receive the information is the student. The student uses the grade to make judgments about his or her achievement, the amount of effort needed to achieve, progress toward graduation or promotion to the next grade. This type of information is communicated regularly in assignments but also in a more summative way in a report card grade.

The second group that uses grading information is parents. Parents are entitled to know the level of progress their children are making toward promotion to the next grade. This is where grading is inextricably tied to report cards. Although parents, for any number of reasons, might not receive feedback on each individual grade their child earns, they will almost always get a report of the aggregate achievement on a 6-

week or 9-week report card. For this reason, grades for individual assignments have
to be aligned with the aggregate communication that goes home to parents.

Teachers and school officials compose the third group that uses grading information to make decisions about pupils. Grades are part of the information used to make
decisions about the types of programs in which students can participate. We can
quickly recognize sorting functions associated with high schools: class rank, tracking
placements, National Honor Society recognition, and valedictory designation. Elementary schools also employ grades as a sorting mechanism. For example, admis-
sion into ability groupings for math and reading is sometimes dependent on a student's
past grades in the subject area. Decisions made about entering programs such as
federally funded programs or gifted education can be influenced by the use of grades.

Calculating a Student Grade

We have discussed several methods by which to calculate grades. You have learned how teacher decisions
about grading comparisons influence a student's
grades. Since teachers and teacher candidates have
firsthand experience with receiving grades and report cards, there is a tendency to
carry over the practices and procedures of our prior experiences with grading. Although in most cases a teacher modeled effective grading practices for us, occasionally the procedures we experienced were not "best practice." Below are suggestions
for how elementary teachers can avoid the traditional pitfalls inherent in the calculation of student scores.

Judge or Child Advocate?

A grade is meant to reflect the achievement of a student in a subject area. Measurement experts suggest that achievement is the purest measures to use when calculating students' grades. Research, however, suggests that teachers use a combination of
adjustments when calculating a grade (Brookhart, 1991). This is due in part to the
dual role required of teachers in arriving at a grade. First, grading requires that teachers be judges of student performance. In that role, teachers want to be as fair as possible; however, many of these judgments are difficult, emotional, and unpleasant. As
O'Connor (2002) points out:

> Grades are as much a matter of values as they are of science—all along
> the assessment trail, the teacher has made value judgments about what
> type of assessment to use, what to include in each assessment, how the
> assessment is scored, the actual scoring of the assessment, and why the
> scores are to be combined in a particular way to arrive at a final grade. (p.
> 19)

Second, teachers are required to be child advocates. An important part of elementary teaching is being caring and compassionate toward children. Teachers want to

see children succeed, especially children who are working at their highest capacity but nevertheless struggling academically. It is difficult to give a student a failing grade when you realize that he or she is working to maximum capacity. Teachers often internalize the child's perception: "If I am trying as hard as I can and I still get an F, why should I continue to try?" As a child advocate the teacher hopes that by helping the student to achieve a measure of success that is indicated in a grade, the student will continue to try.

Because of the dual role, teachers generally use achievement as the basis for the final grade but also recognize and award effort, ability, and attitude. This makes across-the-board comparisons of grades impossible and affects their validity (Brookhart, 1991). Research on the grading habits of practicing teachers suggests that you try to isolate achievement as the measure of choice when developing a grading plan for students.

Although it is generally accepted that elementary teachers use effort, ability, and attitude to calculate grades, one area should definitely be discouraged from affecting a student's grade: classroom behavior. The purpose of a grade is to communicate student achievement in a particular subject area. Report cards are usually composed of two areas: academics and behavior. Achievement in social studies, for example, should not be based on whether an individual remains seated, follows classroom rules, or blurts out answers. These areas of student behavior certainly should be addressed, but the academic portion of the report card is not the place in which to address them. Classroom behavior reports and grades based on achievement in a subject area should be kept separate.

The Use of Zeros in the Calculation of Grades

We stated earlier that averaging percentage grades can be influenced by extremely high or low scores. One of the practices sometimes involved in the calculation of percentage grades is the penalty of receiving a zero grade for an incomplete assignment or some other classroom infraction. Teachers should be aware of the unfair numerical disadvantage that students must overcome if zeros are used in the calculation of percentage grades. If we look at the range of scores for each grade in a typical percentage scale, it is easy to spot a numerical disadvantage:

100–90	A	Excellent	11 possible scores
89–80	B	Good	10 possible scores
79–70	C	Average	10 possible scores
69–60	D	Below Average	10 possible scores
59–0	F	Failure	60 possible scores

Using a zero in the calculation of an average has a punishing effect on the student's final grade. The numerical range penalizes the student for a single assignment but also negatively reduces all other scores because of its effect on the student average

(Canady, 1989). School districts have adopted policies that discourage the use of ze-ros in calculating grades. You will have a better understanding of why school districts have taken such actions after reading the following example.

A student receives three test scores: 80%, 90%, and 70%. When we average these scores together we find that the student has an 80%, which is typically a B. If the student then receives a 0 for an assignment and it is calculated into the average, the student's grade is reduced to 60%, or a D—two letter grades lower! If the student had received a 50%, which is still an F but maintains the 10-point range of all the other grades, the percentage for the student would be 72.5%, or a C, which more adequately captures the general effort and achievement of the student.

The Use of Extra Credit

One of the most common questions teachers face near the end of a reporting period is if students can submit additional work in order to raise their grade. This is such a common practice that even parents or primary caregivers will ask on behalf of their children. One solution, especially with upper-grade children, is to permit students to complete a project that is linked to the curricular area currently being studied. Should this be desirable, maintain a clear understanding with students that they can also *lose* points if the project is not completed with a high standard of quality. The point value and indicators of quality should be agreed upon prior to giving the assignment. Students can sign a contract to complete the extra credit project, which should be completed before the end of the grading period. In this way, extra credit is not an inflationary practice used to eliminate a poor grade, and, more important, it ensures that the work is linked to meaningful learning.

Is there a way to keep students and parents informed about how you calculate the grades of your students? Can you see how parents might be confused about the grades their children bring home?

Grading Students With Exceptionalities

Grading students identified as having exceptionalities has never been easy and continues to be an area of difficulty for teachers. It is always a sound idea to ask your principal about school or district policy on this issue. A frequent district policy is to ask teachers to use the typical A, B, C, D, F letter grade and an additional indicator that the student's grade has been modified. According to Monk and Bursuck (2003), the use of an indicator does not necessarily mean that the grading system has been modified for a particular student. They suggest more complete adaptations that include reporting progress on the individualized education program (IEP) objectives and altering the grading scale and weights. Because grading systems used in general education classes are usually ill equipped for individualization, it makes sense to follow the Individuals With Disabilities Education Act (IDEA) and discuss this with peers and other school professionals.

Calculating a Weighted Grade

Although much has been said about grades in this chapter, little has been devoted to the actual calculation of the student scores that result in the student's grade. Several grading procedures will be discussed and the calculations explained. First, let's answer a few questions so that we can make some decisions about our grading plan:

- Which of the three possible comparisons should I use?
- What types of assessments do I intend to use that will be part of the grade calculation?
- What content and skills have been most important in my teaching and the student's learning?

Suppose that we intend to use the comparison that grades according to standards. That is, we will score each assignment, calculate its percentage correct, and average all the scores in a summative manner. We will then compute the average for each student and assign a grade based on the average score as it compares to a fixed standard of letter grades. There are a few problems with this approach, so we will use it to explain the simple calculations and discuss the problems later in this chapter. The calculation of the grade will come from three tests, one oral presentation, two performance projects, and five homework assignments. This variety of assessments should provide us with an expanded sense of what a student knows and how the student can apply the information. Thus, we can set up our grading plan by using the following:

Test scores (three at 40 points each):	30, 38, 32
Oral presentation (30 points):	28
Performance projects (one 30 points, one 25 points):	20, 20
Homework assignments (five at 5 points each):	5, 5, 3, 3, 4

When we calculate the averages for each we get the following averages:

Tests:	83.33%
Oral presentation:	93.33%
Performance projects:	72.72%
Homework:	80.00%
Total:	82.34% = B

What you should notice from this example is that even though the tests total 120 points, the tests are reduced to one score that has the same amount of influence on the grade as the homework score of 25 points, the presentation of 30 points, and the performance projects of 55 points. As a teacher, can you justify assigning the same value to your homework assignments and your tests? Should two performances have the same power to influence the grade as three tests? Your answer should be no, but you would be surprised how many classroom teachers use grading systems that are not dramatically different from what has just been described.

How Can We Change This?

One method we can use is to weight the different assessments, which means to alter the influence of each so that they do not have an equal influence in determining the final grade. That is, we make some assessments more powerful determiners and some lesser determiners. Given the four types of assessments we described earlier, how might you place them in order of importance? Let's say that tests, performance projects, the oral presentation, and the homework assignments are the order of importance that we choose. There are a few important rules to remember when weighting grades using percentage scores.

First, change all raw scores (number correct) to percentages. Thus, 4 out of 5 correct is 80%; 13 out of 15 correct is 86.66%.

Next, decide the weight of each area, keeping in mind that the sum of all weights must equal 100%. You should not give any area more than 40%; that will result in one area being too powerful. Let's assign some weights to our scores. We want to assign the more important areas the greater amount of the total weight, so, let's make tests 40%, performance assessments 35%, the oral presentation 15%, and the homework 10%. The 10% weight guarantees that the homework score will be less of a determiner of the grade than the other components. This is important because it's impossible to know exactly who completed the homework assignment. Depending on parental involvement, children receive uneven amounts of assistance with their homework. The difference is so great sometimes that we might be unaware of whether the student or the parent completed the assignment. We do not want to discourage parental help with homework, so we use a lower value to limit the effect that homework scores have in determining the final grade. There is also an argument that homework is practice, so students should not be graded on content that is relatively new to them.

The calculation of the grade requires that we average all scores and multiply the average times the weight.

Tests	$83.33\% \times .40 = 33.33\%$
Oral presentation	$93.33\% \times .15 = 13.99\%$
Performance projects	$72.72\% \times .35 = 25.45\%$
Homework	$80.00\% \times .10 = 8.00\%$
Totals:	$80.77\% = B$

Notice that the unweighted calculation was 82.50% and the weighted one is 80.77%. The student did not do anything different; the change is due to the teacher's decisions about the importance of certain assessments. Which score is the "right" score? There is no right score, but the second score is more defensible based on the relative importance of the different types of assessments.

Let's try one more calculation. The idea is not to confuse you with a variety of different means of arriving at a grade but instead to provide another way to justify your grading decisions. In this grade calculation, we will compute the percentage of total points earned by the student divided by the total possible points. An advantage to this method is that if the teacher controls the point values of the assessments, then balance among the assessments can be achieved. Let's look at the example we have used:

Tests	30/40, 38/40, 32/40	100 out of 120
Oral presentation	28/30	28 out of 30
Performance projects	20/30, 20/25	40 out of 55
Homework	5/5, 5/5, 3/5, 3/5, 4/5	20 out of 25
Total		188 out of 230
		81.7% = B

Notice that the procedure used to calculate the grade changed the score again. This is why you must be careful in planning how to grade students. (Also be sure to check your math!) In each of the three examples used in this chapter, the score has changed very slightly. It is easy to see, however, that a score change of a few points could make a difference in the letter grade. Make sure when you begin your grading strategy to consider the type of comparison you want to make, decide how to weight the assessments, check your calculations, and share the scores with your students.

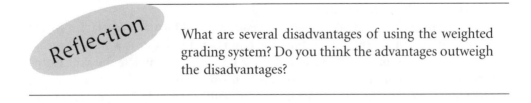

Reflection   What are several disadvantages of using the weighted grading system? Do you think the advantages outweigh the disadvantages?

Different Opinions on the Use of Averages

Another option as the basis of calculating a weighted grade is to employ the median score rather than the mean score. The value of using the median is that, unlike the mean, it is not as vulnerable to scores that are exceptionally high or low. This is especially valuable when teachers use zeros in the calculation of grades. Averaging grades can have a detrimental effect on student motivation. Students who earn a low score on their first or second major assessment might quickly realize that regardless of any future efforts, they are unlikely to achieve a high grade. Although the idea of using the median in place of the mean has been suggested for years (Guskey, 1996, 2002; Wright, 1994), there is increasing consideration of this practice based on the shift to more standards-driven grading requirements.

Report Card Formats

The format of report cards has undergone significant change over the last decade. In the past, grades were typically reported in subject areas using a mark (A, B, C, D, F) to indicate the judgment of the teacher in reference to student success in an academic area. For example, the report card might have the following subjects: math, reading, health, science, social studies, and handwriting. In each of the areas the student would receive a letter grade indicating the level of success or achievement. Most of the grades were calculated with percentages, which were then averaged. A reporting period usually consisted of 6 or 9 weeks, giving teachers a good opportunity to assemble grades in each subject area. Although these types of formats still might be continue to be found in upper elementary and middle schools, their use at the lower elementary level has diminished greatly.

There has been a variety of changes in lower and some upper elementary school report cards. One of the more common changes is a departure from single subject areas to a subject area augmented with a list of subskills. This has come about because of a need to describe the achievement of students in primary reading and language arts with more expansive and precise indicators. Another area in which the use of subskills has become more widely used is mathematics. Report cards now show mathematics progress in problem-solving ability, calculation, and basic facts, among others. The advantage of this is that both parents and the child are made aware of the child's areas of strength as well as areas in which the child may need help. The importance of collecting data to report this progress over a 9-week period in each of the subareas cannot be overemphasized.

Another change that has taken place in the report card format is to place students on a developmental continuum and use the report card to indicate a student's mastery of a skill, incomplete mastery of a skill, or inability to complete the skill. Comments like these emphasize a child's progress compared with his or her previous work. These reports are conducted for a number of skills, often requiring accurate and comprehensive testing prior to completing report cards. When reporting skill attainment, it is necessary to report the current level of achievement instead of the average of level of attainment during the reporting period. For example, if a teacher was reporting the reading fluency of a child, it would be more important to report the current fluency rate rather than the average of all the fluency rates that were assessed over the reporting period.

The shift to standards-driven teaching has resulted in school systems abandoning former report card formats for ones that represent the particular standards adopted within their state. This has come about largely because school professionals realized that if the standards were to be the focus of student achievement, then recording and documenting success by other means would simply lead to operating a dual system. Teachers and principals are too busy to devote time to reporting student success through two separate and sometimes exclusive systems. For example, a fifth-grade teacher might be participating in comprehensive reform efforts to align her teaching to the state standards, and so she is effectively documenting the children's progress toward achieving those standards. She feels comfortable that her teaching is facilitating the students' achievement of the standards. At the end of each marking period she must complete a report card that is structured around subject areas (e.g., social studies, math, science) rather than the standards. It is apparent to her that the report card is lagging behind the curriculum reform practices of the district as well as the teaching and assessment in her classroom. The result is that she must maintain one set of data to report on how well the students are achieving the standards and another set of data to accurately complete the report card. The investment of time in the two systems becomes a point of tension.

A sample report card for the Millcreek Township School District (Figure 6-1) is provided for your examination. The purpose of this sample is not to indicate that it is a perfect report card, for there is no such thing, but to show some of its high-quality features.

The instructional reading level of the child is reported. This provides an opportunity for parents to get a sense of the level of their child's reading and, over the course of the year, what progress is being made toward reading increasingly difficult text. It might also suggest that care is taken to fashion reading instruction that is appropriate to the child's capabilities. Each instructional reading level is also matched to a grade level to ground the understanding for people who are not aware of the actual ability levels.

The major comparison upon which the child's grade is based is his or her performance with the grade-level expectations. This suggests that the grade-level standards are the targets for instruction and that the grades (marks) are not generated by an average of work that might be casually or not at all related to the achievement of the standards. Some might believe that this is a narrowing of the curriculum, but given the current emphasis on accountability, focusing teacher and student effort toward desirable targets appears to be very logical.

Another feature that is worth noting in this report card sample is the breakdown of subskills in both math and reading. The subskills of reading are not exhaustive but are reasonable for communicating success without being overwhelming to parents. Remember that the purpose of the report card is to communicate levels of achievement to an audience. As educators become more informed about teaching and learning, there is a tendency to want to pass that information along to parents and others. If the information is of a technical or complicated nature, it can be more damaging than helpful. This report card avoids using highly technical language and exhaustive lists of subskills. If it is necessary to discuss in more detail what you want parents to

Student Name: _____ School Year: _____
School: _____ Grade: 1
Teacher: _____ Principal: _____

*Indicates your child has an Individualized Educational Program Plan (IEP) or Student Service Plan (SSP). Grades in these subjects reflect programs based on goals and objectives outlined in his/her plan.

Instructional Reading Range | A B C D E F G H I J K L M N O P Q R S T U V W X Y Z
Grade Level Range | K   1st   2nd   3rd   4th   5th   Beyond 5th

Instructional Reading Range:
Q1 _____ Q2 _____ Q3 _____ Q4 _____

3 : Exceeding Grade Level Standards	2 : Meeting Grade Level Standards	1 : Not Yet Meeting Grade Level Standards (Area of Concern)

Language Arts Standards	Q1	Q2	Q3	Q4
Reading:				
Reads fluently				
Understands what is read				
Word Study/Phonics:				
Uses strategies to solve new words				
Recognizes high frequency words				
Spelling:				
Learns required words				
Uses correct spelling in other areas				
Writing:				
Writes a simple sentence				
Writes a series of related ideas				
Uses punctuation and capitalization				
Prints legibly				

3 : Exceeding standards	2 : Meeting standards	1 : Not yet meeting standards

Math Standards	Q1	Q2	Q3	Q4
Computation				
Basic addition facts				
Basic subtraction facts				
Problem solving				

The following subjects are done as group activities and students are assessed based on participation.

SP=Satisfactory Participation   UP=Unsatisfactory Participation

	Q1	Q2	Q3	Q4
Science				
Social Studies				
Art				
Music				
Physical Education				

3 : Exceeding expectations	2 : Meeting expectations	1 : Not yet meeting expectations

Academic and Social Growth	Q1	Q2	Q3	Q4
Follows rules				
Works well with others				
Practices self-discipline				
Returns completed homework				
Shows effort in work				
Completes assignments during class time				
Listens and follows directions				
Participates in class				
Works neatly				

Figure 6-1. Millcreek Township Report Card
(Used with permission of the Millcreek Township School District.)

understand about their child, then a parent conference is a better choice than relying on a report card.

The Union City report card (Figure 6-2) offers a number of contemporary features. The report card is effectively linked to the qualities of effective student writing.

In some states, student writing samples are scored by teachers and state officials using rubrics that assess focus, organization, detail, content, conventions, and style. A report card that communicates this information to parents and students makes them aware of the vocabulary that is used by the state. Using these terms develops a common language that can result in an improved instructional focus by individual teachers, grade levels, and entire schools. It makes sense that if students in every grade are working toward common goals, they are more likely to achieve them than if each teacher is defining the elements of effective writing.

The purpose of this report is to communicate your child's academic progress in meeting grade level, district, and state expectations.

Performance Level Descriptors   Describes quality of student performance

4	Advanced, Exceeds Expectation	3 Proficient, Meets Expectation
2	Basic, Partial Understanding, Limited	1 Below Basic, Beginning, Not Yet
NA	Not assessed at this time	Incomplete

Reading Workshop (1st, 2nd, 3rd, 4th)
- 25 Book Goal — Number of books read: 1 __ 2 __ 3 __ 4 __
- Genre/Text Knowledge — Reads non-fiction, fiction, poetry, etc.
- Word Solving — Applies word skills to gain meaning
- Comprehension/Response
- Reading Level — Independent progress: 1 __ 2 __ 3 __ 4 __

Writing Workshop (1st, 2nd, 3rd, 4th)
- Author's Craft/Revision (Applies craft techniques)
- Traits of Quality Writing (Focus, Content, Organization, Style)
- Conventions of Writing (Spelling, Grammar, Punctuation)

Math Workshop (1st, 2nd, 3rd, 4th)
- Concepts, skills, and strategies
- Otter Creek Program — A structured program for sequential practice and mastery of basic facts.
- Addition: Levels A-Z
- Subtraction: Levels A-Z
- Multiplication: Levels A-W
- Division: Levels A-X

Speaking and Listening (1st, 2nd, 3rd, 4th)
- Expresses ideas clearly
- Listens with understanding

Environmental Studies (1st, 2nd, 3rd, 4th)
- Applies knowledge & skills through class work & projects

PERFORMANCE KEY: S= Satisfactory   U= Unsatisfactory

Media/Technology (1st, 2nd, 3rd, 4th)
- Demonstrates understanding and competency in grade level work and personal expectations

Physical Education (1st, 2nd, 3rd, 4th)
- Demonstrates understanding and competency in grade level work and personal expectations

Music (1st, 2nd, 3rd, 4th)
- Demonstrates understanding and competency in grade level work and personal expectations

Art (1st, 2nd, 3rd, 4th)
- Demonstrates understanding and competency in grade level work and personal expectations

Learner Qualities (1st, 2nd, 3rd, 4th)
4 Consistently   3 Most Often
2 Seldom   1 Never
- **Self-Directed Learner:** Sets goals, self-motivated, takes personal responsibility for behavior, completes daily work, and returns homework
- **Collaborative Worker:** Cooperates with others, constructively resolves conflict, contributes to the classroom community of learners.
- **Problem Solver:** Exercises self control, uses reasoning skills, makes decisions, efficiently solves problems.
- **Responsible Citizen:** Practices safety first, respects others & environment, follow classroom procedures.
- **Quality Producer:** Self monitors for accuracy, exhibits neat and legible work, produces quality work.

Figure 6-2. Union City Report Card
(Used with permission of the Union City School District.)

Compare the report cards in Figures 6-1 and 6-2. How are they different, and how are they alike?

Summary

Grading and the assignment of summative marks to a report card is a complex activity for all teachers. Teachers need to understand the purposes, comparisons, and influences of grading students in elementary and middle school classrooms. Because grading has many subjective aspects, teachers also need to understand how to render grades that are fairly calculated and accurately communicate student success. Changes in report card formats make it essential that teachers plan to collect data that can be efficiently used to reflect student achievement, effort, and behavior. Increased accountability measures that are reflected in standards-driven teaching have impacted grading and report cards. Understanding how the report card can be used effectively in a standards-driven environment is critical to becoming assessment literate.

Teaching Activities

1. Collect several different primary report cards from surrounding school districts or school systems. Focus on how each one reports success in reading and language arts. Some districts are likely to use grades and subskills, whereas others might use developmental continuums or letter grades. The value of the activity is for you to recognize the variety in how student success in reading and language arts is reported across school systems. Also consider how this report card might impact teaching in that school district.

2. Find a report card that uses a developmental continuum to report student success. These often report the student's success as developing the skill, maintaining the skill, mastering the skill, and so forth. Develop a rubric specifically for one area that will provide data to complete the report card.

3. Ask your colleagues whether grading is a subjective or an objective teacher activity. You might be surprised to find out how many persons think that grading is objective. Start a list of subjective decisions that teachers make on the way to determining a final grade. The length of the list can be enlightening. For example: decisions about the comparisons, standards versus curve, letter calculation versus percentage calculation, class participation. All of these make for wonderful discussions and show the subjective nature of grading.

Standardized Testing: Literacy in an Era of Accountability

1. To understand the purposes of standardized testing

2. To be able to interpret the derived scores associated with standardized testing results

3. To understand the various uses of standardized test information in school districts

4. To be able to employ sound practices for the administration of standardized tests

The Purpose of Standardized Tests

Elementary and middle school teachers are usually required to administer annual comprehensive examinations to their students in a wide range of subject areas. The purpose of these exams is to compare the performance of your students to that of students across the nation and to identify areas of strength and weakness. For that reason these examinations are administered, scored, and interpreted in the same fashion. The directions for the test, the amount of time given for students to complete each subtest, and the manner in which each test is scored and reported are as precisely controlled as possible. These standardized tests are commercially developed and usually identified by an acronym, such as ITBS (Iowa Tests of Basic Skills) or CAT (California Achievement Test). According to Reynolds, Livingston, and Willson (2006), the most widely used standardized group achievement tests are produced by three publishers: CTB McGraw-Hill publishes the California Achievement Test and two forms of the Terra Nova, Harcourt Assessment publishes the Stanford Achievement Test, and Riverside Publishing produces the Iowa Tests of Basic Skills, the Iowa Tests of

Educational Development, and the Tests of Achievement and Proficiency. These standardized achievement tests all require strict adherence to administration guidelines.

Standardized tests differ from classroom tests in a variety of ways. It is critical for teachers to understand the differences and to communicate that information to students and parents. The two greatest differences are the purpose of the test and the degree of difficulty of its items. Table 7-1 shows the differences between standardized tests and classroom teacher exams.

Table 7-1.   Differences Between Classroom and Standardized Assessments

Uniquely Standardized Assessment	Uniquely Classroom Assessment
Strives to *document* achievement	Strives to *increase* achievement
Informs *others* about students	Informs students about *themselves*
Provides assessment *of* learning	Provides assessment *for* learning
Reflects *standards* themselves	Reflects *targets* that underpin standards
Produces *comparable* results	Can produce results that are *unique* to individual students
Teacher's role is to *gauge* success	Teacher's role is to *promote* success
Student's role is to strive for a *high score*	Student's role is to strive for *improvement*
Motivates with the promise of *rewards and punishments*	Motivates with the promise of *success*

(Used with permission of the National Education Association.)

The reason for maintaining rigid consistency throughout all aspects of the standardized testing process is to make the test results (student scores) consistent with the scores of other students who have taken the same test. For example, if I test two groups of students on their ability to compute 20 multiplication problems, it would help my comparison if both groups were given the same directions, problems, and amount of time to complete the problems. Obviously, if I give one group of students 10 minutes more to complete the problems, then my comparison of the groups will suffer because of the advantage of extra time. Designing and administering the test with as many similarities as possible provides an opportunity to draw comparisons among diverse groups of students.

Testing that maintains this high degree of control attempts to approach the measure of student achievement in a scientific manner. Developers of standardized tests have spent significant time and resources to ensure that the results of standardized tests are generated from similar testing situations. Understanding that the primary purpose of standardized testing is to compare the students in your classroom to a group of students with similar characteristics is of central importance for interpreting the results. Despite negative impressions toward standardized tests among members of the education community, for the purpose of national comparison, standard measures maintain a clear advantage over teacher-made tests, grade point averages, and other summary classroom data.

Reflection   What comparison problems would you have if students were administered standardized tests with different formats? For example, what if one group takes a multiple-choice test and another group is given an essay format?

Inference Development from a Comparison Group

Because comparison with other students is so important in the process of external testing, it makes sense for teachers to understand the selection and composition of the comparison group. For example, suppose your third-grade students were being compared to a nationally derived group of gifted sixth graders. Short of a miracle, your students are probably not going to appear to have learned very much. On the other hand, if we compared the test results of a classroom of eighth graders to the test results of third graders, it would appear that they have experienced great success in learning. The composition of the comparison group is significant in determining the quality of the inferences we make about our students. The comparison group that is used by the makers of standardized tests is known as the *norm group*.

Although the selection of the specific standardized test battery is seldom left up to the individual classroom teacher, it helps teachers to understand test scores if they know the criteria for judging an appropriate norm group. Thus the testing company should provide information that describes its norm group. Three Rs are generally accepted as evaluative measures of quality norm groups: relevance, representativeness, and recency. *Relevance* means that the norm group is a group to which you would want to compare your students. *Representativeness* means that the norm group has a carefully planned sample that includes a cross-section of students from different subpopulations. Subpopulations that are gaining increased attention due to the recent accountability measures of No Child Left Behind Act include ESL students, ethnic minority students, students with IEPs, and students who live in poverty. *Recency* means that the norm group data is up-to-date. Think about how kindergarten students today would score if they were compared to kindergarten students in the 1960s. Students who attended kindergarten then would not have had the benefit of educational television, academic preschools, and the emphasis placed on early reading to children. Clearly, if norms are not recently developed, the comparisons can be misleading, thereby making the inferences incorrect.

Assuming a high quality of standardized test, the results can provide data to school district personnel to use for a variety of purposes. Kober (2002) states that standardized test results can do the following:

1. Provide information that is more standardized and consistent from school to school or district to district than the results of measures based on an individual teacher's judgment

2. Be used to compare achievement across different classrooms, schools, or districts, or between various racial, ethnic, income, and other subgroups of students

3. Provide valuable summary information about student performance by subject, skill, and knowledge area

4. Be collected, analyzed, and reported efficiently and at a relatively low cost

All these purposes are important to schools and school districts. Teachers often fail to realize that the purpose of standardized tests is not centrally focused on their small group of students or their individual classrooms. With increased accountability from state and federal agencies, classroom teachers will have to realize that standardized test data not only reflect on their classrooms but also reflect on their schools and school districts.

What Teachers Need to Know About Standardized Tests

School districts usually assign the selection of the standardized test to a committee of school personnel, key administrators, and/or assessment specialists. Once the test is selected and purchased, school districts tend to retain the same test for a number of years. There is a cost factor that makes the continued use of the same test desirable. The purchase of a standardized test battery that will assess elementary students in a variety of subject areas is a major investment by a school or school district. Using the same test assists district personnel in making comparisons about the school or district results from one year to the next.

Maintaining the same test also facilitates the comparison of individual student results from one year to the next. The accumulation of test data over several years provides schools with the opportunity to use the results to plan curriculum changes. School districts might complete a curriculum-test match prior to the selection of a test to make sure that the content of the curriculum matches the constructs being tested by the examination. Although the inherent value of doing so is obvious, unfortunately not all school districts invest the time and money to complete a matching activity.

Inexperienced teachers are not typically chosen to participate on committees that adopt standardized tests or conduct curriculum-test matches. Novice teachers or teachers new to a specific grade have limited exposure to the curriculum and to the sophisticated measurement concepts associated with standardized testing. All teachers, however, are expected to be able to administer standardized tests and interpret their results. In fact, Standard 3 of the AFT et al. (1990) clearly states that responsibility: "The teacher should be skilled in administering, scoring and interpreting the results of both externally produced and teacher produced assessment methods." Let's discuss these responsibilities in the next two sections.

How to Administer Standardized Tests in Your Classroom

The type of standardized tests that are most frequently administered to elementary-age children are group achievement tests. The purpose of group achievement tests is to obtain a measure of what students have learned prior to the testing date. Group achievement tests are administered to the entire class in the same setting, except in cases of absenteeism or special circumstances. These tests, frequently called *test batteries,* are composed of individual subtests that focus on different subject areas. For example, the Iowa Tests of Basic Skills (ITBS) has two separate subtests under reading: vocabulary and reading comprehension. Be sure you understand the concepts of group achievement tests, test batteries, and subtests. The administration and interpretation of achievement tests is built on an understanding of their purpose of achievement tests.

As you prepare for the administration of standardized tests, you will probably remember taking them throughout your own school career. Chances are you don't remember them as being a fun experience. There are not many ways to make the taking of these tests pleasurable, but there are some suggestions for making it more bearable for your students.

First, follow the suggested schedule that breaks the administration of the test battery into several different days of testing. Tests usually come with a schedule of suggested subtests that are to be administered on certain days. This schedule tries to ensure that students are not fatigued from overtesting while also ensuring that the test doesn't take up too many instructional days. Testing companies usually provide a recommended schedule, but individual school districts sometimes modify the administration schedule to fit the needs and pacing of the school. If you have never administered a standardized exam, you should consult a teacher or principal to find out how the administration of the test is structured.

Second, try to keep homework and classroom assignments light on the days of standardized testing. Students do not need to be mentally challenged on the days they are taking tests; the tests provide enough challenging opportunities for them. This is a wonderful opportunity for plays, choral readings, art projects, gross motor activities, and other noninstructional activities.

Third, be sure to prepare your students for the degree of difficulty they will encounter on the test. Teachers typically have high expectations for the performance of students on their own in-class tests; it is not uncommon for teachers to expect students to attain mastery (80%) or even a perfect score on an in-class exam. Questions on standardized tests, however, are selected to provide a degree of variability in scores, so not everyone is expected to get all the items correct. In fact, item selection in the development of standardized tests is usually dependent on a 50% degree of difficulty; that is, each question on the test was chosen because generally about half of the people missed it in the test development stage. The degree of difficulty may cause your students to sense uncommon levels of frustration and hopelessness. Young students need to be prepared for the inevitability that they are not going to correctly answer every item. They might also discover that the questions seem more difficult than usual. Encourage students to do their best despite the fact that they don't know the answers to some of the questions or that they think they have missed more than they usually miss on a test.

Fourth, communicate with the parents. Announcements can be sent to parents requesting that they make sure that students get enough rest on the night before the testing and breakfast on the day of the test. A more reasonable suggestion is to ask parents to maintain whatever schedule they have had in place all year with their children. A student who does not usually eat breakfast cannot suddenly be made to eat breakfast because he or she is taking a standardized test later in the day. You might also want to inform parents to avoid making dentist or doctor appointments during the times the tests are scheduled. This will help to reduce the number of makeups that have to be completed. School districts usually require that all students take the tests and that all the tests are processed to be sent to the scoring facility on the same day. Administering numerous test makeups is not a pleasant task.

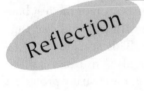 As a classroom teacher, you can prepare your students for the exam using some of the above suggestions. Are there any other ways you can prepare students and their families? It is also helpful to visit the Web site of your state and research the testing accommodations that are prescribed for the state-mandated tests.

We are going to skip scoring, the second standard mentioned in AFT et al. (1990). It is now more the exception than the rule that standardized tests are hand-scored by classroom teachers. If you must hand-score a standardized test, the directions for doing so can be found in the literature that accompanies the purchase of the test battery. Information of that nature can also be acquired by directly contacting the testing company.

How to Interpret the Results of Standardized Tests to Parents, Teachers, and Other School Professionals

In order to be able to interpret standardized test scores (and, yes, it is your responsibility), you must have a basic understanding of how the test results are generated and be able to report student results. Earlier we said that the purpose of the tests is to permit summary comparisons of individual student achievement in subject areas with students in the same grades nationally. In other words, we can compare how Jonathan or Michelle, two students in our fifth-grade classroom, scored compared to a national sample of persons in the same grade who took the test at the same point in the school year.

You will recall that the group to which your students are compared is referred to as the norm group. Norm groups consist of a large cross-section of students nationally who took the exam; their scores were compiled to gain a perspective of what the range of achievement appears to be in a particular grade. Each grade has its own norm group. In fact, to make more precise comparisons, norm-group data is available three different times of the year. Should your district decide to administer the test in the fall, winter, or—the most typical testing time—the spring, the testing companies can provide comparison norms.

Therefore, your interpretations will always be based on how well the test taker (Jonathan or Michelle, or any other person in your class) scored compared to the national sample group. The number of questions Jonathan or Michelle answered correctly on any of the subtests is referred to as his or her *raw score.* For example, let's imagine that there are 30 vocabulary words on the vocabulary subtest. If Jonathan correctly answers 25 of the questions, his raw score is 25 on that particular test. Should Michelle answer 27 of the questions correctly, her raw score would be 27. The interpretation of both of these scores would depend on how they compare to the raw scores of the norm group.

Interpreting the scores is your job, but in most school districts the scoring and the calculation of how your student compares is completed (for a fee) by the testing company that developed the examination. So far, with only two raw scores, we cannot make any interpretation of Jonathan or Michelle's achievement on the vocabulary subtest.

In order for us to make some interpretation of the standardized test results we use *derived scores.* The testing company generates these scores immediately after the tests have been scored. The test results are returned to school district personnel and come to the classroom teacher on a form that lists the individual scores of each child and provides a collective class summary. The derived scores tell us more about how to interpret the achievement of our students. Let's see how they might help us to understand more about our two fifth graders, Jonathan and Michelle, and their respective raw scores. Remember that Jonathan got a raw score of 25 out of 30 and Michelle got 27 out of 30 on the vocabulary subtest.

Three types of derived scores are important for teachers to understand in order to be able to interpret scores for their students, themselves, and the parents of their students: national percentile rank, stanine, and grade equivalent scores.

National Percentile Rank

The first score that helps us make sense of a raw score is the national percentile rank. In this case, it helps us to imagine that the norm group (all those fifth graders who took the vocabulary test at about the same time in the school year) is reduced to a national sample of 100 fifth-grade students. Jonathan's and Michelle's raw scores are compared to the scores of the norm group's performance, and a national percentile rank is calculated by the testing company. Suppose that Jonathan scores at the 83 national percentile rank. This means that out of a possible 100 fifth graders who took the same vocabulary test at the same time of year, Jonathan scored as well as or better than 82 other fifth graders. Do you see how this comparison would help teachers and parents further understand Jonathan's raw score? With a raw score, we know only how many questions Jonathan answered correctly, but with the percentile rank we have a better understanding of how his score compared with others from a national sample population.

Let's examine Michelle's score and see if we can make a similar interpretation. Michelle's raw score was 27, which is easily recognizable as a good score, but how good is her score compared to other fifth graders? Michelle's national percentile rank is 92. This means that out of a possible 100 fifth graders who took the same test at the same time of year, Michelle scored as well as or better than 91 other fifth graders. This also helps us to understand how her score compares to Jonathan's. Her raw score was higher, so her national percentile rank is higher, too.

Can you infer from this what a local percentile rank would be? The student's raw score is compared to the raw scores of other students from the same school district. For example, suppose our two students reside in a district where there are three elementary schools with seven fifth-grade classrooms. The local percentile rank would be derived from comparing Jonathan's and Michelle's raw scores with the students from the seven fifth-grade classes in the school district. Local percentile ranks therefore help district officials to make comparisons of achievement levels among schools within a local education unit.

Stanines

Another descriptive statistic is the stanine score. *Stanine* is short for "standard nine" and is used to provide additional information for interpreting the raw score. Usually stanine scores follow national percentile rank scores. Let's continue with the above example. If Michelle's percentile rank is 92, it would appear in a summary report displayed as 92-9. The 92 is the national percentile rank, and the 9 is the stanine score.

There are nine levels of stanines:

Stanines 9, 8, 7 indicate high achievement.

Stanines 6, 5, 4 indicate average achievement.

Stanines 3, 2, 1 indicate low achievement.

If Jonathan's vocabulary score was 83-8, that means his national percentile rank was 83 and he is in the eighth stanine, which is in the middle of the high achievement range. There is nothing secretive or perplexing about stanines and their use. They are intentionally direct and simple descriptions of student achievement levels. One of their major purposes is to eliminate the overinterpretation of test results. In the case of explaining to parents what the national percentile rank means, the stanine score provides additional explanation about its comparability. It is especially helpful in the area of middle-range scores. Because standardized test questions are designed at a 50% degree of difficulty, the range of average achievement includes scores below the midpoint, or 50th percentile. Because of the difference between classroom tests and standardized measures, this may be difficult for some parents and teachers to understand and accept. The stanine score helps to explain that a score below the 50th percentile can actually fall within an average range of ability, due to the intentionally developed difficulty of the test questions.

Notice that each of the three levels can be further divided into high, middle, and low portions. For example, a student who scores in the fourth stanine can be described as a person who has scored in the low portion of the average range. Similarly, a person who scores in the sixth stanine has scored in the higher portion of the average range.

Grade Equivalent Scores

Grade equivalent (GE) scores are the most misinterpreted of the three derived scores covered in this summary. The importance of understanding GEs is to limit their misuse and to help clarify their meaning to uninformed groups.

GEs are composed of two numbers. The first number indicates the grade level, and the second number refers to the month of the school year. For example, a 46 means that the student's GE is fourth grade, sixth month. Remember that the months are numbered according to the academic year, not the calendar year, as follows:

September	0	February	5
October	1	March	6
November	2	April	7
December	3	May	8
January	4	June	9

What would be your guess as to the meaning of K7? If you guessed that it refers to a kindergarten student in April, you would be correct.

Let's take a moment to discuss the use of months in this derived score. It is important to use months to describe student age or achievement, especially in the primary grades, because each month is a significant portion of a child's life. For example, if a child is 5 years old, he or she could be 5 years and 1 month old or 5 years and 11 months old. The difference of 10 months is significant when you are talking about a youngster who is only 5 years of age. The major significance of this is that our learning and testing expectations for a 5-year-old differ greatly from that of a child who is 5 years and 11 months old. As children get older, the use of months becomes a less critical variable in determining learning expectations.

Now that we have a preliminary understanding, let's discuss how the GE is supposed to be interpreted. The best answer is very carefully! In the cases of Jonathan and Michelle, we know that they have high national percentile ranks and stanine scores on the vocabulary subtest. We can expect their GEs to be high as well. Jonathan's GE is 72, and Michelle's is 81. This means that Jonathan got the same number of items correct on the vocabulary test that we would expect of a seventh grader in the second month of school. Michelle's score means that she answered the same number of items correctly as a student in the first month of eighth grade.

Because these are such impressive-sounding scores, we must be cautious in how they are interpreted. In the course of your career you will have parents suggesting to you that scores similar to Jonathan's and Michelle's warrant consideration for promotion to a higher grade. There are several cautions that you must be ready to discuss with them.

First, recall the first principle of sound assessment from chapter 1: the need to employ multiple measures in order to make sound decisions. Recommending the promotion of a student to a higher grade would depend on an examination of considerable amounts of additional information. Second, we would be basing our decision on the strength of a single test that required a student to select the correct definition of just 30 words. Thirty vocabulary words are not enough evidence to support a promotion in grade. Third, the test is a fifth-grade vocabulary test. If we were to administer the seventh- or eighth-grade vocabulary test to the student in question, it's likely that he or she would not perform nearly as well. Finally, there are social and developmental issues that suggest the utmost caution in promoting a child to a higher grade in school. We would want to take all of these factors into consideration prior to making any decision to promote a student.

Reflection   The examples in this chapter (Jonathan and Michelle) scored well. Is it possible that GE could be misinterpreted and misused with lower achieving students?

In summation, let's consider how to phrase the GE score so that parents and others might gain a clearer and more complete understanding of its meaning. Example: Here is how the GE score of 39 in arithmetic concepts for a second grader named Amy might be interpreted: Amy answered the same number of items correctly on the arithmetic concepts test as what we might expect of a third grader in the ninth month of school.

Should you find that someone still does not understand this concept, try this explanation: Amy answered the same number correct as a third grader in the ninth month of school, if the third grader would have come back to take the second-grade test. (If the person you are attempting to explain this to scratches his or her head and asks if that happens very often, you can assure them that it almost never happens, but that's how GE scores make you think and talk!)

A summary of Jonathan and Michelle's scores are shown in Table 7-2.

Table 7-2. The Interpretation of Sample Test Results

Name of Student	Name of Score	Score	What Does It Tell?
Jonathan Michelle	Raw score Raw score	25 (of 30) 27 (of 30)	Number of correct responses
Jonathan Michelle	National percentile rank National percentile rank	83 92	Placement per 100 students compared nationally
Jonathan Michelle	Local percentile rank Local percentile rank	78 86	Placement per 100 students compared locally
Jonathan Michelle	Stanine Stanine	8 9	Achievement level of the student's score
Jonathan Michelle	Grade equivalent score Grade equivalent score	72 81	Score's meaning in a school or (grade) reference

Reflection

Now that we have covered what are the most frequently used derived scores, use the classroom report of the Iowa Tests of Basic Skills (Figure 7-1) to test your abilities to understand the scores. Consider how you might present this information to parents and/or other school professionals. Additional information about presenting this to parents can be found in chapter 11.

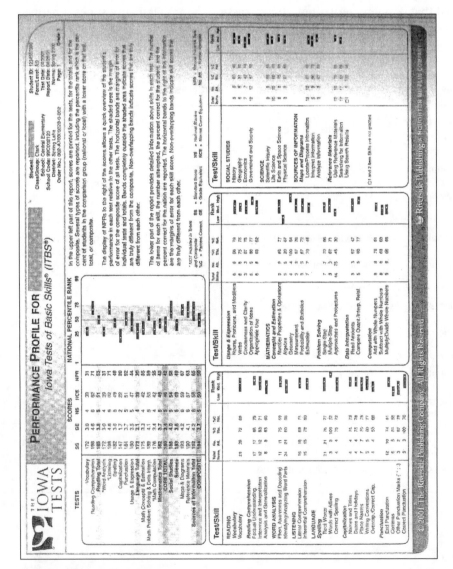

Figure 7-1. ITBS Profile

Achievement Tests Versus Intelligence Tests

Achievement tests are the most frequently administered standardized tests in American schools, but they are not the only ones. Another type of standardized test is the intelligence quotient (IQ), or aptitude, test. The major difference between them lies in the purpose for which teachers and other school professionals use them. Achievement tests are administered to determine how much a student has learned up to that point; IQ tests are used to predict a student's capacity to learn. Intelligence tests generate a score that is used to predict the degree of success the student should or will have in an academic environment. There is some basic information you should know about IQ tests before we discuss their use in schools.

1. The average IQ score on most measures is 100.

2. A minimum IQ score is used in many states as one of the entrance requirements for gifted programs.

3. IQ tests are normally not administered in every grade, but instead they may be given in the lower grades (1–3), again in the intermediate grades (4–6), and once again in middle school, depending on the school district.

4. IQ tests can be administered to groups of students as well as to individuals.

IQ is measured more reliably as the student grows older. Part of the difficulty in measuring early intelligence is separating it from developmental factors. Let's consider the different groups of children who come to kindergarten. First, there is probably a group that has attended preschool for at least 1 year (or more likely 2 years). A second group did not attend preschool at all but did not miss a single episode of children's educational television. A third group comes to school with none of the above and has never even had a book read to them. Can you predict how these students might score on an IQ test? Do you think the test is likely to measure their innate cognitive ability or the environmental factors that characterized their early years? The influence of environmental factors is always present, but it is especially prevalent when measuring intelligence in young children. You can now see why school districts administer another IQ test in the intermediate grades.

Can you understand why the IQ score of a student in grades 1–3 might be significantly higher than the IQ score of the same student in grades 4–6?

Standard Error of Measurement

All exams have a standard error of measurement. That is, all tests or assessments fail to measure with complete accuracy what students know. For any number of reasons—cheating, guessing, illness—the score is contaminated and is not a correct indication of what a person knows. The test score that is likely to be generated consistently and with confidence contains a calculated standard error of measurement. Knowing this is especially helpful when discussing IQ tests. The standard error for an IQ test might be as great as +3 or −3 points. This can be interpreted to mean that a person who attains a score of 125 might, on a retest, score as high as 128 or as low as 122. This concept is especially important to teachers who must face placement decisions that utilize IQ scores. Teachers must understand that an IQ score of 128 does not necessarily disqualify a student from gifted education; it merely suggests that more data should be collected and perhaps an additional IQ test given.

Who Uses Standardized Assessment Data?

On January 8, 2002, President George W. Bush signed the No Child Left Behind Act (NCLB), the reauthorization of the Elementary and Secondary Education Act (ESEA). This incorporated significant regulations on how to determine the instructional quality of America's schools. Externally developed tests became the central tool for measuring the success of students, schools, and school districts. NCLB signals a dramatic shift to increased accountability placed on teachers and other school professionals.

The following statement might be released by a school district as the reason for administering a standardized test: "These tests represent one of the district's primary ways of monitoring the academic success of the student body as a whole as well as the performance of specific schools, classrooms, and individual students." One might infer from this statement that the data generated by standardized measures are used for a variety of purposes. Very often elementary and middle school teachers fail to realize the secondary uses of standardized test data within a school district. Assessment-literate teachers must recognize the importance of the data as it pertains to their students and their teaching, but it is even better if they understand the wider uses of the data.

Below is a discussion of the different people who might use standardized test data and why.

Superintendents

Superintendents are usually concerned with aggregated data, which appears in the form of totals for an entire school district. Your scores are often combined with the scores of other teachers in the district to generate a total score of the district for a certain grade. Much of this data is then turned into generalizations about the status of the school district's instructional success. Because the scores of each school district must be reported for each grade, such scores can affect the public's perception of the quality of its schools.

Curriculum Specialists

Curriculum specialists have the direct responsibility of overseeing the quality of the curriculum in the school system. Because the standardized test data provides scores for the entire district and for each grade, decisions concerning textbook adoption and new programs are often based on these measures. Developing a match between what is taught in the curriculum and what is tested by the standardized exams is an important responsibility of these specialists. Not only are they concerned with whether the curriculum needs of the district are being met, they must also be attentive to the success of certain subpopulations. The school system has a responsibility to address achievement gaps between the aggregated data and the individual scores of these groups. Local norms can provide helpful data for this process.

Principals

Principals are sometimes referred to as the instructional leaders of buildings in which they are the administrator. Serving as an instructional leader is an important role among all the other responsibilities of a principal. If a principal accepts the role of instructional leader, then making decisions about the successes in teaching and learning that are occurring in the building are based in part on the interpretation of external test scores. There is an increased amount of accountability thrust on principals as the public depends more on achievement scores to gauge the quality of a school. NCLB requires that the scores for each school are published for the parents and the public every year. The scores indicate whether the school has met the adequate yearly progress (AYP) goals of the state, and they also report on how the individual school compares to the state average. You should not be surprised to find that there is greater emphasis on preparing students to take achievement tests than there was when you were a student.

School Psychologists

School psychologists are more likely to use individual test scores than aggregated data. A licensed school psychologist is the only person in the school district who is authorized to make special education placements for students. For that reason, if you suspect that one of your students is in need of services for exceptionalities, you will probably have to meet with the school psychologist and other members of a pupil personnel team. In addition to interpreting the standardized test information, the psychologist will probably be interested in classroom performance, social and emotional behavior, habits, routines, and any other information that you can provide. You can see that the use of multiple assessment measures would facilitate this important decision-making process. The standardized test information will be part of a larger referral process for students who are in need of special education services; the data from the standardized tests alone are not usually sufficient to make a placement. In-depth tests, as well as anecdotal classroom records and teacher and parental input, are required to make an informed decision.

Teachers

Teachers use standardized test data to make general judgments about the relative success of students individually and as a group. The scores generated from group achievement tests are not sufficient to make an accurate diagnosis of specific problem areas but can provide a broad profile of student strengths and weaknesses. Teachers also review the test data of a student's previous schooling to gain an idea of whether the student's performance this year is relatively the same as it has been in previous years. Severe drops in an individual student's achievement scores should be questioned.

Parents

Parents use standardized test data to confirm what they already think about their child. Standardized test scores for upper-grade students tend to remain reasonably consistent. Not surprisingly, parents become more interested in an explanation of the data if it appears to run counter to their beliefs or to the performance of the student in the past few years. This is the parents' right, and they should inquire if there is a particular drop in scores. They should be equally interested in scores that increase, but it has been my experience that elevated scores do not attract the same interest and require the same degree of explanation that low scores do.

Information About Tests That Teachers Should Know

In light of the No Child Left Behind legislation, teachers must become more knowledgeable about what tests can tell us and what they can't. Many state accountability systems treat test scores like precise calculations when they are really more like estimates. As an informed classroom teacher, you should be able to recognize some of the following limitations of tests, the reasons they can fluctuate that have little to do with student achievement.

Standard error of measurement. Every large-scale test has a standard error of measurement similar to the margin of error in an opinion poll, which is intended to give people an idea of the test's accuracy. It will be important for you to know the standard error of measurement on the tests of the state in which you work.

Sampling variation. A test is a sample of all possible questions that could be asked about a subject. A test is also a sample of a student's behavior at a single point in time. As states make alterations in the tests that are administered to children, the specific knowledge and skills that are sampled change.

Score inflation. Teaching to the test can raise scores without students actually learning more. If we intentionally focus on only the learning targets that appear on the state tests, are we really preparing students with a well-rounded education?

Changes in the test-taking population. Yearly changes in student population can cause fluctuations in the average test scores of a class or a school. The variation of student abilities, behaviors, and dispositions from one class to the next can have significant impact on cumulative scores.

Summary

Standardized measures of school achievement are going to be a part of the elementary and middle school environment for years to come. Because of legislative mandate, the success and failure of teachers, schools, and school districts are now measured by the scores from standardized tests. For teachers to successfully participate in assessment-driven environments, it is of vital importance for them to be able to administer and interpret standardized tests scores. The interpretation of scores requires that teachers understand the importance of norm groups, test development, and the meaning of derived scores. Teachers must also be aware of how achievement and aptitude tests differ and how their information can be used collectively to help make decisions about children. Finally, teachers need to be test savvy enough to know when scores are being inappropriately used by individuals inside as well as outside the school or school system.

Teaching Activities

1. Try to recall the last time you had to take a standardized test. Perhaps you had to take the SAT, the ACT, the Praxis I, or the Miller's Analogy Test. Think about how you felt going into the test. Did you experience any test anxiety, or were you fairly confident? Discuss how the emotions of students might impact the results on a standardized test.

2. Role-play a parent-teacher conference using a set of derived scores from a standardized measure. Along with a partner, prepare a script of how you might inform the parent of the child's success. Complete one for a student who has done well, one for an average student, and one for a student who has not done well. Is your language similar? Do you approach the discussion of

the scores in the same way with each student performance? After completing that part of the exercise, have a colleague role-play the part of an understanding parent and one who is less understanding and perhaps a bit more difficult. Examine your responses and discuss suggestions for dealing with a difficult conference.

3. Interview a school psychologist and a building principal and ask them how they use standardized testing information in their school duties. Interview a teacher and compare the use of scores by the teacher to the other school professionals you interviewed.

Assessment
in the Context
of the Classroom

Chapter

8

August: Making Greater Use of Assessment to Begin the New School Year

Goals of the Chapter

1. To recognize the types of assessment preparation that will help you organize for a new school year

2. To understand the importance of setting up your grade book and management plan prior to the arrival of students

3. To decide on the types of communication you intend to use during the school year

4. To be able to link assessment activities to the contextual needs of your classroom organization

Preteaching Activities

Teachers enter each new school year with the intention of being caring and fair to each student and competent in all that they do in classrooms. The excitement of a new year usually accompanies a resolve to improve their practice and to be respected classroom teachers. As they grow in their professional development, they evolve into teachers who are comfortable with a wide range of actions and responsibilities that accompany the complexity of teaching. The purpose of this chapter is to provide suggestions that enable teachers to organize the assessment aspects of their teaching and to contribute to their pursuit of becoming accomplished and competent teachers.

Before we begin a discussion of what we might do to organize our assessment practices, let's recall the guiding principles that were emphasized in the first chapter of this book. The development of assessment competence should be grounded on sound assessment practices that require teachers to be cognizant of the following:

1. Employing multiple measures to facilitate decision making about students

2. Matching assessment tools with the instructional objectives and procedures for the lessons

3. Effectively communicating the results of assessments to pupils, parents, and other school professionals

In most states, August is the month in which teachers are busy preparing for the start of school but have not yet begun to teach. Regardless of when school starts in your state, it makes sense to devote a chapter to preteaching activities that can influence your teaching success. This chapter therefore addresses preparing communications to parents, setting up a grading plan, and developing a classroom management plan that is supportive of your report card.

Preparing Communications to Parents

Communicating assessment information should begin before children arrive at school. It's critical for elementary and middle school teachers to recognize the importance of communication as a means of developing a cooperative spirit with the caregivers of their students. It is the teacher's responsibility to initiate clear and frequent interaction with the students' primary caregivers. A welcoming letter may be sent to parents or guardians about 2 weeks before school begins. Some school districts, however, require teachers to make telephone contact or even visit the homes of the children before the first day of school. Personal contact has an advantage over written communication because the latter requires precise wording and can be vulnerable to misinterpretation. Unlike written communication, personal interaction allows face-to-face discussion, eases awkwardness, and promotes a rich understanding of the child's background. Unfortunately, home visits and telephone contacts prior to the beginning of school are generally impractical or even impossible. As a result, getting the first written communication to say what you want it to say is extremely important.

The welcoming letter can take a number of forms and include different types of information. Think through how this letter fits your intention to communicate with parents or guardians for the school year. For example, examine the following sequence of letters that one elementary teacher sends home in the first months and decide how your initial letter might be constructed to fit within this framework. Although some of these letters have nothing to do with assessment issues, they are, nonetheless, essential contributions to the teacher-parent assessment connection, and they typify the context of elementary teaching.

Purpose	Approximate Date
Introductory Letter	August 15
Discipline Policy Notification	First Friday after Labor Day
Homework and Grading Policy Letter	Middle of September

Letter Seeking Parent Volunteers	October 1
Halloween Party Directions	October 25
Invitation to Parent Visitation	November
Notification of Thanksgiving Play	November

You can see from the above list that it is unrealistic to develop an introductory letter that attempts to clarify the entire range of possible topics that elementary teachers will need to communicate. Therefore, let us focus first on the development of a welcoming letter and then form a second letter designed to explain our homework and grading policies.

Essential Elements of the First Communication

What writing style should be used in the welcoming letter? An important consideration in the development of the letter is to make sure that we use language that is positive, encouraging, and professional yet conversational in style. Beginning teachers often attempt to convey their expectations to parents in a style that sounds like a philosophy of education treatise that they penned for a course in their undergraduate preparation. Although it is reasonable to say that you will "attempt to meet the needs of your students," it's probably overkill to say that you intend to "draw on the students' background knowledge to construct pedagogically sound experiences that appeal to a variety of learning styles." You might recall from the fundamentals of writing instruction that the consideration of your audience is of extreme importance. The letter's purpose is to open a communication line between the teacher and the caregivers. If you use language that is unfamiliar to your audience, you have defeated the primary purpose of your communication before it is even sent.

An important component of the letter is a list of times that parents can contact you. You should compose an informational piece that ends up posted on the refrigerator in each student's home. To facilitate the letter's use, make sure that the contact information can be cut from the letter if necessary. A parent informed me that since she had three children attending different schools, it was necessary for her to cut out the contact information from the letters in order to post them all on the refrigerator. Figure 8-1 shows a sample letter with cutout information.

September 5

Dear Parent,

Now that the school year has begun, I would like to introduce myself. I am Julie Heiser, and I will be teaching your child's third-grade class. This is my first year teaching at Cleveland Elementary. I completed my undergraduate degree at State University and am completing my master's degree at Northern University.

I am eager for the chance to work with your child this year. To make it a successful year for your child, I feel that it is extremely important for teacher and parent to work together. Therefore, you can contact me with concerns by calling Cleveland Elementary School at (570) 555-5555. I am available after school from 3:00 p.m. to 4:00 p.m., or you may email me at jh@cleveland.com at any time.

Throughout the year, I will be sending home newsletters to provide you with information about classroom activities. I will also offer you ideas on how you can work with your child at home to promote your child's best work in the classroom. The newsletter will also contain field trip information. This year I hope to get the students out of the classroom for some great experiences. So far I have two day trips planned, to the zoo and to the City Historical Museum.

Together we can make this a successful year for your child! Please feel free to contact me at any time; I value your input and concerns and would be happy to discuss them with you anytime throughout the year.

Sincerely,

Julie Heiser

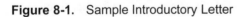

Ms. Heiser's Contact Information
Cleveland Elementary School

School Phone: (570) 555-5555   School Day Times: 8:30 a.m.–3:00 p.m.

School Email: jh@cleveland.com   Times to Contact Me: 3:00–4:00 p.m.

Figure 8-1.   Sample Introductory Letter

Additional content includes the following:

- Something about yourself that might connect you with parents
- How often you intend to communicate
- An encouraging statement and a willingness to address any questions or concerns parents or guardians might have

If necessary, address the needs of any non-English-speaking families with children assigned to your classroom.

Reflection   Examine the sample welcoming letter. Are there any changes you might make? How might this letter be constructed differently if you were a middle school math, science, or social studies teacher?

It is most important that you do not attempt to address everything that you want to accomplish for the year in this letter. Multipage letters that attempt to lay out the entire school year can send a subtle message to parents that you want to put all the information in one letter so that you don't have to be concerned with the bothersome task of frequent communication. Finally, make sure that your first communication to parents is error free. Have a colleague or a family member proofread your letter before you send it out. Don't trust the spellchecker that is part of your word processing package to catch spelling errors.

After years of reviewing opening letters, I would also offer the following advice:

- Be careful not to start too many sentences with *I.* A letter I recently reviewed contained seven consecutive sentences that began this way. Besides being poor writing, it sends the message that you are slightly egocentric.

- Check that you use proper agreement. Avoid sentences that say, "My goal is to make your child become all they can be." The noun *child* is singular, but the pronoun *they* is plural. This type of disagreement is a frequent error because the writer shifts back and forth from referring to one child versus an entire class of children, or because the writer wants to avoid using a gender pronoun when speaking of a child in general.

- Avoid informal language such as "If you want to get a hold of me, call this number." Instead say, "If you need to contact me during the day, I can be reached at this number."

- Although it is important to provide the school telephone number and perhaps your home number in the letter, I would avoid including a cell phone number. As a professional, you have the responsibility to offer a means for parent contact, but you also have the right to a personal life away from school. Offering your cell phone number might result in invasive calls that ultimately frustrate the relationship you are trying build.

Remember that the welcoming letter is the first opportunity for parents to form perceptions and judgments of you. Store the letter in a retrievable spot so that you can change or reword parts of the letter for the next school year.

Using Web Pages to Facilitate Communication

Communication between home and school has greatly increased due to the Internet. School districts are making homework assignments and students' grades available for examination by accessing district-developed sites. Using a Web site as a means to communicate with parents (and former students) can be effective, but you will need to know about your audience. How many of your families have Internet capability? In areas of socioeconomic stress, it is unlikely that all the families of your students have convenient or consistent access to computers. If you are unsure who has the necessary technology, proceed cautiously about putting essential information on your Web site. The first communication is so important as a greeting and an opening to the year that it should be sent through the postal system. You can then be certain that all households have received your welcoming communication. If you determine that all the parents have Internet access and are comfortable using electronic communication, then subsequent communications can be sent to parents by e-mail and Web site postings. If you designate your Web site as a means by which students and parents can contact you, then you have a responsibility to check it frequently and respond to their inquiries.

Creating too many means of communication can be problematic. For example, if you have e-mail and voicemail at your school along with all the traditional means of contact—notes from parents, parent calls to the office, and stop-in visits—you might want to ask yourself if you really should open yet another line of communication through a Web site that will require additional management, time, and effort. The decision rests with the individual teacher, but it might be prudent to limit the number of contacts that one has to check each day. There is an obvious downside to having to check five sources of possible communication each day. Time is essential to elementary and middle school teachers, and how you use your time will determine your overall efficiency as a professional.

Reflection

Think about the community in which you teach. Are there modes of communication that are more effective than others? Should you attempt to add more, or should you delete some of the means you currently use?

Developing a Letter Explaining Grading Policies to Parents

In developing a letter to explain homework or grading policies, you should keep your purpose squarely in focus. Your purpose is to communicate information about aspects of homework and/or policies that determine how you calculate students' report card grades. The tone of this communication is official, but again it is critical to use language that is understandable. You might want to start the letter with important information on the school district's grading and homework policies. It is possible that the parents of your students are unaware of or misinformed about school policies. For example, some school districts have recently enacted policies that forbid the use of zeros in calculating percentage grades for students. As an employee of the school district, you must comply with the policy, so it is helpful to share with parents the official guidelines you are following. For parents who are new to the district, this could be their first encounter with the policy.

The following is an informational report on changes in grading procedures that one school district provided to its parents and residents (Hall, 2004):

> Issuing report card grades is a delicate and complicated process that is not taken lightly at the Elizabeth Forward School District (EFSD). Letter grades (A, B, C, D, and F) are meant to be a reflection of a student's academic performance over an accumulation of past months of instruction. More recently, that performance is to reflect a student's understanding of the academic standards as set forth by both State and National Departments of Education. Ultimately, the goal is to present, in a single unit, how much of a subject area a student has actually learned after a period of 9 weeks of instruction and, finally, over a period of 9 months of instruction. (p. 8)

After a brief explanation of the variety of factors that might influence grades and the presentation of a standard percentage scale to be used in grades 4–12, the informational report discusses the important change in the grading process:

> Recently, however, some changes have been made in the calculation of failing grades. These changes have been made as a result of an examination of all the possible factors that influenced grades as well as an understanding of what it would take for a failing student to achieve future success. When a student earns a failing grade that is below 55%, that student will receive an F on his/her report card. However, the percentage assigned will be 55% regardless of what the actual percentage earned might be. In addition, this 55%, and not the actual 45%, will be used to calculate the final grade for the year. For example: In combining Nikki's scores over the first 9 weeks, it is determined that she has earned 90 points out of 200 total possible points, or 45%. On her report card she will receive a letter grade of F. However, the computer will assign 55% instead of the actual 45% that she has earned. Furthermore, [to] calculate[e] Nikki's final grade for the year, 55% and not the actual 45% that she earned during the first 9-week period will be combined with her other three 9-week scores (55% + 68% + 70% + 74%). Consequently, she would receive a D (66.8%) for her final grade.

In the previous example had she not been assigned the 55% as the lowest possible failing grade, Nikki would have had little chance of earning a passing grade regardless of how much her grades had improved throughout the year. Having established a future of failure so early in the year would most likely have serious implications for Nikki's future as a student. (p. 9)

(Used with permission of the Elizabeth Forward School District.)

This school district report is an example of how a districtwide communication can be used in conjunction with a teacher's personal grading policies. The combination helps to inform parents about how grades are calculated and ensures that communication about student success is open and well coordinated. This report could be attached to your letter.

The completion of homework is often an element in the calculation of student grades. You might decide to include in your grading letter a brief discussion of your homework guidelines. It is always a good idea to advance the notion that teamwork contributes to the successful completion of homework. Children who complete their homework generally take responsibility, seek help from their teachers, and are supported at home in their efforts. It is advisable to mention the importance of homework as an additional practice that helps to reinforce the information that you taught during the day. Extra practice ensures that students develop increased levels of facility, fluency, or understanding. Be careful to assign homework that does not involve the learning of new skills or concepts. Parents or caregivers do not want the responsibility of "teaching" their child new skills; they are much more comfortable reinforcing skills. In diplomatic, nonthreatening language, explain the consequences of consistently unprepared homework.

As you address the grading information, briefly share your beliefs about fairness and judgment in grading issues. Use several sentences to explain district or school policy if it provides background for how you have developed your procedures or practices. You might also include an explanation of how behavior is reflected in a section of the report card. If you intend this communication to be a two-page informational letter, include a section that provides frequently asked questions (and their answers). Conclude the letter with an invitation to call you with questions about anything that was confusing or unexplained.

Do you see how communications to parents can be altered according to their purpose? Can you think of other messages that would require specific attention and careful wording?

Table 8-1 summarizes the elements of two types of communication to parents.

Table 8-1.   Elements of Two Communications to Parents or Guardians

Introductory Communication to Parents

Length:	One or two pages
Spacing:	double
Font:	12-point Times Roman is easy to read
Style:	Professionally conversational, encouraging and inviting
Critical Information:	A welcoming statement
	Something about yourself
	Times you can be contacted
	School phone number
	Boldface contact information
	Information about frequency and form of your subsequent communications
	One or two highlights of the upcoming school year
	Error free
Additional Optional Considerations:	Don't attempt to include everything in one letter.
	Provide the critical communication information in an area that can be cut from the letter and posted.
	Adaptations for non-English-speaking persons

Explaining Homework and Grading Policies to Parents

Length:	One or two pages
Spacing:	double
Font:	12-point Times Roman is easy to read
Style:	Professionally conversational but technically clear (Ask a friend to read it)
	Sent well ahead of first report card
Critical Information:	Homework policy statements
	Team effort: teacher, parent, student
	Rewards and consequences
	Homework and its impact on grading
	Grading policy (district)
	Personal beliefs
	Comment or questions
	FAQs
	Error free
	Adaptations for non-English-speaking persons

Organizing a Grade Book Prior to the Start of Classes

Another activity that can help you organize your classroom is to prepare a grade book or place the names of your students in an electronic grade program. Classroom rosters are usually completed by the middle of August, so you have an opportunity to set this up prior to the first day of school. Consider the layout and contents of the report card you will be using. If you haven't had an opportunity to view elementary and middle school report cards in the last decade, you will notice significant changes from the format you remember. The nature of what is reported and the form in which it is reported have changed dramatically. (See chapter 6 for samples.) There are several commercially available grade-book programs that can assist teachers in the completion of their grade books. School districts often purchase one of these programs and encourage teachers to use it. As school districts develop more Web-based grading practices, it is likely that the sophistication of grading programs will increase. Several grading programs are available at the following Web addresses:

My Grade Book	www.mygradebook.com
ClassAction Gradebook	www.classactiongradebook.com
ThinkWare Educator	www.thinkware.com

Preparing a grade book or program that will allow you to easily convert the grades to a report card will be to your advantage. For example, setting up a grade book to calculate percentages may be appropriate in some grades, but in other grades the content-area (or school-district) skills are reported in more absolute terms (advanced mastery, proficient mastery, basic mastery, and below basic mastery). A bit of preparation here can save you considerable confusion and time later. If you are teaching in an area that uses levels of mastery to report subskills, it is clearly advantageous to evaluate student work using a scoring rubric that lists the mastery levels appearing on the report card. This eliminates awkward conversions of scores from one marking scale to another. Imagine that as a beginning teacher you have been scoring your third graders' work using percentages for the first half of a grading period, then you find out that the report card is constructed around absolute values. Converting percentages to absolute levels of achievement can be an odious task. Explaining the conversion formula to parents or school professionals could be compromising.

In the upper elementary grades you might want to determine in advance the kinds of activities that you intend to use to generate grades for the first marking period. Sharing this information with your students sends a message that you are not attempting to blindside them with an assignment. Should you decide to weight certain activities in the calculation of the 9-week grade, this also provides you with the time to think through the weights and share the process with your students.

It is also important to consider the social aspects of the report card. Teachers some-times begin the school year with a management plan but fail to link it to the information that is reported to parents. Figure 8-2 shows two sample social areas of report cards that describe student behaviors by different means. The reporting differences create different approaches for guiding and ultimately reporting student classroom behaviors.

Millcreek Township School District

3 : Exceeding expectations	2 : Meeting expectations	1 : Not yet meeting expectations

Academic and Social Growth	Q 1	Q 2	Q 3	Q 4
Follows rules				
Works well with others				
Practices self–discipline				
Returns completed homework				
Shows effort in work				
Completes assignments during class time				
Listens and follows directions				
Participates in class				
Works neatly				

Union City School District

Learner Qualities 4 Consistently 3 Most Often 2 Seldom 1 Never	1st	2nd	3rd	4th
Self-Directed Learner: Sets goals, self-motivated, takes personal responsibility for behavior, completes daily work, and returns homework				
Collaborative Worker: Cooperates with others, constructively resolves conflict, contributes to the classrooms community of learners.				
Problem Solver: Exercises self control, uses reasoning skills, makes decisions, efficiently solves problems.				
Responsible Citizen: Practices safety first, respects others & environment, follows classroom procedures.				
Quality Producer: Self monitors for accuracy, exhibits neat and legible work, produces quality work.				

Figure 8-2. Social Behavior Portions of Two Report Cards
(Used with permission of the Millcreek Township School District and the Union City School District.)

The first sample is the academic and social growth section of a second-grade report card from the Millcreek Township School District. (The contents of the entire report card can be found in chapter 6.) This sample shows how you can develop a management plan that parallels or at least approximates the behaviors that are reported to parents. Teachers in that school district use three numbers (3, 2, 1) to indicate the intensity or frequency of a student's behavior. Although this report card heading is "Academic and Social Growth," one can quickly see that the majority of the reported behaviors are social and behavioral rather than academic.

Teachers who use this report card are required to complete them quarterly (every 9 weeks) during the school year. To more effectively plan for the beginning of school, classroom teachers could link their classroom rules and management plans to the areas that they ultimately report to parents each 9-week period. Unfortunately, from a national perspective this connection is often not completed by practicing teachers, and therefore the report card is ineffective as a means to communicate the social and behavioral progress of students. A problem that frequently occurs with new teachers is that a student will manifest a behavioral problem and the teacher will check the report card to see if there is an area in which this can be reported to the parents or caregivers. Instead, we should more effectively align our behavior or management plan with elements of the report card before the beginning of school.

In the second sample, taken from the Union City School District, you will notice a subtle difference in how student behavior is framed. Each teacher must complete this report card quarterly and report on the frequency or intensity of student actions with four numbers (4, 3, 2, 1).

The student behaviors that are described in this report card are listed under the heading "Learner Qualities," which are identified by five different areas. Each of these subareas is defined by criteria statements. For example, a self-directed learner sets goals, is self-motivated, takes personal responsibility for his or her behavior, completes daily work, and returns completed homework. The value of this type of format is that it discusses how the behavior is directly associated with desirable classroom activity. Teachers who use this report card work with students from the first day of school to understand each of the learner qualities and the types of behaviors that are associated with each. This may take place with formal group instruction or individual conferencing with students. If students understand the behavior that is required of them, that makes the instructional goals of the teacher easier to meet. Teachers can also plan to report the student behavior with an instrument that is directly aligned with the instructional activities of the classroom.

Developing a Classroom Management Plan Prior to the Arrival of the Students

Deciding What Type of Classroom You Want

Assessing and reporting the behaviors of students is part of being an effective classroom teacher. The absence of a thoughtful and well-articulated management plan makes the assessment of student behaviors more subjective and your decision making more vulnerable to criticism. The classroom management plan that you create should allow you to teach children in a personally comfortable manner and support effective instruction. In order to meet those two goals you should reflect on past practices that have been effective, acknowledge student behaviors that have been distracting or disruptive, and consider new techniques that you want to employ in your classroom. This begins with clarifying your own beliefs about management. Following are several questions to assist you in understanding how you want to approach classroom management:

> What is the goal of your classroom management?
>
> Who has the primary responsibility for managing student behavior?
>
> How would you like students to relate to each other in your classroom?
>
> How much choice will students have in your management system?
>
> How do you intend to handle student misbehavior?

It would be impossible within the framework of this chapter to cover all the contingencies that might be associated with the answers to the above questions. The purpose of the questions is to allow you to think about the development of a management plan. For example, teachers who consider the question of student choices must consider whether they are going to provide consequences and rewards. These decisions contribute to the overall tone and atmosphere of the elementary classroom. As the teacher answers each question, the framing of the overall classroom management plan becomes clearer to understand. From an assessment perspective, referring to the academic and social part of the report card can assist the teacher in answering some of the questions. For example, the question of who has the primary responsibility for student behavior can be answered in part by the school district report card. Phrases such as "practices self-discipline," "listens and follows directions," and "respects the rights, property, and opinions of others" imply that the primary responsibility for behavior lies in the student. In the Union City report card, primary responsibility for behavior is overt in the description of the learner qualities. Referring to the classroom report card can assist teachers in forming a classroom management plan.

Organizing the Physical Arrangement
of the Classroom

Prior to the beginning of school you will usually have an opportunity to see the class-room in which you will spend the majority of the instructional year. This provides you with an opportunity to be proactive about situations that can have an impact on your management. In effect, you want to make sure that you do not create situations that cause students to be tempted, thereby contributing to their misbehavior.

The following example will help to clarify this point. When I was an elementary principal I had the opportunity to visit the classroom of a newly hired and quite conscientious teacher. She was at school weeks ahead of the starting date in order to prepare her classroom, and I noticed that most of the student desks and chairs were moved to the front of the class, resulting in a large empty area at the back of the room. When I asked about the arrangement, she smiled and said that elementary students need an area in which to express themselves through activity and dance. I acknowledged her response, and we talked about a wide range of other issues. After the first week of school, I noticed that the student desks and chairs had been reorga-nized, and the large area at the back of the room had disappeared. When I asked the teacher why she had rearranged the classroom seating, she said that the children's expression had been the kind demonstrated by participants in the World Wrestling Federation. The teacher had therefore created a situation, through the placement of the student desks and chairs, that tempted or encouraged the students to exhibit unac-ceptable behavior. On a report card, this situation would be reported as "the student did not demonstrate responsible behavior" or "the student failed to practice self-discipline." In the case of the Union City learner qualities, a "responsible citizen" practices safety first, respects others and the environment, and follows classroom procedures. It is easier, how-ever, to be a responsible citizen when the classroom arrangement supports your efforts.

There are generally accepted guidelines for the physical arrangement of an effec-tively designed classroom. First, make sure that your classroom seating arrangement provides adequate pathways so students can move easily from place to place. In fact, about one-third of your classroom should be devoted to pathways. Second, remove large empty spaces that encourage students to engage in unacceptable physical be-haviors. Make sure that the teacher's desk is placed in a location that allows the teacher to see the entire classroom. This includes making sure that any barriers between the students and the teacher are removed so that students will not be hidden from the teacher's sight. Most important, however, is that the arrangement of desks and chairs facilitates the teacher's instructional intentions. For example, if the teacher intends to frequently use cooperative learning strategies, then it makes sense for the classroom seating arrangement to be in clusters of desks instead of straight rows.

Classroom arrangement can take one of four classic configurations: desks in rows, circles, semicircles, and clusters. Each of these arrangements has its advantages as well as its disadvantages. These are outlined in Table 8-2.

Table 8-2. Typical Classroom Seating Arrangements: Advantages and Disadvantages

Seating Arrangement	Advantages	Disadvantages	Comments
Rows	Offers classroom control features because each student is isolated from another. Lends itself well to lecture formats and individual student tasks.	Does not allow for group work. Isolates students from being able to share information or solve problems collectively.	Creates pathways that can easily allow students to get from one place in the classroom to another. More likely to be associated with upper-grade classrooms.
Circles	Puts teacher at center or provides for a sharing of information where each student can see all others. Facilitates group discussions.	Students can choose to "disappear" easily by non-participation. Difficult to easily use assistive visual technology.	Difficult to maintain for all teaching activities. Pathways are troublesome; generally does not make good use of classroom space. Used in primary classroom for small-group instruction.
Semicircles	Provides for discussion when there is a central person who is discussing. Facilitates presentations.	Limited because it takes up so much space unless used concentrically.	Pathways are difficult to maintain. Generally contributes to wasted classroom space. Permits audience participation and can be novel in its application.
Clusters	Facilitates group work and provides opportunities for students to develop collective positions on topics.	Not appropriate for individualized assessments. Difficult to use visual presentation media.	Pathways can be arranged and maintained easily. Can usually be formed from a row configuration without much effort. Different desk heights can be a problem in elementary grades.

Establishing Classroom Rules and Consequences

Much of your management plan can be completed (or at least thought out) prior to the arrival of students in your classroom. The establishment of classroom rules should intentionally involve students so that they can experience a sense of ownership. Their involvement, however, does not inhibit you from thinking through the main rules to have in place and the intensity of the consequences to follow student actions. This decision-making process takes us back to the report card. As you think about the rules and consequences, consider the most important items on the social and behavioral portion of your report card. For example, if you think that "respects rights, property, and opinions of others" is most important, then your classroom rules and consequences should specifically address that area. This provides you with an opportunity to share with students the reasons for the rule, the consequences, and how it can be reported to parents. Naturally, your classroom plan to effectively control the teaching environment will be much more specific than the general terms used on a report card, but the two should have some common areas. Aligning the daily rules with an overarching plan linked to the report card can be a powerful beginning to classroom management. The Union City report card uses the learner qualities as a basis to structure the classroom rules. Discussing rules that require students to be self-directed learners, collaborative workers, problem solvers, responsible citizens, and quality producers can bring a sense of clear expectations to students.

Managing Chronic or Persistent Behavior Problems

Every classroom teacher will encounter students who will challenge the limits of the management plan. This can occur through an unexpected outburst or a dramatic event, but more likely it will occur through a consistent repetition of misbehavior over time. The difficulty in this situation is that although no single event causes a reaction on your part, the sum of continual misbehaviors erodes your patience and can affect your decision making. For example, students who were sent by teachers to see me when I was a principal would often say that they were sent to the office because they "got up in the middle of class to sharpen their pencil." I was keenly aware that that behavior was not enough to warrant a trip to the principal's office. The teacher's reaction was caused by a series of small misbehaviors that collectively pushed the teacher beyond a reasonable judgment. On a different day, or perhaps at a different time of day, this teacher would not have sent the child to the office for sharpening a pencil during the middle of class. The teacher simply did not have a plan for dealing with chronic or persistent misbehaviors, nor was there any record of ongoing student behavior and teacher response. With a strategy for addressing chronic misbehavior, the student would have had to work his or her way through the plan and face the consequences. It might then have been a similar disruption that forced the teacher to remove the student, but the student would know that he or she was being sent to the office for persistent misbehaviors.

The anecdotal record in Table 8-3 indicates how a teacher recorded shouting behavior, her responses, and the efforts to eliminate the behavior.

Strategies that can be used to extinguish misbehaviors are self-monitoring, behavior contracting, applied behavior analysis, contingency contracts, and home-based reinforcement. The description of these and their specific procedural guidelines are beyond the scope of this text, but it is important to note the data collection aspects of these and how assessment can be part of a good classroom management plan. In the case of home-based reinforcement, the report shown in Table 8-4 is completed by the teacher and sent to the parents or guardians.

Table 8-3.   Anecdotal Record for Shouting Behavior

Student Name		Target Behavior	

Date	Student Behavior	Teacher Action	Initials
10/6	Shouting out answers to questions in class.	Signaled interference Peer reinforcement Reminded student of rules	
10/8	Shouting out answers	Signaled interference Peer reinforcement Reminded student of rules Met with student	JDC
10/10	Shouting out answers	Reminded student of rules Shared log of anecdotal records, explained purpose	JDC
10/11	Shouting out answers	Signaled interference Student signs log	JDC
10/12	Shouting out answers Student raised hand	Signaled interference Called on student for answer	JDC
10/13	Shouting out answers Student raised hand	Reminded student of rules Reminded student of success Called on student for answer	JDC
10/16	Raised hand consistently	Called on student appropriately Shared log with student	JDC
10/17	Raised hand consistently	Called on student, ended log contingent on continuing appropriate behaviors	JDC

Table 8-4.   Daily Behavior Report for Home-Based Reinforcement

Jeremy's Daily Report			May 18			

Class Period	Behavior			On-Task Behavior			Teacher
Reading	3	2	1	10	5	1	Mr. Schwa
Math	3	2	1	10	5	1	Mrs. Slope
Physical Education	3	2	1	10	5	1	Ms. Dribble
	3 Excellent			10	100% on task		
	2 Good			5	50% on task		
	1 Poor			1	10% on task		

Total Score: Specific or Overall Comments:

Summary

Effective classroom teachers are ones who enter the classroom with specific plans and goals in mind for themselves and their students. Assessing students involves plans that are devoted to the academic and social aspects of the classroom. August provides a time for teachers to plan and determine how they intend to collect and represent evidence of student learning, provide a structure for positive classroom behavior, and establish reasonable and effective communication lines with parents. It is important to have a design for communicating with parents, a classroom management strategy, and a plan for grading the academic and social behaviors of students.

Teaching Activities

1. Prepare a letter that includes the components suggested in the chapter. Share the letter with another student or students. Discuss the positive aspects of each and also what changes should be made to the letters. If you have the opportunity, have a person who is currently teaching also review the letter.

2. Develop a classroom management plan that includes the following components:

    - Goals for the plan
    - Classroom organizational plan
    - Rules and consequences
    - Handling of persistent problems

    In four-person groups, have each person design a plan for a specific grade. Discuss the commonalities and the essential differences among the grades.

3. Using a report card from a local school district, choose a subject area and lay out several possible assessments that could contribute to the generation of a grade within a 9-week grading period. Discuss what types of scoring instruments could be used to aggregate the data for the grade. Identify another subject area and discuss what assessments would be helpful to the development of a grade. How are the two areas different?

September: Focusing on Reading and Mathematics

Goals of the Chapter

1. To understand the types of assessments that support components of effective reading instruction

2. To understand how to select instructional practices that assist in the improvement of achievement on externally generated tests

3. To understand the types of assessments that support effective mathematics instruction

The Importance of Reading

The first days of any school year are exceptionally busy times for teachers and children. The daily events of September move quickly and require a high level of energy from all teachers. In the absence of a high degree of planning and organization, the first days and weeks of the school year can be exhaustive and frustrating. While you begin to organize your classroom and establish routines, you should not be losing sight of your purpose. Your first order of business and the reason for which you were hired is to provide high-quality instruction to students.

Although this text is not designed to comprehensively cover effective instruction in all areas of the curriculum, it would seem appropriate to spend time discussing two areas that are highly valued in our schools: reading and mathematics. In elementary and middle school classrooms there is no more important subject area than reading. The ability to read might be the most important determiner of student success in American schools; thus, developing the reading skills of all the students in your class is of extreme importance. In classrooms today, the teaching of reading may be integrated with writing instruction and referred to as *literacy development*. Any mention of the development of reading skills in this text should not be considered as a suggestion that reading be taught in isolation from the other language arts.

The Challenge of Developing Literacy in Children

Reading is the incorporation of knowledge and skills by an individual to make sense of print. Although this description sounds fairly simple, teaching children to read is one of the most complex tasks that teachers encounter each day and throughout their careers. Designing effective instruction that will assist each child in making sense of print is difficult. Assessing their abilities in the area of reading has grown more complex. Paris and Hoffman (2004) indicate that the numbers of commercial tests available to teachers increased from 20 in 1990 to 148 in 1999. Meisels and Piker (2000) collected information from teachers and educators that identified 89 types of noncommercial literacy assessments that measured 203 skills. Assessing student literacy levels has become increasingly sophisticated.

This chapter is designed to assist your efforts in planning reading instruction based on the sound use of assessment planning and instrumentation. It is not designed to substitute for deep theoretical explanations of the purposes of reading instruction. That understanding must be developed from other sources of professional development. Every teacher has a responsibility to improve and develop his or her understanding of how students learn to read. Much of your professional career will be spent seeking improved strategies to promote literacy learning.

The most effective teachers of reading apply a variety of strategies to meet the individual literacy needs of children. These strategies frequently require different types of instruction and therefore different types of assessment. The importance of assessment to reading instruction lies in the measurement and diagnosis of children's abilities and misunderstandings. From the data generated by the assessments, teachers can prescribe effective teaching activities that address students' literacy needs.

Differences in Ages and Grades

Although there is a distinct difference between teaching reading in the lower elementary grades and the upper elementary grades, *Put Reading First*, a publication developed by the Center for the Improvement of Early Reading Achievement (Armbruster, Lehr, & Osborn, 2001) cites the following important components of reading instruction across grade levels: phonemic awareness, phonics, fluency, vocabulary, and text comprehension. With these components in mind we will discuss a variety of assessments that can be used in the development of literacy in children.

Phonemic Awareness

Phonemic awareness is the ability to identify and work with the individual sounds of spoken words. *Phonemes* are the smallest parts of sound in a spoken word that make a difference in the word's meaning. For example, changing the first phoneme in the word *hot* from /h/ to /p/ changes the word from *hot* to *pot*. In order for students to be able to read, they must recognize the sounds that are associated with the printed symbols (letters).

Designing assessments that confirm the student's level of phonemic awareness gauges the student's ability to do the following:

- Recognize words in a set that begin with the same sound
- Identify the isolated first or last sound in a word
- Recognize rhyming and the production of rhymes
- Form or recognize combinations and blends that make up words
- Break or segment a word into separate sounds

Assessment methods used to determine a student's phonemic awareness are mostly observational in nature. This is primarily because phonemic awareness is often the target of designed instruction for the development of beginning readers. A structured program that assesses phonemic awareness as well as other early reading behaviors is the Dynamic Indicators of Basic Early Literacy Skills (DIBELS) program (Good & Kaminski, 2001). Teachers who are interested in assessing phonemic awareness might be seen using a checklist as they circulate among students and asking them to respond to different word configurations. Another assessment technique might be to require students to complete different tasks at several learning stations. The students rotate through each learning station while the teacher collects evidence of student competency. This usually requires the teacher to have assistants who are able to collect the important data at each of the stations. Computer-generated programs are often helpful in providing practice and recording student success in this area.

Phonics Instruction

The purpose of phonics instruction is to ensure that children understand the relationship between the letters of written language and the individual sounds of spoken language. Knowledge of these relationships contributes to children's ability to read words both in isolation and in sentences. With phonics instruction we begin to see the student using pencil and paper to indicate responses more frequently than we do with phonemic awareness. Phonics instruction should be linked to the direct application of reading a passage as much as possible. This helps to teach children to apply the knowledge of phonics for its intended purpose and avoids suggesting that phonics work is isolated. Teaching approaches that enhance the students' understanding of phonics include but are not limited to the following activities:

- teaching students to convert letters and combinations of letters to sounds
- requiring students to blend sounds together to form recognizable words
- enabling students to recognize and use word families
- teaching students to use syllabication in saying and reading words

The assessment of phonics skills, as in the case of phonemic awareness, requires the use of keen observational skills on the part of the classroom teacher. Teachers who want to assess phonics often use miscue analysis or running records of children reading passages. This is a more authentic use of phonics skills than isolated drill and practice sheets. Other typical assessment measures include letter identification, high-frequency words, and DIBELS activities. Search and sorting activities can demonstrate student knowledge and skills in this area. Written evidence of students being able to correctly respond to letter-sound relationships is especially helpful, and it provides rich support for observational data. Student writing samples can be a powerful indicator of how the student is applying phonemic awareness skills in direct literacy application. Student writing assists teachers in assessing the student's success in carrying over the auditory skills to print.

Notice the similarities between assessing phonemic awareness and phonics. Think about how they differ.

Fluency

Fluency is the ability to read print accurately and at a pace that facilitates the reader's understanding of the text. Fluency is present in the reading of effective readers and is sometimes missing in the reading of poor readers. The relationship between reading fluency and reading comprehension is well documented in the literature. The mental effort expended in decoding each word in a sentence directly affects the possibility that the reader can focus on the meaning of the word or its relationship to other words in the sentence.

Teaching strategies that support the development of fluency are based on repeated reading techniques, paired reading, and independent reading. Make sure that students are reading material that is at an appropriate level, which can be determined by pretesting. Repeated reading requires students to reread a text a certain number of times, until fluency is reached. The most effective repeated readings have teacher guidance and feedback as part of the activity. Encouraging students to practice independent reading at their own level is also an acceptable means by which to develop fluency in student reading. The more time students spend reading, the more likely they are to increase their reading fluency. We should make sure that we are developing fluency that facilitates the student's understanding of the text, not fluency just to develop speed. The use of a stopwatch to gauge the student's fluency rate might trigger a misinterpretation that "faster is better." Instead, we are looking for a rate that allows the student to comprehend the material; that is the purpose of reading. It will serve no legitimate purpose to encourage students to read with a high rate of fluency at the sacrifice of comprehending the text.

Table 9-1 shows a rubric for the evaluation of fluency.

Table 9-1. Rubric for Fluency Evaluation

1. Very little fluency; all word-by-word reading with some long pauses between words; almost no recognition of syntax or phrasing (expressive interpretation); very little evidence of awareness of punctuation; perhaps a couple of two-word phrases but generally disfluent; some word groupings awkward.

2. Mostly word-by-word reading but with some two-word phrasing and even a couple of three- or four-word phrases (expressive interpretation); evidence of syntactic awareness of syntax and punctuation, though not consistently so; rereading for problem solving may be present.

3. A mixture of word-by-word reading and fluent, phrased reading (expressive interpretation); there is evidence of attention to punctuation and syntax; rereading for problem solving may be present.

4. Reads primarily in larger meaningful phrases; fluent, phrased reading with a few word-by-word slowdowns for problem solving; expressive interpretation is evident at places throughout the reading; attention to punctuation and syntax; rereading for problem solving may be present but is generally fluent.

Adapted from NAEP's Integrated Reading Performance Record, Oral Reading Fluency Scale. Used with permission of National Center for Educational Statistics.

Teaching activities that promote fluency include the following:

- Teacher-student reading with structured feedback
- Modeling the reading of a passage with fluency and then asking the student to read and reread the same passage until fluency is attained
- Teaching students to see phrases rather than individual words
- Correct use of punctuation
- Reciprocal reading
- Choral reading
- CD-assisted reading

The purpose of fluency assessment is to decide if the student is reading at a pace that permits comprehension of a passage written at a certain reading level. Take a baseline of timed sample reads in order to develop a sense of the student's success. Increases in the degree of difficulty of the text are sure to impact fluency. Most reading programs provide approximations of fluency rates for beginning readers. Miscue analysis and running records can also provide assessment information that supports a teacher's inferences about a student's fluency rate. Remember that fluency is less about time and more about phrasing and comprehension.

Running records indicate more than just fluency; they are powerful indicators of a student's reading ability. They are most often used in the lower grades. Figures 9-1

Student Name __Benjamin Dover__

Date __11/30__

Text __Level C__

Error Ratio _____   Accuracy Rate _____

Page	Title	Words	E	Self-Corrections
	Wake Up	67	(5)	
pg 2.	✓ ✓ ✓ ✓ ✓ ✓ ✓ ✓ ✓			
pg 4	✓ ✓ sleeping / asleep		I	
pg 6	✓ ✓ Get/wake ✓ ✓ ✓ ✓ sleeping/asleep		I I	
pg 8	✓ ✓ Get/wake ✓ ✓ ✓ ✓ sleeping/asleep ✓ ✓		I I	

Teacher Comments:
In this sample, the student's attempts are meaningful—"get up" instead of "wake up," "sleeping" instead of "asleep." The student has also developed a beginning reading vocabulary—*is, up, said*. One-to-one matching appears to be in place. Instruction can now be focused on teaching the student to notice the mismatch in visual information, making sure that the reading make sense and also looks right. Paying closer attention to how words start is a good first step for early readers.

Courtesy of Laura Schaaf

Figure 9-1. Running Record and Teacher Comment, Sample 1

and 9-2 display running records that have been generated from students who have been asked to read a short selection. In each example the information shows the recorded reading performance of a student and the interpretation of that reading performance by the child's teacher.

The use of running records requires the teacher to use a coding system to assess student accuracy in word recognition as well as the reading strategies students use

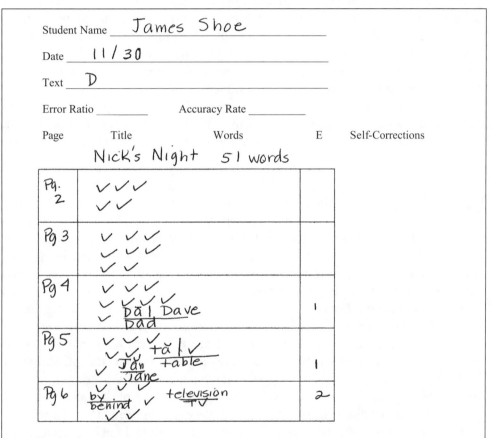

Teacher Comments:
This student understands that reading needs to make sense. The reader is able to quickly identify a number of high-frequency words with little effort—*have, you, your, said*. This record shows that some attention to vowel sounds on the part of the student may be necessary. Page 5 is a good example—here the student tried a short vowel sound for "table" but then was able to correct the attempt. In the next line, the student again uses the short *a* sound, but this time the attempt makes sense, so no further work was done. Page 6 provides evidence of where further instruction could occur. The student is using meaning and the first letter to read, but a further search of the visual information is necessary in order for the reading to make sense and look right.

Courtesy of Laura Schaaf

Figure 9-2. Running Record and Teacher Comment, Sample 2

when confronted with unknown words. As a student reads aloud, the teacher uses this coding system to indicate reading behavior such as accurate reading, rereading, self-correcting, and sounding out. The teacher then calculates the percentage of total words read accurately, and a reading level is determined.

If a student performs at 95%–100% accuracy, the text is considered easy for that student. Easy texts can be used to develop fluency in reading, to build sight vocabulary, and to allow students the opportunity to orchestrate all they have learned about reading. If a student performs at 90%–94% accuracy, the text is considered instructional. Instructional text is appropriate for guided reading or tutoring situations in addition to classroom instructional opportunities. Instructional text allows students to read independently while continuing to have to do some reading work in order to make sense of the text. However, should a student perform at an 89% level or below, the text is too difficult, and the reading behaviors that are usually in place begin to disappear as the student becomes overwhelmed by the unknown content of the text. There is little evidence to support the use of difficult text for instructional purposes.

Vocabulary
Vocabulary is the words that students must be able to understand when they read and speak. Vocabulary develops in children through direct instruction, but it can often be enhanced through independent reading. As a classroom teacher, I came to the realization that the children who were hooked on reading independently needed less frequent and less intense vocabulary instruction. They had developed strong vocabularies from having read extensively and from other environmental influences (being read to, having discussions with their parents or guardians). More important, they had developed their own strategies for figuring out the meanings of new or unfamiliar words. This is not to suggest that we can satisfy the need to develop vocabulary in students simply by developing avid readers. Instead, it suggests that the need for direct instruction in vocabulary development is uneven across classroom populations. Not all students will need the same amount of direct instruction in vocabulary development. This example also suggests that the value of developing independent readers should not be overlooked.

Instructional Strategies for the Development of Vocabulary

Vocabulary development, as it relates to formal reading instruction, can be classified as whatever is specific to understanding the words in a story and whatever helps students as they encounter words they do not know when reading material outside class. For example, if you are requiring students to read a selection, it is quite possible that there will be several words in the assignment that are new or unfamiliar to the students. Teaching the meaning of these words prior to the lesson is important for the student to be able to comprehend the story. Teaching vocabulary to students prior to their reading of a text can take several forms: discussion, group work, and resource materials that include dictionaries and online services.

The other type of vocabulary development provides students with the skills that they will need when they encounter new words outside school. Using reference materials to locate words that appear in a story should be a skill that students will employ voluntarily. The most important part of teaching the use of reference materials is not in finding the specific word, but in teaching the children to utilize these resources as part of their independent development as readers. Other strategies that readers can use when they encounter new words include contextual clues and word knowledge. For example, children can use sticky notes to mark new or unfamiliar words and then use strategies they have been taught for defining the words. In this case less preteaching of vocabulary takes place.

Three common forms of assessing children's vocabulary utilize matching and multiple-choice formats. These are perfectly acceptable gauges of students' understanding of words. Employing a matching test to assess vocabulary words from a story should be done with great care. Suggestions for the development of effective matching formats can be found in chapter 3. In some cases the vocabulary words from a story will lack homogeneity, and the assessment of the word meaning can be completed without complete understanding. The multiple-choice format, which is very popular in standardized measures, assesses word meaning but, like matching, fails to indicate what type of word skills are used to arrive at the meaning of the word. For that reason other types of assessments are necessary to assess the skills students use when they encounter unfamiliar words.

One possible exercise requires students to predict the word meaning using context clues and/or word analysis skills and then confirm the accuracy of their prediction with a resource. A second means of assessing vocabulary development can be a word log that students use when they encounter new words. In it they write the word, the method they used to derive its meaning, and the actual meaning of the word. A third method is to collect dated samples of student writing. Although this may not show immediate growth, it is nonetheless important and gratifying to observe that students are using a richer vocabulary and more complex sentence structures at the end of the school year than they were at the beginning. Students' writing is almost always a reflection of their reading vocabulary development.

Text Comprehension

All reading instruction deals with two major intentions on the part of the teacher: having students decode unfamiliar words and having them make sense of what they are reading. Decoding is important as a means to an end: comprehension. The purpose of teaching reading is to have students understand print.

To begin to understand how to teach comprehension, recall some of the ways in which reading comprehension was taught in previous decades. I can recall being "taught to understand" the text by answering the questions at the end of the story or chapter. The assessment of whether I comprehended the text was based on my answers to the questions, but, unfortunately, answering the questions was in no way instructive to the development of my comprehension skills. The assessment actually took place long after I had read parts of the story or chapter. Today's instruction in comprehension strategies makes students more active in monitoring their own understanding *while* they are reading. There are distinct differences in these approaches. First, there is a shift to students accepting an active role in monitoring their own reading, and second, there is an emphasis on understanding the text during reading rather than after the story or chapter is completed. These are just two of the major premises that guide the development of reading comprehension instruction.

There are specific text comprehension strategies to make students active and aware in their reading of text. Armbruster et al. (2001) suggest the three comprehension strategies described below.

The use of graphic and semantic organizers. These include webs, diagrams, and charts. Their value is that they reorganize the story from the one that is presented in the text to an abbreviated version that presents the story in a more visual display. The reduced representation helps students to more easily see the relationships among concepts. It can also help the student to make connections to the text by visualizing.

Answering questions. Having students respond to questions about their reading has long been an effective means by which to judge their comprehension of a story. Effective questioning can be used to gauge comprehension as the students read parts of the story rather than waiting until they have read the entire piece. The type of questions that students are asked is also important. For example, different levels of student understanding of the text can be noted by asking questions that require literal or inferential interpretations. For information on asking questions that require higher level thinking, see chapter 3.

Generating questions and text predictions. Having students generate their own questions about the story prior to and during reading helps to make the student become active in responding to the text. Here the student is "going to" the story rather than having the story come to him or her. The students should check their questions or predictions about the story at certain intervals. As the story or reading assignment changes, students can confirm their predictions or recast what they think is going to happen next. Breaking the story into smaller sections can assist slow readers who might be overwhelmed by having to read what they perceive as a long story. To further your own personal development, investigate some directed reading comprehension strategies to gain a deeper understanding of this area.

There are a range of assessment activities that can be used to monitor the ability of students to comprehend text. Comprehension can be gauged with student writing that includes a graph or visual that represents the structure of a story, or by having students complete a written retelling of the story. Another written assessment might require the student to describe a character, the plot, or the problem in a reading assignment. In the lower grades, oral questioning strategies are a mainstay in the assessment of student comprehension. Students can be called upon to answer literal and/or inferential questions or participate in retellings. Making sure that students can draw inferences from what they read requires teachers to actively pose questions of that nature to students. The difference between literal and inferential comprehensive development lies more in the nature of the questions than the types of instructional activities that are required of students. With inferential questioning, the teacher is trying to get students not to simply sustain the meaning of the story but to extend it beyond its literal interpretation.

Table 9-2 shows an anecdotal record of a student's reading skill development.

Table 9-2. Anecdotal Records of Reading Skill Development

Teacher Comments	Skills Observed and Noted
10/04 Level 4 Early reader books. No spacing between words when writing. Use of strong phonetics. Mixture of capital and lowercase letters. Fluency choppy and comprehension low. Uses picture clues. Does not choose appropriate books at level for independent reading—needs guidance, needs one-to-one instruction.	Emergence of writing Phonetic ability Fluency Reading strategies Decision making Student confidence
11/04 Level 8 Enjoys pattern books. Is trying very hard to improve skills. Likes one-to-one attention. Writing skills improve when in group, not independent, practice every day.	Writing skills Student confidence Group and independent behaviors
12/04 Level 12 Light is beginning to flicker on about the reading. Is taking pride in her success. Independent work is beginning to falter as time is taken by extra help. Needs more independent practice. Fluency and comprehension improving. Strong use of phonetics—beginning context clues.	Fluency Purpose for reading Comprehension Phonetics Group and independent behaviors
1/11 Level 14 Good handle on putting sounds together to make words. Fluency is coming. Beginning to really enjoy books. Likes to verbally respond—very enthusiastic. Needs to pay attention to endings.	Fluency Purpose for reading Comprehension Self-monitoring Phonetics Group and independent behaviors
2/8 Level 16 High frequency words need emphasis—"this," "then," and "would." Uses capitalization and punctuation in dictation. When writing responses needs to internalize using these strategies.	Writing skills Fluency Instructional needs
3/8 Level 17 Has gained confidence. Sometimes overly confident—forgets use of strategies in writing skills. Needs more practice. Reading is coming. Will move up to level 18—will try this.	Self-monitoring behaviors Writing skills Applications of reading strategies Independent reading
4/1 Level 18 Good fluency in oral reading. High frequency words still need work. Is able to express ideas in a meaningful manner. Often in a hurry—needs to take more time. Enjoys one-to-one work.	Fluency Instructional Needs Comprehension Expression Self-monitoring Student-teacher inaction

Used with permission of Susan Cumming.

Using Table 9-2, think about the observational assessments that were conducted. What are the specific components of reading that were assessed?

Preparing Students for State Reading Tests

Crocker (2003) suggests that as school accountability increases, effective teachers will need to know how to prepare their students for assessments. Specifically, teachers must be prepared to teach *for* external assessment and not simply *to* a particular test. This refers to teaching that prepares students to demonstrate their acquired knowledge and skills on multiple types of external assessments conducted by others beyond the individual teacher.

Such is the case with state measures of reading achievement. Statewide measures of children's ability to read are present in every state. The passage of the No Child Left Behind Act mandated the standardized testing of reading achievement by all states in grades 3 through 8. The responsibility of preparing students to demonstrate their reading abilities on externally developed measures has heightened pressure and anxiety among teachers and school professionals.

Teachers who are able to prepare their students for state reading tests must have knowledge and skills in the five areas described below.

Defining the Reading Standards and Interpreting Their Instructional Intent

Despite claims that state standards are clearly written goals for student achievement, there can be considerable room for interpretation and, unfortunately, misunderstanding. For that reason, it is suggested that teachers engage in what McTighe and Thomas (2003) refer to as "unpacking the standard." In other words, teachers uncover the key skills or ideas that are not explicitly stated in the standard and come to an agreement about the intent of the standard language. Clarifying the intent of the standard helps to ensure that teaching activities will be adequately aligned to support student learning. It also assists in developing assessments that generate valid and reliable data. For more details on working with standards, see chapter 4.

Designing Instructional Activities That Provide Students With Opportunities to Learn the Knowledge and Skills Described in the Standard

From an ethical perspective, if we intend to assess students on their ability to master the standards, each child should have adequate instruction in order to develop the knowledge and skills that facilitate such mastery. This is more easily suggested than accomplished. For example, "being able to distinguish fact from opinion" is an essential skill that is found in the reading standards of nearly all states. Although teachers and other professionals can agree that students should have the opportunity to learn to distinguish fact from opinion, not all opportunities are equally effective. Providing instructional activities that develop a student's opportunities to learn must be sensitive to reading level, contextual difficulties, student interests, and availability of resources.

Developing Classroom Assessments That Effectively Assess the Student's Mastery of the Standard

The development of classroom assessments that assess the student's ability to master the standard (based on our instruction) involves elements of sound instructional practice that are covered in the first chapters of this book. We want to be especially careful to employ multiple measures that are congruent with our instruction. Let's return to the fact and opinion example. A student's ability to distinguish fact from opinion is better assessed by providing opportunities for students to express their thoughts through written and oral processes than through correct answers to questions. Without an assessment of students' decision making, fact and opinion exercises can be reduced to true/false exercises.

Recognizing the Main Themes Tested by the Standardized Reading Assessment

State tests that are designed with the purpose of measuring students' ability to read are generally built around a test design framework. The framework is a set of broadly stated goals that describe desirable reading abilities for the student body of a particular state. For example, suppose that a state-mandated test in reading is based on four major goals, or stances, that include making sense of the text, making connections across content areas, personally responding to the reading, and critical thinking. The value of teachers and other school professionals recognizing these stances lies in the opportunity to shape instructional practice toward the stances. Here is an example of how knowledge of the state stances can assist in the development of focused instructional activities by the classroom teacher.

The purpose of the third stance is to ensure that students are making personal connections to what they are reading. Readers who make personal connections with a text often have increased levels of comprehension and satisfaction with reading. Throughout the year there are many opportunities to have students role-play characters and write about how they behaved when they were in similar situations as the story characters. Other types of activities might include writing about specific major and minor characters. An example of how students can make personal connections with another person is modeled in the following exercise:

> Everyone has experienced disappointment in his or her life. Disappointment is not the same as tragedy. Tragedy might involve the loss of a friend or family member, diminished health, or financial ruin. Disappointment is not quite as serious but still has a quality of discomfort. In our story the character was disappointed because . . .
>
> Tell how the character in the text was disappointed.
>
> - Tell about a time when you were disappointed.
>
> - Explain how your experience is similar to the character in the story.
>
> - Use information from the story to create a paragraph that summarized how you both were disappointed.
>
> Check your answer:
>
> I was able to describe a disappointing time in my life.
>
> I connected my ideas with the character in the story.
>
> I wrote about both and used information from the story.
>
> Use a graphic organizer:
>
> How I Describe Disappointment
>
> How the Character Described Disappointment
>
> The character and I are the same in this way:
>
> The character and I are different in this way:

Developing Classroom Assessments That Are Congruent With State Assessments

There are several reasons for developing and using classroom assessments that are congruent with your state's assessment program. First, in such high-stakes testing situations, students ought to have experienced similar types of assessment formats. You are attempting to remove any influence on the test score that is derived from the student being unfamiliar with the format. For example, if you are teaching reading for the greater part of the school year and have never asked your students to use written composition to account for comprehension activities, then you should expect several of your students to feel anxious about having to complete such a process on a state test. Naturally, a few students will feel anxiety or worry from a lack of confidence in their own writing skills, but we should try to avoid having such feelings influence more students because of a basic unfamiliarity with the assessment process.

The second reason for using congruent assessment measures is that children need sufficient practice to maximize and/or maintain skill development. If we limit our students to a cram session of assessment processes in the week or so immediately preceding the test, a number of students will not have sufficient practice in gaining familiarity with the assessment process. We want to eliminate or at least minimize the chance that the students will know the material but not perform well because the process is awkward or new. An example would be students who can compare and contrast characters, plots, and settings but have had no formal training in Venn diagrams, so they cannot respond to a question that requires the interpretation of a Venn diagram. The failure of students in responding to the question has implications for the school and the teachers who have failed to provide the students with critical information.

Teaching literacy development to students is the most important task that teachers face. Its importance is exemplified by the correlation of reading ability to the success of students. This text is not designed to substitute for deep understanding of reading processes and assessments. However, a failure to acknowledge the importance of reading assessment would effectively ignore a wider, more inclusive definition of assessment literacy. If a teacher is assessment literate, he or she must at least have a basic understanding of how to teach and assess children's literacy development.

Reflection

How can your understanding of assessment help your students to become more successful lifelong readers while improving their reading achievement on state-mandated tests?

Teaching and Assessing Mathematics

Children today are more likely to experience a need for understanding mathematics than any previous generation. We live in a world where the understanding of mathematics enriches all aspects of our lives. Mathematics competence plays a part in normal everyday applications, in workplaces, and in career decisions that determine the very direction of our lives. Our sociotechnical reliance on mathematical understanding has expanded with the acceptance of computers in our lives, and our future dependence on them will very likely increase. The preparation of students to meet future challenges relies in part on our ability to deliver effective mathematics instruction.

Groups such as the National Council for the Teaching of Mathematics (NCTM) have established the content areas, the standards for student achievement, and the suggested practices that best address quality mathematics teaching in American classrooms. Areas of mathematics instruction that should be a part of all school programs are prescribed by NCTM (2000). The areas that NCTM recognizes as being essential to the promotion of mathematical skills in all students include the following:

- Content standards, or what to teach
- Numbers and operations, algebra, geometry, measurement, data analysis, and probability
- Process standards, or how to teach
- Problem solving, reasoning and proof, communication, connections, and representation

The scope of this text makes it impossible to describe all these topical areas and the appropriate assessments for each. Nor is it possible to discuss the effective process of teaching mathematics, which, in addition to content, has a profound effect on developing students' understanding of mathematics. The remainder of this chapter will focus on four of the most common topical areas in elementary mathematics instruction: numbers and operations, measurement, problem solving, and communication. A brief description of each area will be followed by suggestions or examples of appropriate assessment methods. Different forms of assessment can be implemented for all the mathematical content standards.

Numbers and Operations

Competence in the area of numbers and operations means that students understand numbers, their representations, and number systems. Students should also understand the operations, compute fluently, and make estimations. This is not an exhaustive review of this content area but just a starting point for discussing mathematics instruction and assessment.

In the lower grades teachers spend considerable time developing one-to-one correspondence, counting, and number representation. Central to facilitating understanding of these is the use of concrete examples. The range of materials that can be used to assist student understanding ranges from expensive, commercially made materials to used coffee cans filled with lima beans. Addition and subtraction are the operations emphasized in K–3, along with the beginning of multiplication and division. In general, teaching mathematics in K–3 requires active hands and minds. Children need a variety of explanations, plenty of repetition, opportunities to use numbers in meaningful situations, and corrective feedback.

Assessing K–3 students' understanding of numbers and operations presents a range of teacher options, but the most common practices utilize the observation of children. Anecdotal observation and record keeping is important in determining student success but also critical in tracking student development of mathematical competence. By first grade, students are completing tasks that indicate their facility with numbers, however, assessing their deeper understanding of place value and number systems requires probing questions and the attention of the teacher. This involves teachers interacting one-to-one or in small groups in order to assess students' understanding. Learning and play centers can provide insight into children's ability to complete operations and to use vocabulary accurately. Computer programs such as Meridian Math are available as additional assessments, and they can effectively record students' efforts over time.

At the higher elementary and middle school levels, numbers and operations take on an increased understanding of number representations, such as fractions, decimals, negative numbers, and percentages. Operations focus on multiplication and division and their inverse relationships. At this age students are likely to begin to effectively use calculators to extend their math understanding.

The assessment of upper elementary and middle school children may differ in sophistication from lower elementary children, but all forms of assessment can be used across grade levels. The expanded capability of the students creates an opportunity to enhance the difficulty level of an assessment. Students can develop complex models, schematics, or other representations to indicate their depth of understanding. The use of calculators makes possible assessments that require a longer period of time to complete. For example, older students can be asked to complete multistage problems because calculators free them from the burdensome task of slower manual calculations. The increased use of calculators, however, requires that our students have the ability to estimate effectively. Students who use calculators must be able to reason that the answer they generated with the calculator is a reasonable one.

Measurement

The teaching of measurement to primary-age students requires that they understand the concepts of length, volume, and time. Children need to be able to measure using standard and nonstandard units and to know which instruments are appropriate for different measurement tasks. It is important for instructional tasks and assessments to have a high degree of authenticity. When children can make effective connections to real-life situations, the content becomes more meaningful. This content area requires children to effectively connect mathematical knowledge and skills in order to be successful. Understanding that 1 yard is equal to 3 feet is important but of limited value if one cannot apply that information to problems of linear measure inside and outside the classroom.

Students must be provided with multiple opportunities to measure as well as the presence of suitable materials to facilitate measuring. Having an adequate number of meter sticks, balances, trundle wheels, scales, measuring cups, and a host of other materials increases the opportunity to learn. Teachers can improvise when they do not have adequate supplies. For example, in the absence of meter sticks, an old clothesline can be cut into sections of 1 meter in length and used by each student to measure physical items in the classroom. The capacity of the school district to provide essential measurement materials will contribute to the effective teaching of measurement skills.

In the lower elementary grades, measurement activities can be developed around play or learning centers. Checklists and anecdotal records are helpful assessment tools when they are developed around the specific skills that teachers want to develop in their students. A combination of checklists and written records can also be used. If you want to record student success at a center, you might observe the student work independently, then ask a series of probing questions to assess the student's depth of understanding. Here is an example taken from a K–3 learning center.

Observations: Can the student (given a 6-inch ruler, a 12-inch ruler, and a yardstick) choose the most appropriate measuring device to measure a 40-inch piece of material? Does the student employ a measuring strategy that will guarantee successful measures? Can the student effectively measure the perimeter of the material?

Probing questions: Why did you choose the yardstick to measure the length of the piece of cloth? Do you think your measurement of the cloth is correct? Are there any other ways to correctly measure the length of the piece of material? Can you calculate the perimeter of the piece of material with fewer than four measurements?

Meaningful observations that lead to accurate inferences are time-consuming. They require patience and a high degree of accurate record keeping. In K–3 classrooms it is often important for the teacher to utilize other adults to assist with the management of children so that focused and detailed observations can be completed. Parents, high school volunteers, paraprofessionals, instructional aides, and other groups are all sources of effective help. Teachers are not turning over the assessment of the children to the other adults, but merely using them to monitor the other children as they focus their important observations on an individual or a small group of students. The information gained from these observations is necessary to determine the instruction for individual students and/or small groups of students who possess the same instructional needs.

In the higher elementary and middle school grades, students can be exposed to more sophisticated types of measures and measurement activities. Three-dimensional figures are introduced and require students to be able to calculate volume and angle. It is equally important at this level to provide students with opportunities to measure and to apply measurement to real-life situations.

Assessments that are congruent with instructional practices designed to develop measurement skills require the use of scoring rubrics or checklists. The activities that involve precise measurement generally conclude with a single correct answer. The assessment of measurement skills often requires multiple enabling tasks that are logically completed to generate a correct measurement. The decision making and the skills that are applied to the measurement task are equally important in the assessment process. In order to provide effective feedback, it is important to address all aspects of the measuring process, not simply a correct or an incorrect answer from the student.

What do you see as the most significant differences in assessing K–3, 4–6, and 7–8 students in the areas of numbers and operations and measurement?

Problem Solving

Teaching problem solving in primary grades begins with listening to students. Each day, in every classroom, there is an opportunity to teach problem solving, its process, and its vocabulary to children. As problems arise in classrooms, teachers can discuss the problem with students and request that they think about possible solutions. Listening to the solutions generated by students provides meaningful insight into their ability to solve problems. It is equally important for students to see incorrect responses and to clarify missteps or misconceptions. Of course, the classroom culture should be one in which students can speak freely and openly without fear of criticism. Talking about how they solved problems helps students to gain a deeper understanding of the mathematics they are learning. These daily occurrences can be unstructured, but they are nonetheless important instructional information.

More structured arrangements can be organized through direct instruction and play and learning centers. Play centers can be constructed around themes that include visits to a grocery store, restaurant, or service station. Additional themes might include environmental awareness, diet and health needs, or care of a pet. The purpose of presenting these center themes is to show the importance of integrating math, and specifically math problem solving, into curriculum opportunities for young children. Procedures for assessing a student's abilities to problem-solve are very much akin to those mentioned in the measurement section. Keen observation, checklists, scoring rubrics, and anecdotal record keeping are the most efficient and effective means of assessing problem-solving skills in lower elementary classrooms.

In upper elementary and middle school classrooms, problem solving can take on expanded forms that include the use of multiple stages, the development of strategies, and increased complexity. Like measurement, problem solving is a process that requires students to apply knowledge in a logical sequence of actions to determine a solution or an answer. It is extremely important to develop the problem-solving process with children. Assessing student progress in problem solving requires that teachers assess the process the students used to arrive at the solution. This can be done through oral and written responses to tasks and probing questions.

Oral questioning of responses in order to gauge students' understanding can be recorded anecdotally, but that process takes time and organization on the part of the teacher. Written responses are desirable because they provide for easier record keeping. For problems that have a limited number of possible solutions, a rubric that is aligned with the solution process can be beneficial to assessing student success. For example, if a student is required to interpret a graph, use the data to construct a graph that is a more powerful explanation of the data, and defend his or her choice, then a rubric can be structured emphasizing these three main areas. Sharing the rubric with the student before scoring the student's work helps to focus and direct his or her efforts toward the completion of the task. The student will need additional corrective feedback in addition to the rubric score, which will advise the student about his or her success but will not be informative enough to assist the student in reaching the next level. This provides an opportunity for the teacher to compile information about what skills each of the students can complete and what instructional activities are necessary to assist students who are having difficulties.

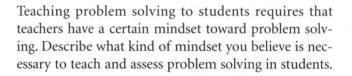

Teaching problem solving to students requires that teachers have a certain mindset toward problem solving. Describe what kind of mindset you believe is necessary to teach and assess problem solving in students.

Communication

It should be clear from the previous discussions that teaching students to communicate their thoughts about mathematics is an essential part of effective mathematics instruction at all levels. This is especially important to develop in children during their K–3 experiences. Most children come to school wanting to talk and share information about what they know. Giving them opportunities and developing oral speaking skills in shy and reserved children is a necessary part of early schooling. Although the writing skills of students in the lower grades lag behind oral speaking skills, written communication can be a powerful indicator of what students understand. Student's drawings can be interpreted in much the same manner as oral language. With the increased development of written skills, math journals become an effective means of documenting students' perceptions, understandings, and dispositions. Journaling can be used as a means for student expression, as a review of critical material, or as a personal communication between the student and the teacher.

Table 9-3 sums up content area assessment options for elementary students (K–3 and 4–6).

Table 9-3. Content Areas of Math Instruction and Assessment Options

Content Areas (K–3)	Assessment Options	Comments
Numbers and Operations Understand numbers, representations, and number systems Operations, addition and subtraction Fluent computation Estimation	Observation and anecdotal records of student responses is vital. By first grade students can calculate using pencil and paper formats. Learning centers as well as play areas can serve as assessment areas. Technology can assist in the development of skills and providing repeated practice.	Exercise care in interpreting students' understanding of number concepts. Probe for clear understanding by asking follow-up questions. Memorization of facts can be misleading when drawing inferences about student understanding.
Measurement Understand the concepts of length, volume, area, and time Use correct terminology when making comparisons Understand how to measure using standard and nonstandard units Use appropriate measuring instruments	Measurement involves conceptual understanding and skills. Observation and anecdotal record keeping is important. Opportunity to measure concrete objects is important. Centers provide opportunities to check measuring skills. Checklists can be used to assess the development of important skills in measuring.	Opportunity to learn can be crucial to the development of measuring skills. Children need to have multiple experiences measuring the same attribute. For example, measuring linear distance requires different standard measures and a variety of objects. Skill development is contingent on the complexity of the task.
Problem Solving Solve problems using a variety of strategies Use metacognitive skills to judge the quality of responses and strategies	Play centers provide children with opportunities to develop "real-life" problem-solving skills. Observation is important. Listening to students explain how they arrived at solutions is important. Checklists can assess skill application.	Observing students utilize problem solving skills outside the math classroom is important. Application of the skill to areas outside the instructional block is highly desirable.
Communication Clearly communicate thinking through oral or written expression Utilize precise mathematics vocabulary in explanations	Student pictures and written text are important assessment measures. Verbal responses can be scripted by teachers as evidence of understanding. Journaling can begin as writing skills emerge.	Care must be given to ESL students in order to develop math communication skills. Modeling the use of precise vocabulary can assist students in the use of correct terminology.

(Continued next page)

Table 9-3. Content Areas of Math Instruction and Assessment Options (Continued)

Content Areas (4–8)	Assessment Options	Comments
Numbers and Operations Understand numbers, representations, and number systems Operations, expand to multiplication and division Fluent computation Estimation	Pencil and paper calculations Development of models, schematics or webs Story problems using operations Calculator estimation problems Speed versus power tests	The prevalence of calculators in everyday life makes estimation skills more of a necessity. Students must be able to know that their answers are reasonable. Expanded thinking of students enables the use of a wider variety of assessments.
Measurement Select appropriate measures for units—i.e., weight, area, length, volume, and angle. Complete conversions within a given system. Understand the formulas and compute area, perimeter, and volume.	Assessment can be longer in duration and be more sophisticated in detail and process. Three dimensional figures can be used in developing models for assessment. Performance assessments requiring rubrics or checklists can be utilized. Formulas or computation can be more sophisticated with the use of calculators.	Student abilities differ so it will be important to assess students within their grade and age expectations. It will be equally important to develop assessments that contribute to measurement understanding for both slow and accelerated learners. Accommodating student need is challenging in this area.
Problem Solving Solve problems using a variety of strategies Use metacognitive skills to judge the quality of responses and strategies	Problems can be developed that require multiple stages. Greater focus can be given to the employment of problem-solving strategies. Rubrics, checklists, and models are effective assessment instruments.	Care must be given to the interpretation of the student thinking. Using rubrics and checklists are helpful but having the student expose his or her thinking is more critical than calculating a correct answer.
Communication Clearly communicate thinking through oral or written expression Utilize precise mathematics vocabulary in explanations	Written procedures to the solution of problems. Development of models. Written calculations with supporting explanations provide keen insight into student thinking. Journals are also effective instruments.	Written and oral solutions are especially helpful to diagnosing student misconceptions and errors. As the knowledge and skills increase, so does the importance of being able to express mathematical literacy.

After reviewing the section of this chapter that discusses preparing students to take state-mandated reading examinations, think about the types of planning, instruction, and assessment that would best prepare students to take similar mathematics exams.

Summary

Literacy and mathematical development in elementary and middle school children is a critical function of any teacher. Teachers who understand the basic targets for instruction in both reading and math can begin the process of developing sound assessments. Assessments that support the development of reading and math are linked to the essential teaching activities, and they vary according to the purpose of the assessment. Teachers who are assessment literate understand the need for a wide variety of precise assessments that are linked to important instructional activities in reading and mathematics.

Teaching Activities

1. Find a partner or a colleague with whom to work. Each person should design an assessment to use with students in one of the essential areas of reading instruction. Field-test the assessment by using it in a general education classroom and collecting samples of student work. Analyze the generated data to check for reliability. Revise the assessment as necessary. This activity can also be completed for mathematics with the same procedure.

2. Most basal reading textbooks are advertised as "balanced approaches to reading instruction." Examine a basal reading text for the presence of the essential components of reading instruction. Try to categorize the emphasis of the text. You might find a wide variance in the definition of *balance* by publishers. This activity can also be completed for mathematics instruction by noting the number of pages devoted to certain skills and concepts. If you check the alignment of the pages of the text with NCTM (2000), you can determine the emphasis of the text.

3. Reading instruction has constantly been discussed in journals. There is no less of an emphasis these days on what constitutes quality reading instruction. Find three articles that address the components of quality reading instruction. Construct a grid indicating what the authors suggest are the most important aspects of reading instruction. How does this information correspond to the basal examination in activity 2?

Chapter 10

October:
Building Tests to
Gauge Student Success

Goals of the Chapter

1. To be able to effectively plan a test that measures a wide range of instructional targets and is sensitive to the limits of time

2. To be able to employ methods that ensure content validity and the use of higher level questions when developing tests

3. To identify and be able to create accommodations and modifications of classroom tests for students with exceptionalities

The First Summative Assessments

When you turn your calendar to October, you realize that you have completed your first month of school. It probably seems to you to have flown by, but there remains so much more to do. You should be acquiring a sense of what works with your students and where you need to make modifications. By now, some of the routines are falling into place and you are collecting information about the individual capabilities and actions of your students. By now you can also gauge the accuracy of some of the advice of your experienced colleagues and their perceptions of students. You have probably made several informal assessments and keen observations, but after teaching for the first 3–4 weeks you are ready to assemble several summative assessments. In self-contained classrooms these are most likely to be in the areas of math, science, social studies, or health. If you are teaching in a middle school, you probably want to administer one of your first major assessments.

You might not believe that you have any more time left in your day as you focus on your teaching and interactions with other faculty, but remember to consider others who also have a stake in the education of your students. Parents, administrators, and other school professionals might seem a distant concern compared to the urgencies of each day, but they require some of your time. You should be asking yourself the following assessment questions:

- How are you addressing the needs of the exceptional students in your classroom? Are they meeting with success?

- Are you aware of any students who are struggling and in need of a formal placement? What accommodations are you making for them in your instruction? Have you tried to work cooperatively with the parents to gain extra help?

- Are you providing an adequate number of assessments to justify the accurate grading of a student's achievement as it appears on your report card?

- Is there a project that you can initiate with the students that will permit them to participate in a performance assessment?

- Are you communicating with the parents of your students?

- Is the pace of your instruction realistic for a successful year?

All of these questions can help to gauge your success and progress through the year. Answering them depends in part on your ability to develop valid and reliable tests that generate data concerning student success.

Despite years of experience with different types of tests, teachers need to improve their abilities to effectively develop and administer classroom tests. Crafting and assembling questions to create a good test requires careful thought. Test formats in elementary and middle schools differ widely because of student developmental differences, content areas differences, and the difficulty of material. Changes in the composition of student populations in general education classrooms has also resulted in an increased need for teachers to be skilled at employing testing accommodations and modifications. This chapter discusses test assembly, makes suggestions for appropriate accommodations in testing situations, and presents possible modifications to test questions.

Table of Specifications, or Test Blueprint

The development of high-quality tests requires attention to the issues of adequate content sampling and the use of higher level questioning. A procedure that addresses the development of these qualities in a test has been around for years; it is known as a table of specifications, or a test blueprint. Generating a test blueprint requires that teachers create a matrix of identified content to be tested and the cognitive levels assigned to the questions to be asked (Table 10-1). As the teacher creates a question and tallies its position on the matrix, the visual display helps the teacher to determine if he or she is asking an equitable number of questions about each part of the lessons that were taught. This enhances the content validity of the test (you should remember that concept from the first chapter). By assigning the appropriate cognitive level to each question, the matrix helps to remind the teacher to design higher level questions, thereby avoiding a test that is entirely devoted to lower level recall questions.

Table 10-1. Test Blueprint

	Know/Comp	Application	Analysis	Synthesis	Evaluation
Goal 1, Question #s					
1	X				
2	X				
7	X				
16	X				
17	X				
Goal 2, Question #s					
6			X		
12	X				
13	X				
14	X				
15	X				
22				X	
Goal 3, Question #s					
3	X				
4	X				
8	X				
9	X				
18	X				
21	X				
Goal 4, Question #s					
5	X				
10			X		
11	X				
19	X				
20	X				

The motives behind developing a test blueprint are commendable, and the overall quality of teacher-made tests would be improved if teachers around the country subjected their existing measures to the rigor of a test blueprint. Unfortunately, it has been my experience that many teachers are simply too busy to complete a test blueprint for many of their tests. An elementary teacher working in grades 4–6 in a self-contained classroom might easily generate 100–150 tests within a single school year. Even the most conscientious teacher does not have time to prepare a table of specifications for all of those tests while juggling the daily urgencies of teaching. This is not to suggest that we abandon the development of the test blueprint; instead, we must simply make it more usable and less time-consuming. Ensuring adequate content sampling and the assessment of higher level thinking should not be sacrificed in test development practices.

Keep in mind the purposes of the test blueprint when creating a test. We want to make sure that we develop questions that comprehensively assess the desired targets that were planned in the unit. You might recall, from your own experiences as a test taker, occasions when you studied material in three chapters only to find that all the questions were from the material in the first chapter. Your experience is an unfortunate example of what can happen to students when the teacher is guilty of poor content sampling. The inference drawn by your teacher about what you (and all the students in your class) knew about all three chapters was questionable, because the only material adequately assessed by the exam was the material found in chapter 1.

Guskey (2003) claims that this type of improper test preparation results in two unfortunate consequences. First, students come to believe that the time and effort spent studying has little or no effect on their test results. Second, they learn that they cannot trust their teachers. In order to avoid the same mistake, review the objectives of your lesson plans, which guided the teaching of the material you now intend to test. Try to develop questions that assess critical content and student understanding from each of the lessons. Also look for skills (usually appearing as verbs in your objectives) and vocabulary that you think are important enough to test. If you make this a habit, you can begin to develop a sense of good content sampling based on tangible evidence derived from your teaching.

Another action that might help you to develop good content sampling (especially in the upper grades) is to question your students after the test about what they expected on the test that was not tested and what questions were unexpected or tricky. For example, a middle school teacher uses a four-point scale, asking students to anonymously rate the fairness of her tests. She contends that her students respond honestly to her inquiry. Her students are also provided with an open-ended section in which they can comment, complain, or explain. Reflecting on the quality of your test and asking students for their input can help your future test development efforts.

Another purpose of a test blueprint is to make sure that some questions require higher level thinking. Although this is a desirable goal for all teachers, it is not easily achievable in middle school classrooms, where the testing format largely consists of objective item formats. Designing objective test items that require students to employ higher level thinking skills might be beyond the test-making capabilities of most teachers, without sufficient training. Multiple-choice formats can be used to assess higher order thinking skills, but efforts to achieve that goal often result in the question being overly confusing to elementary-age children. Rather than giving up on the idea of testing higher level thinking in these children, it might be best to shift formats. Including an essay question on the test will give you an easier opportunity to assess higher level thinking. The essay question format, you will recall, provides us with an opportunity to assess higher level thinking.

Now that you realize that the table of specifications frames the development of your test, there are other important elements to consider when assembling questions for the purpose of summative assessment. These are discussed in the following sections, with guidelines that will help your test construction.

Test Length

One consistent question that teachers wrestle with is "How many questions should I ask the students?" In order to answer that question you must determine how much time is available to test the students. We must fit the number of questions that adequately sample the content within a reasonable time frame for administering the test. Test length is also dependent on the age and developmental level of the children. If we are testing third graders, a test of 15–20 minutes will probably stretch them to the limit. Grades 4–8 can be tested for longer periods, but in the case of departmentalized teaching, a school's class periods can place finite limits on testing time. Keeping the overall period in mind, we can use the following as a guideline to determine how many questions we should ask on the test: True/false items usually require about 10–20 seconds each, but multiple-choice questions can take 30–45 seconds each. Completion items take 10–15 seconds each, but the time to answer a matching exercise is dependent on its length and complexity. Essay items require much more time for students to formulate their answers.

The following example will clarify how to estimate the time your test will take. Suppose that our sixth-grade class period permits 30 minutes of testing time (after subtracting the time required for the distribution of tests and reviewing any test completion requirements). If we create a test of 10 multiple-choice items, 10 true/false, a matching exercise, and perhaps an essay or two, will the students have adequate time to complete the exam? You can see from the guidelines above that the objective portion of the test will require 12–15 minutes. Depending on the complexity and length of response required by one essay question, you will have to make a good decision about whether to include a second essay question. It might require a little too much time for this testing period. Remember to design the essay items so that the average student will be able to respond to them.

Because the reading levels of the students will affect their speed in taking this test, we should allow an adequate amount of time for all children to complete the exam. If you are in doubt about the length of your first test, always err on the side of making the test too short. Construct an exam that allows you to be confident that all students can easily complete your test within the time limit. If you make the test too long for students to complete in one class period, you will have to decide how to deal with the students' unanswered questions. This can be an especially tricky situation with conscientious students who took extra time to provide details and examples in their answers to your essay questions. Be cautious with your first attempts; you want the first test of the year to be a successful experience for you and your students.

Numbering and Weighting Test Items

As you develop different question formats—for example, five true/false questions, five multiple-choice questions, and a matching section—make sure that you number the items sequentially instead of starting over in each category. Numbering sequentially gives you a sense of how many items are on the entire test and helps to limit confusion when you are reviewing the exam after scoring it. Try not to overwhelm the students with any one particular test format. If your tests are 90 percent true/false items, you need to rethink your approach to test development. Students perform (and, more important, perceive that they do) differently on one question type than another. Their perceptions are very closely tied to their history of success with the various test item formats. Using a variety of question formats allows all students to be optimistic about at least one part of the exam.

The weighting of questions is important to make the test fair for all students. You might want to double the weight of an item format if you think it's more important than other areas of the test. For example, each multiple-choice item might have a value of 2 points, whereas each true/false item might be worth 1 point. Make sure to explain this to students when administering the exam. Another important consideration of weighting is to make sure that the overall weight of one area of the test does not disproportionately affect a student's final test scores. For example, suppose your constructed test includes 25 objective test questions worth one point each and two essays worth 20 points each. The students who perform best on essay questions will have an easier time scoring well on the test. If fact, the students who prefer objective questions and generally don't perform well on essays might be in danger of failing the exam. A more reasonable distribution of points would allow for each part of the test to contribute equitably to the student's final score.

Reflection

How does the amount of time allowed for the test and the distribution of test items affect student success? How can those two elements create unfair assessments of students?

Developing
Objective Questions

Constructing objective test items can be perplexing and frustrating if you approach it without a plan. A method that helps teachers to develop objective items efficiently is described below.

Let's suppose you are teaching fifth-grade social studies and intend to develop a summative chapter test. You have reviewed your lesson plans and intend to match your questions to the important content of the chapter. You determine that one of the important points of the chapter is that Abraham Lincoln issued the Emancipation Proclamation, which abolished slavery in the United States.

If you intend to design an objective question, you have three options: true/false, completion, or multiple choice. The first option is an easy one; if you use the statement as is, you immediately have a true/false question. If you want to make the item false, you merely change a critical part of the statement, as shown:

> Abraham Lincoln issued the Emancipation Proclamation, which abolished slavery in the United States.

> Abraham Lincoln issued the Declaration of Independence, which abolished slavery in the United States.

For the second option, completion, you simply reword the statement and place a blank at the end of the statement:

> Abraham Lincoln abolished slavery in the United States by issuing the
> _____.

> The Emancipation Proclamation, which abolished slavery in the United States, was issued by President _____.

Here you are attempting to test the same item, but you are asking the students to recall two different facts. It is your choice whether you want them to recall the Emancipation Proclamation or Abraham Lincoln. The choice has much to do with the context of the teaching and the content of the rest of the test.

Your third option, a multiple-choice question, could appear as follows:

> Abraham Lincoln abolished slavery in the United States by issuing the
>
> A. Gettysburg Address
>
> B. Emancipation Proclamation
>
> C. Declaration of Independence
>
> D. Missouri Compromise

This is how a fact or concept that was emphasized in your instruction can be developed into one of several different types of objective questions. Students all have what they consider to be their favorite (and sometimes, least favorite) type of test question. You might hear students say, "I hate essay questions" or "I don't feel confident taking true/false tests." This should appeal to your sensitivity about student differences. First and foremost, we want to match the instruction with the most appropriate type of assessment, but we also want to consider varying the assessment format to address student strengths and weaknesses. These are important issues in the development of a test.

If you are unclear about the advantages and disadvantages of various types of test questions, consult the guidelines for the construction of sound questions in chapter 3.

Developing an Answer Key

There are several ways to develop an answer key that will help you to score student tests. Let's consider the objective item format first. If we are working with objective tests and the students are generating one answer for each numbered test item, then we can make an answer key sheet that requires the student to transfer the correct letter to the answer key and not write directly on the test. Having a separate answer sheet facilitates the checking of student papers because the teacher does not have to turn the individual test pages. The downside is that it enhances the ability of a student to copy answers from another person's paper. If you suspect this is happening, you can put more space between your students or create two forms of the same test.

Another way to develop an answer key is to simply run another copy of your test and write in the answers. You can instruct your students to write directly on their tests, and you then check each test. The scoring of the tests is most easily completed by checking all of the page 1s, then all the page 2s, and so on. Although it is a bit more time-consuming, this action permits you to view the students' responses to the questions. The net result of this method is that you get a better sense of how the students did on a specific question.

There is a natural inclination among test makers to place the objective item formats at the beginning of the test and the essay questions at the end of the test. The reasons for this are probably time and difficulty. The students can complete the objective items quickly and then effectively budget their time to complete the essay question(s). It is always advisable to place easier questions at the beginning of the exam in order to avoid overwhelming the students and adding to test anxiety. In the case of elementary-age students, especially those with reading and writing difficulties, it makes sense to defer the essay question to later in the test.

Suggestions for scoring and providing feedback on essay formats can be found in chapter 3 and chapter 15.

Accommodating and Modifying the Test for Students With Exceptionalities

The law is clear about the inclusion of students with exceptionalities in regular education classrooms and the proper validation of assessments to meet their needs. Students have a right to be tested in an appropriate mode with appropriate modifications to accommodate their exceptionalities (Siskind, 1993). This chapter cannot provide all the suggestions that could be made for you to accommodate and modify teacher-made tests. Instead, suggestions are offered that can be applied across the board with the hope that you will adapt them to your own classroom. It is of extreme importance that you, as a teacher, know and understand the accommodations and modifications that are permitted by law for students with exceptionalities.

It is important to make the distinction between test accommodation and modification. Pitoniak and Royer (2001), define *accommodations* as changes that remove or limit the student's disability and allow for a more valid assessment of the construct being tested. *Modifications,* on the other hand, involve a change in the construct itself, or an alteration in the questions making up the test.

An example of an accommodation is to use large print for a student who has a visual disability. This accommodation does not change the content of the question, and it allows the student with the disability to answer the questions in the same manner as all the other students. Accommodating any testing situation can be approached from an organizational structure. The guidelines listed by the Pennsylvania System of School Assessment (2003–2004) include the following major areas:

- Test preparation
- Test administration
- Test response
- Timing and scheduling of the test
- Setting
- Assistive devices

More than 50 suggestions are included under these main headings. All of the accommodations are designed to manipulate aspects of the questions while retaining their integrity. In other words, the question format and wording is not altered in any manner. For example, suggestions under the heading "test preparation" address accommodations that assist the student in understanding the directions to the test. Another area, "test response," indicates that students with exceptionalities can be permitted to use enlarged answer sheets.

Additional accommodations for the day-to-day assessment of students with special needs include the following:

Reading the test orally

Allowing open-book tests

Allowing the use of a study guide during the test

Adapting the format and/or length

Allowing printing

Allowing extra time to complete the test

Retesting one-to-one

Taking dictation for essay answers

Giving advanced notice of a test

Not penalizing for spelling or handwriting if that is not the focus of the test

Administering the test with special education teacher by appointment

Although these suggestions are offered for the administration of state tests, the accommodations are certainly reasonable to use in everyday classroom assessment.

Modifying Day-to-Day Assessments for Students in Your Classroom

Confusion exists concerning the use of modifications in classrooms. Educational professionals and psychometricians generally agree that modifications, as opposed to accommodations, can generate validity issues.

Following are some reasons for the confusion concerning classroom modifications for special needs:

- Children with exceptionalities are widely diverse in their strengths and weaknesses, making it difficult to construct general suggestions for the modifications of test items.

- Many of the currently applied modifications stretch the indicators of quality (validity and reliability) that are the foundation of measurement. Issues of validity and reliability are grounded in large-scale test design and are important for the purpose of large-scale assessments. Classroom assessments differ in their purposes and their uses.

- The requirements of a student individualized educational plan (IEP) often demand specificity. This need can contradict the guidelines for the development of large-scale test items.

- There is a lack of clear direction by governing bodies and learned societies on ethical decision making for the modification of test items.

Modifying Objective Item Formats

Following is a list of suggestions for modifying objective item formats in the classroom. Teachers should be cautious with the use of these modifications and consult the student's IEP or knowledgeable personnel within the school system when making these changes.

1. True/False Item Modifications

    *   Write the item with the shortest amount of reading that retains the intent of the question.

    *   Avoid using the word *not* in the test item.

    *   Highlight or use an alternate word that might trigger the student's memory of important content.

2. Multiple-Choice Item Modifications

    *   Try to avoid using combinations of response alternatives as the correct response—for example, "both A and C."

    *   Shorten the stem to focus the question and reduce the amount of reading.

    *   Highlight a key word or two in the stem.

    *   Reduce the number of response alternatives from four to three or from five to four. Avoid reducing the number to two because that makes the multiple-choice item a true/false question.

    *   Make sure to present the response alternatives in a vertical arrangement rather than a horizontal arrangement. The vertical arrangement is typically easier to read.

3. Completion Item Modifications

    If you are testing items in a series, provide the first item in order to trigger the student's recall of the next two. For example, "The three branches of government are executive,_____ , and _____." Further modification might include providing two of the three.

    Provide a word bank from which the students can choose the correct response to the completion item. Using a word bank creates a sort of matching exercise and shifts the completion format from recall questions to recognition questions. Validity issues are associated with this modification, and there are rules that govern the sound development of this exercise. For example, proper word bank construction requires that there be more word choices than number of blanks; however, employing a word bank in which the number of word choices is equal to the number of blanks often occurs. This aids the process of elimination for students.

The use of blanks to identify multiple-word answers can also be employed as a modification. For example, if the completion item requires a two-word response, then providing two blank spaces rather than one can be an aid to the student.

4.   Matching Item Modifications

The most common modification in the matching format is to reduce the number of items in order to focus the student's reading and energy. For example, a matching exercise containing 8 premises and 10 responses might be too cluttered and appear to be overwhelming to students with visual discrimination difficulties. Splitting the format into two matching exercises on separate pages can make the activities more easily understood by the test taker.

Another modification that can be used to adapt matching exercises is to simply dismantle the matching exercise and create completion or true/false items with content to be tested. You should recognize that you are making a severe change in the test format and that the resulting student responses will have to be interpreted individually rather than compared to other students' achievement.

Modifying Essay Item Formats

Under the 1997 amendments to the Individuals With Disabilities Education Act (IDEA-97), children with exceptionalities must be instructed and assessed, to the greatest extent possible, in the general school curriculum. Two points should be emphasized. First, the wide range of possible exceptionalities, as defined by IDEA-97, compounded by the influence of the individual student's intellectual, behavioral, and social actions, emphasizes the contextual vulnerability of recommendations offered in this section. Teacher and IEP team decisions concerning the child and appropriate classroom assessments are most important. Second, any modification of the format of the assessment usually generates some consequence to its validity and reliability and ultimately impacts the use of the results.

Given that accommodations and modifications should be completed with thoughtfulness and a clear understanding of the consequences, the following are suggestions for making essay items more reasonable for use with all students.

Teachers can provide a structure for the student answer. Whether the intention is to use a restricted-response or an extended-response essay, providing a scaffold to guide the organization of the answer can be helpful to students. For example, students who are asked to address the following restricted-response question could benefit from a prepared response sheet: "Name and discuss the impact of three events leading to the Revolutionary War." A structure that minimally compromises the assessment includes an answer sheet that contains a 3 x 2 matrix with the word *Events* as the head of the first column and *Impact* as the head of the second. Students who struggle with the organization of their responses could benefit from this framework, and the assessment of content remains valid.

For an extended-response essay, the employment of a modification can be more invasive to the primary purpose of the assessment. This can be illustrated using the following example:

> You are a newspaper critic who has been asked to respond to the current fluoride debate in your city. After reviewing the data, write a column for the newspaper that defends your argument either for or against the addition of fluoride into the city's water supply.

In this essay we are assessing the student's ability to analyze information, synthesize the content into a new format, and compose a written piece for or against the addition of a chemical into the city's water supply. Modifications might consist of assisting the student in one or more of the areas targeted by this question. Teachers can modify the data analysis portion by presenting it differently or by reducing or completely removing extraneous information. If the synthesis portion is an area of concern, the teacher might have the student complete a plus or minus activity that more concretely indicates the position most beneficial to the public. To accommodate the written composition, the teacher can give the student additional time and/or permit the oral submission of the opinion, like a television news report. Each of these modifications of the question assists the students by adjusting the way in which the question is posed. The degree to which the teacher has exceeded the need to modify the question is difficult to measure and must rely on the teacher's professional judgment and understanding of assessment.

Table 10-2 shows the modification of essay questions.

With each modification to the question, there are various degrees of change that affect the teacher's ability to infer the student's achievement of one of the desired targets of the assessment. The determination of appropriate accommodations and modifications requires teachers to consider the special needs of the student as well as the targets and format of the assessment (Criswell & Criswell, 2004).

Summary

Understanding how to develop fair and well-constructed written questions is an important skill for all teachers to possess. However, putting the objective and subjective formats together to complete an effective written examination requires additional knowledge and skill. Teachers who are skilled at developing tests consider elements of time, essential content, and a student's opportunity to learn. Careful thought and planning are also essential in addressing issues of sampling, weighting items, and modifying questions for students with special needs. Teachers who can effectively develop sound written examinations will have clearer perceptions of the strengths and weaknesses of their students. They will also be confident in their abilities to report to students, parents, and other school professionals what students know and can do.

Table 10-2. Essay Questions and Modifications

Type of Question	Required of Student	Modification to Question	Student Responses
Restricted-Response Items	Student knowledge of fundamental information and the ability to express himself or herself in a written form.	Providing a scaffold to the question: (See below)	Orders and cues the response. Compromises assessment of organization, may assist student in recall of essential information.
EXAMPLE	Name and discuss the impact of three events leading to the Revolutionary War.	Name Impact Event #1 Event #2 Event #3	
Extended-Response Items	Student knowledge of fundamental information and the ability to express himself or herself in a written form. Use of higher order thinking skills.	Providing a scaffold to the question:	Orders and cues the response. Compromises assessment of organization skills and perhaps the higher order thinking that is necessary.
EXAMPLE	You are a newspaper critic who has been asked to respond to the current fluoride debate in your city. After reviewing the data, write a column for the newspaper that defends your argument either for or against the addition of fluoride into the city's water supply.	Positives Negatives 1. 1. 2. 2. 3. 3. What do think should happen? If you were a newspaper reporter, how would you report what you think should happen?	

Teaching Activities

1. Using a test that has already been constructed, either one of your own or an off-the-shelf test, modify the items using the suggestions in the chapter. Be sure to make appropriate modifications to the essay items that might help students with organizational difficulties.

2. Using a chapter from an upper elementary or middle school social studies or science text, construct several test questions. Use a variety of formats, including multiple choice, matching, and essay. Share the items with a partner and troubleshoot each other's work.

3. Using the department of education Web sites of different states, find out what the suggested accommodations are for each state's standardized assessment. Check for commonalities and differences among states. Note if there is a discussion of suggested appropriate modifications.

November: Planning an Effective Parent-Teacher Conference

1. To recognize the importance of conducting a well-organized parent conference

2. To be able to organize data in a way that supports communicating student results to parents and other school professionals

3. To be able to approach parent conferences with confidence

The Importance of Parental Involvement

National Education Week occurs in November and involves numerous parent-community activities in many American schools. Inviting parents or guardians to visit their children's schools during the day or organizing a Parent's Night is an expression of the understanding that family-school collaborations is important to student success. Although the activities associated with National Education Week differ according to geographical area, parent-teacher conferences are a common feature. Organizing an effective parent-teacher conference, however, is not restricted to November but is a critical component of the development of strong parent-school relations throughout the year.

Parent involvement is increasingly being recognized as an important feature in the development of schools that care about reaching all their students. According to Christie (2005), 17 states have grant or award programs that encourage schools or districts to involve parents in their children's education. Maryland's Parent Advisory Council recently released two dozen recommendations addressing five themes of parent involvement: accountability, training, leadership, partnership, and communication. In the area of training, it proposes that the state education department should assess the training needs of local school systems with regard to parent and community involvement and funnel resources accordingly. In the area of communication, it recommends that districts use a variety of methods, media, and languages to provide parents with grade-level information on curriculum, school programs, and suggestions for improving individual student achievement (Christie, 2005). Parental involvement is changing in the ways that teachers communicate with parents and also in the ways in which parents can partake in school functions. In view of these expanded roles and responsibilities, an assessment-literate teacher must possess the knowledge and skills to coordinate and lead an effective parent-teacher conference.

According to Tierney, Crumpler, Bertelsen, and Bond (2003), parent-teacher conferences are the site of planning for the future, presenting and reviewing educational goals, solving problems, and creating connections between a student's life at school and life at home. This chapter lists different reasons for parent-teacher conferences, discusses ways to develop positive conferences, and provides guidelines to promote the effective use of assessment data.

Why do you think there is such an emphasis on bringing teachers and parents together? Beyond the apparent student benefits, are there other reasons that schools should seek parental support?

Reasons for Parent-Teacher Conferences

Although districts or individual schools might formally require and designate scheduled teacher-parent meetings, conferences can be requested by teachers or parents for a number of reasons. These conferences may take place at any time during the school year but frequently occur around the time that report cards are issued. Other typical scenarios that trigger the need for a requested parent-teacher conference include the following:

- Parents noticing an extreme change in their child's attitude toward school or willingness to attend school

- A teacher observing unusual types of antisocial behaviors on the part of the child, especially behaviors disrupting teaching and learning in the classroom or affecting the individual child's academic progress

- Parents recommending a conference to discuss their child's grades, test scores, or progress over the course of the year

- Teachers wanting to discuss what appears to be a lack of support from home, such as the child not coming to school or not being adequately prepared; possibly reflected in the child's lack of energy, personal hygiene problems, unkempt appearance, and nutritional deficiencies

There are a variety of reasons for parent-teacher conferences, but the general purpose of such conferences is to promote a clear understanding among participants of how to shape a child's school and home experiences to enhance student success. In the case of formally scheduled parent conferences, which are usually held in conjunction with National Education Week, parents get a chance to sit down with their child's teacher (and perhaps the child) to review evidence of performance. The purpose of these conferences is to collectively review the products of a child's classroom efforts and thereby provide parents with a window on their child's school life. Conferences may also be designed around academic difficulties, classroom behavior problems, intervention strategies, and a host of other more specific reasons. Although each of these conferences has a slightly different purpose, the primary intent remains the same: to make the parent-teacher conference as productive as possible.

Common Logistical Arrangements and Atmosphere

Regardless of the type of parent-teacher conference, part of sharing important information with parents is preparing for their comfort in visiting the school and being part of a team. Most parents visit schools infrequently and usually do not have a sense of comfort in meeting a team of important school personnel. This is especially true for parents who have been consistently asked to come to school to discuss their child's academic or behavioral difficulties. Parents of children coming from other school systems might have had prior experiences where there was only a one-way communication from the teacher and parent-teacher conferences were not a valued part of schooling. Assume, however, that most parents want to know about the learning, growth, and development of their children in your classroom. There are ways to structure the meetings that helps to put parents at ease.

Meet the parents at your classroom door or make yourself available prior to meeting others who are also attending the conference. Although titles are important, it has been my experience that parents appreciate a comfortable degree of formality. For example, I would always introduce myself by saying, "Hi, I'm Mr. Criswell, your daughter's teacher." Make sure to ask their names and let them know exactly who will be attending the conference. When inviting other teachers, indicate your reasons for doing so. For example, "Ms. Murphy will be attending today's conference because she is Benjamin's science teacher."

When you arrive at the meeting location, take time to introduce each of the attendees and explain their purpose for being at the meeting. Seat the parents so that they are on the same side of the table with you. Avoid a seating structure where the teacher sits at his or her desk and the parents sit at student desks. You want to create a sense of the group conversationally facing each other. If you are a K–3 teacher, avoid requiring adults to sit in chairs designed for 6- to 7-year-olds, especially if you are sitting in an adult chair. Setting a tone for the conference cannot change the information that you share with parents, but it might affect the way the information is perceived. Making parents feel welcomed is the first step in saying, "I value your opinion."

All conferences should begin with an attempt to be as positive as possible and a sense that the ultimate purpose is to work in the best interest of the student's success in school. You should take the lead by stating the purpose of the conference immediately. For example:

> We are meeting today at the request of Mr. and Mrs. Duncan, who are interested in gaining more information about their son Slam's scores on the last achievement tests. Our purpose here today is to provide the Duncans with as much information as possible and to answer any questions they might have during the conference.

As the conference develops you might notice that the conversations drift away from the purpose. Always allow parents to pursue questions and other areas of interest, but if you find that the conference is likely to be unproductive due to the time spent on discussing extraneous information, then pull the group back to the original purpose. This can be done by simply suggesting, "Although it has been valuable to discuss Slam's telephone habits, we have gotten off track. Are there any other areas of the achievement scores we need to explain in greater detail?" Not all conferences, however, are as explanatory in nature as discussing standardized test results, and some meetings will require teachers to directly address more specific student strengths and weaknesses.

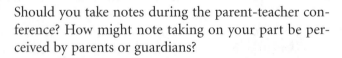

Reflection   Should you take notes during the parent-teacher conference? How might note taking on your part be perceived by parents or guardians?

Discussing Strengths and Weaknesses

Descriptions of student performance should include comments on what the student does well and where the student needs improvement. In too many cases, the focus of the conference is on the need for improvement and so takes on a negative tone. This occurs most often when teachers and school professionals emphasize the academic achievement of low-functioning students rather than considering other important factors such as effort, progress, and disposition to learn. It is important to include student successes as well as areas that require more effort or attention.

When discussing student weaknesses, it is important to use positive or encouraging language. Phrase the suggestion to state what you want the student to do rather than what the student is not doing. For example, "Susan would benefit from completing her homework more regularly" instead of "Susan doesn't do her homework." It then becomes easier to enlist the help of the parents by asking how they might be able to arrange for Susan to complete her homework.

Another technique that can be used with a bit of preparation is the "sandwich method" of discussing strengths and weaknesses. Plan the content of the conference in such a way that you sandwich any weaknesses between the strengths that you intend to discuss. The value of this presentation strategy is that it avoids presenting what might seem to parents as an endless list of weaknesses. This does not mean that the teacher should invent positive aspects or elaborate on unimportant events in order to create positives that match the negatives. Instead, if the student possesses a relatively equal number of strengths and weakness, then consider the sandwich method as an option for presenting the information.

Organizing the Data: A Framework for Sharing Student Work Samples

The order and pace of sharing information is crucial when leading the parents through a review of student work. The conference will be more efficient when it is planned with a structure that outlines the meeting and the sequence of information to be shared. Benson and Barnett (1999) suggest developing a list of work samples to demonstrate a child's progress, areas of concern, and areas of strength. The following organizational framework can be used to shape a conference.

Greeting. This includes introductions, seating, and getting people comfortable. Utilize the information at the beginning of this chapter to address specific areas.

Presentation of material. Organize your materials and student work samples to be presented by subject area, by strength and weakness, or by chronological order of student completion.

Meeting closure. Summarize the important agreements or what was concluded from the conference. Decide on who gets to keep the student work samples and collectively develop a plan to address any areas of concern. Discuss the appropriateness of the next scheduled meeting to include how soon, what day and time is most convenient for all parties, and if additional persons should be present.

How to Indicate Progress Using Student Work Samples

Samples of student work are probably the most effective means by which to indicate student progress in areas of knowledge acquisition or skill development. Central to the idea of showing student growth is making a comparison. Dating the samples helps to create a baseline of student achievement that is essential for comparisons with other work. Growth is measured by noting skill development, increased achievement, or enhanced depth of understanding. However, it is also important to address the idea of progressing in relationship to what are considered acceptable developmental levels in the grade you teach.

For example, in the area of literacy acquisition with K–3 students, you can present dated material that includes the following:

- student writing samples
- the results of fluency checks
- retellings, story maps, other comprehension checks
- measures of decoding success
- dispositions toward reading and reading instruction

Upper elementary and middle school student progress can also be presented to parents or guardians in an organized arrangement. Dated samples that help to inform the conference include the following:

- tests and/or test results, projects, or performance tasks
- writing samples for different literacy purposes, logs, or journals
- homework or other out-of-classroom assignments
- observations of work habits, use of independent time, attention to detail
- observations or other evidence of an ability to effectively contribute to a group project

The emphasis with parents or guardians should be the degree to which the student is progressing in his or her ability to perform at a level suitable to the expectations for that grade. You should call attention to the individual's growth or improvement, but parents will also want to know how well their child is reading compared to other students and the expectations for that grade. Be prepared to indicate both.

Other areas of schooling can also be addressed in terms of progress. For example, you might want to comment on a student who has experienced difficulty with social behaviors and adjusting to classroom routines or rules. Progress toward acceptable levels of behavior is worth reporting to parents. This can be achieved through the use of anecdotal records, summary information of disciplinary actions, and reports of other school professionals.

Refer to the section of chapter 8 that describes the development of a classroom management plan for additional information that can be communicated to parents in a conference setting.

Reflection

Material presented to parents has begun with areas of strengths. Is there any occasion when you think that starting with concerns or weaknesses would be more important?

Areas of Concern or Weakness

Student samples should also show areas in which the child needs more intense work or guidance. For example, if the student is experiencing problems with the addition and subtraction of fractions, it is worth communicating this to parents. Upper elementary and middle school students who have been successful with basic operations (addition, subtraction, multiplication, and division) might encounter difficulty with understanding fractions. Because fractions require abstract thinking, students may need additional time, multiple approaches, and repetition to acquire a depth of understanding.

In order for feedback to be most effective with students, teacher comments and directions should be timely, specific, and corrective. This is also generally true of your conversations with parents. Take time to explain the types of errors that you notice in the child's work. Suggest a means by which the student can improve his or her product or achievement level. In other words, propose a corrective action. The types of suggested action might include increasing repetitions, strengthening understanding, or proofreading the child's work. In the area of increasing repetitions, parents can work with their child on recalling facts, practicing the completion of problems, or rehearsing a speech. Strengthening the understanding of a student might require the parent to provide an example, clarify a meaning, or suggest an outside resource. Proofreading the child's work shows the student that the parent cares about the quality of the work. It is also a powerful modeling tool. Always be sure to suggest these as reinforcement methods and not as substitutes for your teaching. Accept the responsibility for teaching the student, but encourage the additional support of the parent or guardian.

Below is another example of a student weakness and the suggestions that might be shared with parents as corrective actions. Parents are frequently interested in how they might directly assist their child. Keeping the tasks simple but productive helps to ensure the participation of the parents.

In the area of writing, Sarah has improved in her focus and organization. She has started to use more vivid descriptions, and her word choice has grown. She continues, however, to write sentence fragments rather than complete sentences. The following suggestions might be made to the parents:

> If Sarah is working on a draft of a written assignment at home, ask her to proofread it and call her attention to making sure that all her sentences are complete. Please review her writing. Should you find an error, tell her which paragraph contains the error and have her locate the sentence fragment. It might be effective to have her read the paragraph aloud. Reading aloud occasionally helps the student to hear the error that was missed in the silent proofreading. Also encourage her to read independently, which will increase her exposure to practical examples of complete sentences.

Areas of Strength

One of the easier decisions to make as a classroom teacher is the choice of samples of outstanding student work to share with parents. Involving students in the selection process helps to develop pride and meaningfulness in the work they complete. If you have students select pieces to share with their parents, it is a good idea to have them write about why they chose those pieces. The types of evidence usually chosen by students convey deep understanding, outstanding test scores, high degrees of creativity, or the pursuit of personal interests.

Areas of strength can also be used as a means by which to develop increased understanding or promote motivation. Celebrating student success is important and helps to encourage future efforts and increased levels of determination. Sharing the success with parents spreads that encouragement outside the classroom. Make decisions about whether you need to keep the materials that you share with the parents. Many times they will ask if they can keep their child's work. I'd advise you to prepare a least one or two outstanding pieces before the conference that they can take with them. They will most likely share this with other family members and keep it to show to their child later in life.

Concluding the Meeting With a Summary or a Plan

When conducting teacher conferences, provide a written conclusion of what you see as the areas of growth, weakness, and strength. This write-up can be used in conjunction with the student's report card or as a separate attachment that parents or guardians can take home with them. Beginning the conference on a positive note sets the tone for the conference; ending the conference on a positive note sets the tone for the future. This type of conclusion indicates that you are well organized and have a plan that, with the parents' help, will lead to a greater degree of success for the student.

Always provide a clear summary. It is especially important to conclude with a clarification of the issues and points addressed between the teacher and the parents or guardians. After the completion of a conference, the main purpose for the conference is often lost in the discussion of other supporting details and sidebar conversations. Taking several minutes at the end of the conference to develop a plan will tie up the loose ends and provide a meaningful closure to the meeting. If the conference has involved a high degree of tension, the plan is especially important, in order to avoid any misunderstandings between the two parties. It is a good idea to make two copies of the written summation, one for the school's records and one for the parents; it is essential if there were disagreements.

The plan should restate the tasks that each of the parties will work to achieve. For example, if you designed a plan to have a student consistently complete her homework, we might conclude the conference with the following comments:

> In order to make sure that Susan completes her homework, first she will complete the entries in her homework journal and Ms. Sperry [the classroom teacher] will initial the journal prior to Susan leaving the building. Either parent will sign off on the completion of the assignments, and Susan will be responsible for presenting it to Ms. Sperry each morning. Is everyone comfortable with his or her role in this plan?

The Role of Students in Parent-Teacher Conferences

Tierney et al. (2003) outlines three formats of parent-teacher conferences to describe the involvement of the student (Table 11-1). The selection of these is based on your context, personality, teaching style, and confidence.

The first format is the traditional parent-teacher conference in which the student is not invited to attend. The advantages of this format are openness and the ability to discuss sensitive issues. The second format is a parent-teacher conference with the child present. Here the student attends the conference and comments when appropriate to clarify the discussions. The student is an observer and comments on a limited basis only. The third format is a parent-teacher conference with input from the student. Here the student presents selected materials and shares them with the parents. The child then leaves, and the teacher and parents continue the conference. The choice should be made with a consideration of comfort as well as which format offers the best opportunity for a successful parent-teacher conference.

Table 11-1. Parent-Teacher Conference Formats

Type of Conferences	Description	Benefits	Factors to Consider
Format 1: Traditional Parent-Teacher Conference	Parent and teacher meet to discuss student growth and progress. Student is typically not invited to attend.	Open conversations between teacher and parent; sensitive issues can be raised and discussed.	Student not involved in conference, thus no input from student. Child might become anxious about what is being said in his or her absence.
Format 2: Parent-Teacher Conference With Child Present	Parent and teacher meet to discuss student growth and progress. Student is invited to attend and listen to what is being discussed.	The student is able to hear the discussion between the teacher and parent.	Both teacher and parent are guarded in what is being discussed.
Format 3: Parent-Teacher Conference With Input From the Student	The student begins the conference by sharing work samples that have been selected. Student then leaves the conference so the teacher and parent can continue conference.	Open communication between all stakeholders—student, parent, teacher. Parent can hear how child is doing from child's perspective.	Organization and preplanning of supervised activity for the students after leaving the conference. Some type of transition system in place to minimize distractions to others.

Used with permission of Christopher-Gordon Publishers, Inc.

 Can you think of any disadvantages in the types of parent-conference arrangements that have been described?

Frequency of Conferences

Meeting with parents to discuss the progress of a child or to develop a plan for intervention should not be an isolated event. Conferencing is part of an ongoing communication system that provides opportunities for sharing information between the home and school. Consideration should be given to setting up a follow-up conference.

The decision to meet again with parents is based on a number of different variables. The gravity of a conference will make another conference desirable. If the purpose of the conference was to set up a working plan between home and school, then it is necessary to schedule a follow-up conference. Because learning should be a sustained process, it is reasonable to schedule the next parent conference after the suggested actions are in place. Conferences should be scheduled as necessary; no absolute guideline of time can be suggested. In the event that the initial parent conference was informational and its purpose was not to set into motion a series of actions between home and school, then a follow-up meeting is probably not necessary. Instead of another meeting, you can continue to communicate through e-mail, newsletters, personal notes, and telephone calls to keep parents informed. Report cards are a form of home-school communication, but their format is usually rigid and fails to provide the specific types of information that assist parents. A final reason for a follow-up conference is the dissatisfaction of follow-through by either the school personnel or the parent or guardian. It would be misleading to suggest that all parent conferences end with strategies that are effectively implemented and result in a complete solution of a problem. It should be suggested at some point in a parent-teacher conference that both parties have the responsibility for communicating any dissatisfaction they experience with the completion of the plan.

Summary

The nature of parent involvement and the interactions of teachers and communities are expanding the role of the teacher. Parent-teacher conferences are one part of healthy school communications. The purposes for conferences differ greatly, but the need for cooperative and productive exchanges is critical. Planning for the parent-teacher conference is essential and requires the use of multiple forms of assessment data. A welcoming environment and an organized presentation of information will assist in the effectiveness of the conference. Accomplished teachers understand the importance of quality parent-teacher relationships and can organize conferences that focus the efforts of parents and teachers for the benefit of students.

Teaching Activities

1. Using information that provides a profile of a student (a permanent record folder or a portfolio) with all the names removed for confidentiality purposes, develop an outline of how you would conduct a parent conference. After discussing several of the outlines in class, have several students role-play a parent conference. If necessary, the instructor can sway the conference tone by providing role-playing information to the players. For example, provide one of the players with a note indicating that he or she is to play the role of a skeptic and request more explanation of every point that the teacher makes during the conference.

2. Interview a teacher or another school professional about his or her experiences with parent-teacher conferences. Inquire whether the school or district has a formal handbook for conducting parent-teacher conferences. Ask about the teacher or principal's most memorable conferences and why those conferences were unforgettable. Ask for his or her personal suggestions for organizing effective parent-teacher conferences.

3. Investigate Web sites that might provide you with additional information about parent conferences. Check the National Education Association, the National Parent Teacher Organizations, and the National Association of School Psychologists. Create a grid of common elements that each organization suggests as guidelines for effective parent-teacher conferences. How are they similar? What are the greatest differences in their recommendations for effective parent conferences?

December: Using and Assessing Learning Centers and Project-Based Learning

Goals of the Chapter

1. To recognize the instructional value of learning centers and project-based learning

2. To identify the different purposes of learning centers and project-based learning

3. To identify how project-based learning differs from other instructional designs and make adjustments for effective teaching and assessment

4. To be able to develop effective assessment methods to use with learning centers and student projects

Enhancing Classroom Instruction

Instructional days are at a premium during the month of December. Classrooms are busy with holiday season preparations, and the interruptions that are usually characteristic are more frequent during this time. This is a great time to direct student energy and enthusiasm into tasks that are exploratory and motivational yet fundamentally sound academically. Learning centers or project-based learning tasks present opportunities for teachers to use effective instructional strategies during interrupted schedules. Because learning stations can be used to support and enhance classroom instruction, assessment-literate teachers ought to be able to assess what students learn from them. This chapter discusses the different purposes and the instructional value of learning centers and project-based learning. It also suggests ideas for the assessment of student efforts using both instructional strategies.

Learning Centers

According to Schurr, Lewis, LaMore, and Shewey, (1996), "A learning center is a place in or near the classroom where students can go to participate in activities designed to introduce, reinforce, and/or extend their knowledge or skill base as it relates to a particular topic, concept, or interest." There are some important features of learning centers (LCs) that make them a desirable part of classroom instruction.

LCs offer opportunities for students to learn individually. That is, the classroom teacher can defer the learning experience to the student based on that student's interests, abilities, or needs. For example, if the child regularly completes work ahead of the rest of the students, an LC can be designed to challenge that student in the areas of his or her personal interests. The center, however, might require the interaction of two persons, thereby forcing the children to work cooperatively to reinforce skills or discover new information. If we are truly concerned with developing students' ability to be independent learners, then the LC becomes a means through which teachers can model and instruct children in the development of individual learning skills. Another important aspect of the LC is that we get an opportunity to observe how well a child can work with another student and share responsibility for the development of a product or the acquisition of skills.

LCs provide opportunities for teachers to observe, measure, and comment on students' ability to self-guide, work with others without direct supervision, and learn on their own. These areas are not always easy to assess, but LCs used for instructional purposes can shed light on different aspects of student performance.

Kellough & Roberts (2002) offer the following suggestions for the development of LCs:

1. They should be attractive, purposeful, and uncluttered.
2. They should be used for an educative purpose, never for punishment.
3. They should be self-directing and self-correcting.
4. They should contain multilevel types of activities.
5. They must be safe from any dangerous materials or tools.

If we are serious in our intent to assess the results of the LC, establishing the purpose for the center is unquestionably important. Once we are able to establish our intent, we can effectively determine the direction for the completion of the LC and the appropriate types of activities and assessments. If we fail to identify the purpose of the learning center, the product may end up being overly complex and impossible to assess or so simplistic that it fails to justify the student's or the teacher's time. Although there are many different ways to categorize LCs, we will identify them by their possible purposes. The categories below are certainly not exhaustive, but they help to show how a clear purpose for the LC can assist the teacher with assessment decisions. Let's take each one of these purposes and investigate how it is linked to the assessment instruments that might support its use.

Learning Centers That Reinforce Material or Skills in Different Stages of Mastery

A learning center designed to reinforce a concept or a skill is usually implemented after the teacher's initial instruction. Reinforcement, as designed for use in these types of LCs, might take different forms. For example, an LC designed to reinforce math facts could be used to provide students with more practice. Developing a center based on a game that requires students to respond to math facts in order to advance on a board is typical. This LC's purpose is to provide repetitions that lead to the increased quick recall of math facts. The assessment that would accompany this type of LC should measure the acquisition of the math facts and can be completed in several different ways.

A self-assessment can be completed by the students using the LC. This is usually set up so that the students can self-check their work or a student's partner can do the checking. Issues of fairness and honesty can cause the teacher to exercise caution in the use of the results from these assessments. The initial data can be used by the teacher to gain a sense of the entire class's performance, but it also provides information about the skill level of each student. The results can be used to create flexibly grouped mini-lessons. The information gained from the student self-assessment provides baseline data about student competency in an area.

On the other hand, the teacher might administer a short assessment that is focused on the content or skills that were reinforced at the LC. In the example above we would assess math facts and check whether participation in the LC activity contributed to increased facility with the facts. Linking assessment measures to LC activities also helps students to understand that the LC is not a form of entertainment but is designed to assist them in mastering skills or increasing their speed and accuracy. It is sometimes advisable to use a sign-in sheet in order to know which students have been taking advantage of the center to practice facts. The sign-in sheet will inform you of any students who are not gaining access to the practice with the math facts. The sign-in sheet can also reveal important information about how students spend their free time. There are quite a few computer programs that can be used in a reinforcement center for math and reading skills. These programs are excellent with drill and practice and keep wonderful records of students' participation and success. The assessment purposes not only measure students' content knowledge but also evaluate their use of classroom time and their motivation.

Reflection

LCs that are designed to reinforce or provide practice can be helpful, but they don't always have a high level of interest. Think of ways to "spice up" LCs to encourage interest.

Another LC based on reinforcement can be designed for the purpose of maintaining a skill. For instance, a teacher might choose material that has been covered and previously mastered by the students. In order to maintain the mastery of this skill, the students are required to complete a similar activity every few weeks. This is extremely helpful in an age of high-stakes testing, when teachers are being held accountable for the achievement of students. The maintenance of essential skills greatly improves achievement scores. A specific example is an LC that requires students to read several high-interest selections and identify the literary form used in each one. The literary forms have been mastered earlier in the year, but without an occasional reminder, students might not remember alliteration, hyperbole, personification, and so forth. The assessment for this LC would require that individual student success be documented for the teacher's use. This type of student effort can be kept in a literacy portfolio that demonstrates the student's ability to apply the recognition of literary forms in an authentic context. As an extension of this, students can participate in an ongoing newspaper review that requires them to identify different literary elements.

Learning Centers That Provide Students With an Opportunity to Explore Different Topics

The Internet has made the rate of retrieval of information in American classrooms historically unprecedented. Never have students been able to search, collect, and pool information at the current speed and volume. The Internet increases the opportunity for students to investigate a wider variety of topics of interest. Not only does it provide a breadth of information, it also permits an immediacy in the acquisition of that information. For example, if a student is interested in acquiring knowledge about the Native Americans of the eastern woodlands, there are several sites that can provide such information. Should the student, however, be interested in researching a particular tribe of eastern woodland Native Americans, that information can also be researched with relative ease. A learning center that is designed with an exploratory purpose should have Internet capability if it is going to provide students with the skills of the future. It is certainly possible to create an exploratory LC without a computer, but it severely hampers the research abilities of the students.

Not all exploratory LCs have to be linked to the computer. One might permit students to use manipulatives to find the solution to a problem. In the study of electricity, students can be given a light bulb, a battery, wires, and a switch to use in creating a circuit that will result in the bulb lighting up. In order to light the bulb, students will have to use problem-solving skills and explore with the given materials to complete a circuit. Problem solving through exploration is a skill that students will have to employ in real-life situations.

Assessing exploratory activities is not easily accomplished. A reasonable assessment of how much students gained from this LC could be done by requiring students to complete a drawing of a completed circuit. Another type of assessment might require each student to actually assemble the materials so that the circuit was successfully closed. Judgment about which of these assessments is more reasonable depends on available time and resources.

Assessing student ability to use an exploratory LC requires the teacher to think through the desirable skills that are important to develop in children. In the example of students researching information using the Internet, we would first want the students to be able to access Internet sites that pertain to the topic. This requires the student to form a question, word, or phrase that is searchable. This process might require direct instruction linked to the use of the LC. Another desirable skill to assess is the student's ability to assemble multiple sources of pertinent information about the topic. Finally, we would assess the depth and the credibility or accuracy of the information that the student retrieved.

A beginning rubric for the assessment of this type of exploratory assessment would have at least the following constructs:

Presence of a clear topic or question

Quantity and/or quality of the sources of data retrieved

Presence of depth of information addressing the question or topic

Exploratory learning centers are generally the most difficult to grade. For that reason, teachers often avoid grading them and their use is considered to be more for student enrichment. What factors make exploratory learning centers difficult to grade?

Learning Centers for Diagnostic Purposes

A diagnostic learning center is intended to assess students' knowledge, skills, or dispositions. They are used prior to instruction and are designed to sample a portion of the material in an upcoming unit of study. For example, if you are going to teach a unit on magnets and electricity, you might decide to provide students with magnets and perhaps 15 different types of materials. Students at the LC are required to predict the materials they think will be attracted to magnets, test the materials, and verify their predictions. The students are then asked to explain what materials are attracted to magnets. The value of this is that the teacher has activated the students' interest and assessed some of their knowledge and thinking skills in the area of magnets and electricity.

Another instructional strategy that can be employed in an LC is a K-W-L chart. If you are unfamiliar with K-W-L, you will need to investigate language arts instructional strategies. K stands for what you already *know*, W for what you *want* to know, and L for what you *learn*. This strategy allows you to determine what students already know and what they want to learn about the topic you have chosen. The information you collect can guide your teaching.

Here is another example. Your sixth-grade students learned about fractions in earlier grades, but you want to determine how much they recall. Several types of written activities can be used that will provide information you can use to design instruction. These activities include the following:

- Completing a number line that has fractional values missing
- Matching fractional representations with the appropriate fraction
- Determining whether a fraction is closer to 0 or closer to 1
- Ordering fractions by their values
- Comparing groups of fractions to determine whether their sums are less than 1, equal to 1, or greater than 1

Not all of the fraction activities have to be used at the same time in one LC. Each completed activity, however, provides information about what students understand about an aspect of fractional values.

Knowing what the students already understand about a topic and discovering their areas of interest in it allows you to be more precise in your planning of instructional activities. An additional advantage of assessing students at LCs is conserved instructional time.

Assessing Student Dispositions and Behaviors in Using Learning Centers

The decision to use learning centers impacts the issue of classroom management. The idea of students moving throughout the classroom and participating in several pupil-directed activities in the absence of control can be a frightening thought. If we want to take maximum advantage of LCs, then a plan to assess student behavior and appropriate use of LCs is part of our assessment responsibilities. This can be addressed in our preparation in August (see chapter 8). Your classroom management plan should be linked to the report card that you will be using, and directions and expectations for the use of the LCs should be linked to your management plan. For example, the Union City report card shown in Figure 8-2 could list rules for the use of LCs in its category "learner qualities." These might include the following: takes personal responsibility for behavior, contributes to the classroom community of learners, respects others and environment, follows classroom procedures, and produces quality work. These phrases serve as a reasonable starting point from which to develop scoring instruments to assess students' ability to use LCs and to assist others in their effective use.

Table 12-1 presents a rubric for LC behaviors.

Table 12-1. Rubric for Behaviors at Learning Centers

Self-Directed Learner	Always	Sometimes	Never
Sets goals			
Stays on task			
Is organized			

Problem Solver	Always	Sometimes	Never
Seeks solutions to problems			
Shares ways to solve problem			

Responsible Citizen	Always	Sometimes	Never
Follows classroom rules and procedures			
Respects others			
Respects classroom materials and equipment			

Quality Producer	Always	Sometimes	Never
Completes assignments on time			
Completed work neatly			
Takes pride in work			

Project-Based Learning

"Project-based learning is a systematic teaching method that engages students in learning knowledge and skills through an extended inquiry process structured around complex, authentic questions and carefully designed products and tasks," states the Buck Institute for Education (BIE) on its Web site. Project-based learning has potential benefits to students of all ages but can be especially effective in upper elementary and middle school. According to the

BIE's project-based learning handbook, several of most important benefits to students include the increased opportunity for the following:

1. To practice lifelong learning, civic responsibility, and personal or career success

2. To be assessed on performances using similar criteria to those used in the work world, which encourages accountability, goal setting, and improved performance

3. To create positive communication and collaboration among diverse groups of students

4. To understand the difference between knowing and doing.

As with most teaching activities, a fundamental key to the success of project-based learning experiences is careful and comprehensive planning. This is critically important in all cases but even more so when the results of the students' efforts contribute to a student's final grade and/or a high-stakes decision. Because of increased accountability issues, many schools are requiring students to complete and present a project-based investigation in order to advance to the next grade. This occurs most frequently in the movement of students from elementary to middle schools, but it is also commonly used as a requirement to advance from middle school to high school. Many states now require the completion of a senior project as partial or complete fulfillment of high school graduation requirements. The high-stakes nature of the results demands that teachers take every precaution to ensure that the student passes or fails because of the student's performance and not because of a teacher's actions or omissions. Careful planning of the teaching and assessment activities can help teachers to avoid such situations.

Project-based learning differs from other types of student activity in a number of ways. First, performance projects require an element of time that separates them from the normal on-demand tasks or two-day lessons. Projects-based learning may take students as little as 2 weeks or as long as half a semester to complete. The devotion of substantial instructional time to the completion of these projects indicates their importance as a meaningful learning experience. This also helps to explain why planning is such an important component to project-based learning. For example, if a project requires half a semester, such a massive commitment of instructional time should not be squandered by unclear expectations, unorganized activities, and ambiguous requirements.

Second, project-based learning differs from other forms of instruction in the student requirements for successful participation and completion. Project-based learning typically requires students to employ a variety of skills and higher level thinking. The devotion of a large amount of instructional time to the completion of these projects is justified by the unique opportunity to have students engage in the application of skills and thinking that is otherwise impossible in short segmented lessons or abbreviated learning experiences. Part of the teacher approval process for these projects should be linked to a requirement of higher level thinking. If the students can describe what they intend to complete as their project and it is completely void of any higher level thinking, then the project should be redefined to include a higher level thinking requirement.

For example, suppose that a group of students has an interest in finding out more about Custer's Last Stand. This research does not guarantee the utilization of higher level thinking. However, if students were required to investigate the event, propose ways in which it could have been avoided, *and* discuss the event in light of other interactions that Native Americans experienced with American expansion, then the presence of higher level thinking is more predictable. Lemlech (2006) suggests that problem selection has three elements: (a) the problem should provide content that has depth, requires the use of research skills, and is appropriate for the grade level; (b) the problem should be one in which students have an interest; and (c) the problem should be provocative. Ensuring that the question is provocative is another way of requiring higher level thinking on the part of the students.

Third, project-based learning differs in that it can require students to work in teams. (This is not true, however, with graduation requirements for the satisfactory completion of an individual project.) Being able to work with others is an essential skill that is sometimes difficult to develop because of the competitiveness of school rankings. Aside from accountability issues, completing a scholarly group project is desirable from the aspect of learning to work effectively with others. Despite the growing perception that everyone can now work isolated at his or her own terminal and forgo the social aspects of work, the reality is that positive interdependency is becoming more important as the work world requires increased sophistication and levels of teamwork.

Fourth, project-based learning differs from other teaching and learning experiences in its interdisciplinary approach. Schools often organize courses according to disciplines, such as social studies, math, reading, and science. Although this has been an effective means for the study of a single discipline, unless there is an intentional effort by the teacher to work across the disciplines, most instruction stays within one discipline. That is, math is taught in math class and social studies is taught in social studies class. In project-based learning, however, students typically address problems or investigate themes that cross discipline lines. The larger the problem or project, the more likely it is to go beyond the boundaries of a single discipline. An example of this is environmental education. Suppose that a group of your students wanted to know more about the effects of runoff in a watershed. One's first inclination might be to think that this is a subject that can and should be taught exclusively in science class. Nevertheless, there are clearly other areas of investigation that would inform students of the problems associated with runoff. Children should be guided to consider the political nature of the problem, the mathematics necessary to understand the problem, and the writing and reading skills necessary for effective follow-up. If students choose a real-life problem that affects a large number of people, it will most likely require a solution that is not isolated in a single discipline.

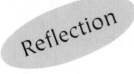

Now that you have read about project-based learning, can you think of a time in your educational experience when you were involved in this type of learning? What were your impressions of its educational value? What types of assessments were used?

Challenges in Assessment of Project-Based Learning

Because project-based learning differs from other types of learning experiences in the four ways described above, their use poses an assessment challenge to teachers who are unfamiliar with employing them in their classrooms.

Extended Instruction Time

Because project-based learning requires extended periods of instruction time, teachers must carefully plan the timing of the project. Report cards, a mainstay of reporting student achievement and progress, are generally issued at 9-week intervals, and teachers usually want to base their grades on a collection of work samples that provide a valid profile of student performance. If a single summative measure is used to assess the project, the time requirement of the project might prevent the generation of an adequate number of grades.

Project-based learning requires that teachers be prepared to assess students at various stages of completion or to accept important parts of the project as evidence of progress. For example, suppose you decide to assign a project to students that requires approximately 6 weeks of collecting data about the growing rates of several types of edible plants. If you decide to postpone any grading decisions until the project is completed, you'll find yourself extremely close to the end of the grading period with a single grade representing the student's effort, achievement, and progress. It would be more prudent to provide students with a schedule of completed parts of the project and grade those individually. Scoring component parts provides ongoing assessment of the project, generates more than a single grade, and avoids having students suffer from the "gotcha" treatment. The "gotcha" treatment can be defined as waiting until the project is completed to tell students that they have an error in the process or in a major component of the project. If we believe that formative feedback is important to learning, why would we withhold important information about the work until its completion? Issues of grading and reporting student progress belong in the initial planning stage of project-based learning projects. Providing feedback to students during the project does not exclude the opportunity to assess the project upon completion. Planning and sharing a clearly defined schedule of periodic assessments is an important key to using project-based learning tasks.

Measurement of Student Thinking

Assessing project-based learning also requires that teachers be prepared to measure the application of student processing skills and/or thinking skills. Providing for the design of this type of assessment begins with students and teachers working closely to identify the project's main focus or the problem to be solved. Otherwise it will be difficult to agree on the types of skills or thinking processes that should be applied to the completion of the project. The skill levels that are required of the students should be sensitive to grade level, the student's opportunity to learn, and the prior experiences of the students. Skills that are required of students engaged in project-based learning include hypothesizing, inferring, calculating, measuring, researching, writing, and presenting. Bloom's taxonomy of the cognitive domain (see Appendix B) can be a resource for identifying thinking skills that students should employ in the completion of the project. The types of instruments that best assist the assessment of projects are associated with performance assessments. Rubrics, checklists, and anecdotal records are appropriate measurement tools for the assessment of skills (see chapter 4).

Cooperative Grouping

Project-based learning can be assigned to students individually or in a group configuration, but using it in collaboration with cooperative learning can increase the value of the experience for children. Cooperative learning is different from simply grouping students. First, it should be designed to promote positive interdependency, the quality of people working together to complete a goal or project. It involves contributing to the group, affirming the contributions of others, and sharing appropriately. Second, students should be assessed by the quality of their contribution to the project. Assessing students in a cooperative learning environment is tricky but not impossible. For a project that is designed with a variety of roles, the roles can be assigned to individual students who are then assessed based on the quality of their completion of the role.

For example, suppose that a project requires four roles: investigator, leader, resource person, and presenter. Each person should be assigned to complete a list of specific tasks. Care should be given to balance the workloads of the participants. After the students have been engaged in working on the project, sit with each group and have each member indicate his or her progress to you and the rest of the group. These progress report meetings help to keep the group focused, and they eliminate situations in which one person completes the work of several members of the group. The teacher can also reinforce prosocial behaviors by recognizing and reinforcing participant behavior in areas such as contributing ideas, participating in the role, and assisting others in the completion of their roles. The power of teacher modeling of cooperative social behavior should not be underestimated.

In preparation for the group meeting, each student should complete an individual assessment form evaluating his or her contribution, the obstacles to completing the assignment, and the quality of the product that has been generated to date (Table 12-2).

Table 12-2. Formative Reflection Assessment for Project-Based Learning

Contributions

I have accepted my role in completing this project and I have begun to work on it. Yes Partially No	Areas I need to address and complete:	Remarks (can be completed by teacher or student):

Obstacles

I am experiencing problems in the following areas that might keep me from completing a quality project:	I can solve this on my own by: I need to work this out with group members or the teacher by:	Remarks (must be completed by teacher and student):

Quality

Currently, the progress of the product is: Qualitative Quantitative	What we need to do to improve the quality of the project:	Remarks (must be completed by teacher and student):

This reflective activity is helpful in three ways. First, it forces students to reflect on their work and, in a small way, turns over judgment to them. Students often see the teacher as the "keeper of the quality" in whom all judgments rest. After years of teachers passing judgment on such work, this deference on the part of students should not be a surprise. Part of the purpose of this reflective activity is to have students put themselves in the role of stepping back from their work and judging it based on their own internal measure of quality. The desired outcome is for students to be able to judge the quality of their own work. Then the teacher's judgment is simply a reaffirmation.

Peer evaluation can also be used to assess cooperative learning. Students tend to put forth more effort when their peers give input for the scoring of the project. Students might rate their peers in level of preparedness, cooperation, ability to assume the designated role, and assistance in the achievement of group goals. Practices that accompany peer assessment in cooperative learning usually involve collecting all rater forms, examining them for reliability, and omitting a disparate rating. If a student is rated higher or lower by all of his peers in relation to his own ranking, conferencing with the teacher is necessary. Completing a self-assessment about cooperative learning should not be a one-time event. Peer assessment and self-assessment require consistent use throughout the school year to be effectively developed.

The second benefit of students completing a formative reflection is that it establishes written evidence of what the student views as progress toward achieving the goal, of the obstacles that threaten the completion of the project, and of the student's perceived quality of the product. This information can be used in conjunction with portfolios to showcase the work of the students completing a process-oriented assignment. When students encounter difficulties, this information provides a way to open up a conversation among the student, the group members, and the teacher for the purpose of problem solving. Teachers can take a direct role in solving the problem for students or can facilitate students' solving the problem on their own. The role chosen by the teacher has much to do with his or her teaching style.

Third, the information serves as a reference for justifying the summative success of the project. Because much of the grading of this project is based on the subjective decision making of the teacher, it is important to have written student perceptions and documented monitoring of the project. Thus, the first two benefits support instruction, and the third one applies mostly to the areas of evaluation, grading, and accountability.

Interdisciplinary Projects

One of the basic problems that confronts teachers who intend to use project-based learning is not how to assess the student's work but rather how to represent the assessment with a grade on a report card. This is especially true for upper elementary and middle school teachers, who must use report cards that are organized by discipline areas. Projects that require a high level of interdisciplinary coordination might be difficult to sort out according to weight by specific subject area. There are at least two options available to teachers who face this dilemma.

First, try to think through how much each subject area contributes to the completion of the overall project. For example, suppose you require a written summary of the project the students chose to investigate. Calculate the effort and time expended by the students in relationship to the completion of all their other activities. If you believe that the written summary accounted for about 25% of the entire project, then score that individually and use it to account for one-fourth of the total project score. You can also directly assign this score to the writing portion of the report card.

A second, more time-consuming, method would be to conference with each student or student group and decide how the project should be scored and to which area of the report card each part should be assigned. There are clear benefits to this strategy. The students and you have the freedom to customize the project components to the report card. The students gain an enhanced sense of ownership because not only do they get to choose the topic, they also get to have input about which areas of the report card will be used in this assignment. This method creates a more instructionally sensitive reporting scheme, but it has a downside. Because you have decided to customize the project to the report card, many students will have to be graded with different numbers of points in each subject area for the grading period. If planned for, this can be achieved without undo stress on your part.

In middle school, the subject areas are often isolated but the teachers are organized in teams. Team teaching can facilitate project-based learning if there is frequent communication among the members of the team. Team members can decide what portion of the project they want to take responsibility for and then include the students' work into the overall grade for the marking period. Team planning for project-based learning is critical to its use in middle school classrooms. Bringing together the creativity and ideas of three or four teachers in the development of a meaningful instructional event can be a powerful way to teach children. The advantage is that middle school students are developmentally ready to accept new challenges, and they appreciate the opportunity to exercise choice and explore new and interesting material.

Summary

In order for teachers to be able to meet the individual needs of all children, they must create situations and opportunities to work with small, flexibly created groups. This means that some groups of students must be able to work independently at instructionally sound learning activities. Two of the most common activities that require individual independent effort are learning centers and project-based learning. Because instructional time is of critical importance to teachers, it is necessary to develop sound assessment strategies, not only to assess the success of the students but also to evaluate the worth of the learning center or the project. Focusing on the purpose of the learning center provides important grounding for making decisions about the value of a student's participation. A variety of assessments can be used with learning centers to assess students' knowledge, skills, and dispositions.

Project-based learning requires intensive planning for successful use in classrooms. This instructional method differs from other teaching activities because it requires more time, a commitment to higher level thinking, increased levels of cooperation, and an interdisciplinary approach to completing the project. These differences all impact the nature of assessment in project-based learning. First, teachers must be sensitive to how the increased time requirements affect assessment processes and the organization of the district reporting system. Second, teachers must focus on assessing the degree to which students successfully applied higher order thinking skills to the project's completion. Third, teachers must learn to assess students in a cooperative setting. Finally, teachers must be willing to adapt the assessment to address the interdisciplinary nature of project-based learning.

Teaching Activity

Locate a database of information that has some appeal to students (and perhaps one in which you are interested). Prepare the data in such a way that you can easily share it with your students. For example, earthquakes seem to be interesting to most people. Find a Web site from which you can draw data and provide access for your students. Create a project that involves the students in the use of the data and requires more than two different subject areas. The options include allowing the students to discover a Web site that they like and that generates data, or allowing the students to choose two discipline areas but requiring all students to generate a written product as a summative assessment.

January: Using Assessment Information to Identify Retention Candidates and Design Effective Interventions

Goals of the Chapter

1. To understand the tensions inherent in the retention of elementary-age studentss

2. To understand the importance of systematic intervention as an alternative to retention

3. To recognize the need to approach retention decisions with caution and thoughtfulness

4. To recognize the importance of a pupil personnel team and its role in the development of a retention and intervention plan

A Fresh Start

January is an exciting time for students and teachers. It is usually free from interruption, and its 20 instructional days make it a very productive month. Children are excited and generally ready for a new start. They want to tell you all about their holiday experiences, what they did over the break, and where they traveled. Use this enthusiasm for the new calendar year as an opportunity to begin anew in your classroom. If a procedure or a strategy has not worked well, perhaps you will want to introduce your students to a change that is part of the classroom's set of resolutions.

This month is also important because most schools are approaching the midpoint of the school year. By now you have a sense of the learning rates and academic progress of the students in your classroom, and you can name the students who might be academically at risk. If you are an elementary school teacher, you might be wrestling with the notion of whether a student has made sufficient progress to advance to the next grade. Whether you ultimately decide to retain a student, this is the month in which you must at least identify those students you believe to be retention candidates and set in motion procedures associated with this action. This chapter will help you to identify children who are at risk of grade retention and develop an effective intervention plan.

The Retention of Elementary School Children

After working with teacher candidates for more than a decade, I have concluded that most textbooks designed for the development of assessment literacy fail to adequately address several of the most important day-to-day issues that confront contemporary teachers. One of the most overlooked issues is the retention of elementary school children. Wells and Miller (1993) surveyed 162 American Association of Colleges for Teacher Education (AACTE) member institutions and found that teacher preparation programs typically do not address retention, and when they do, they address it in a cursory fashion. There are few decisions for elementary school teachers that are more taxing and emotionally difficult than deciding to recommend retention for a student. In order for teachers to be able to make clear decisions about children who are at risk of grade retention, they should understand what the literature has to say about the effects of retention.

Retention and Its Place in American Schools

According to Jimerson (2001), grade retention is defined as "the practice of requiring a student who has been in a given grade level for a full year to remain at that level for a subsequent school year" (p. 420). According to the National Association of School Psychologists (Raforth, 2002), an estimated 15% of American students are held back each year. Two-thirds of these retained students are held back between kindergarten and third grade (Owings & Magliaro, 1998). The increased emphasis on standards and professional accountability that is so much a part of contemporary schooling has resulted in a greater perception of retention as a remedy to academic difficulties. In 2003, for example, 27,000 third graders were held back based on the results of the Florida Comprehensive Assessment Test (Sager, 2005). More important, the ambitious learning rates set by the future adequate yearly progress goals of the No Child Left Behind Act ensure that school professionals will be faced with a large number of students who fail to meet the standards. This text will attempt to offer general suggestions and guidelines; these should be taken as such and not viewed as applicable to all children.

There is substantial and persistent research indicating that retention does not result in student academic improvement. Instead it is strongly correlated to a high student dropout rate and has negative effects on achievement and self-image. Raforth (2002) suggests that the most consistent finding from decades of retention research is the high correlation between retention and students dropping out of school. The same source also reports that retention is associated with significant increases in behavior problems, especially as children approach adolescence.

I do not intend, in this chapter, to endorse or advocate the retention of elementary-age children. This chapter is included because the issue of retention for elementary teachers is a reality, not a theoretical argument. Regardless of whether a teacher believes that retention is harmful to students, the district in which he or she works will likely have a policy that definitively shapes his or her actions. Though undeniably important to the ethics of the profession, the value and impact of retention in the lives of students is a separate discussion best left for another textbook. In summary, I believe that current national and state accountability policies combined with the present level of acceptance ensures that retention will remain a recognizable fixture in American schools. In fact, its use will most likely increase, and thus its position will be secured as one of the most controversial consequences of No Child Left Behind. If so, it follows that teachers and other school professionals ought to make every effort to see that any retention action is a last resort. This book takes the position that identifying students who are not making sufficient progress and developing effective interventions for them is the most professional and thoughtful approach to assisting students who are struggling to learn. Teachers might not have the option of retaining an elementary student, but there is always an opportunity to develop an intervention plan.

Do you have a personal philosophy about the retention of children in elementary grades? Does your stance differ for middle school students?

Critical to thoughtful decision making is the belief that all judgments concerning the promotion of children to the next grade should be made using multiple sources of data. If we recall from Part I, the first principle of sound assessment is that inferences should be based on the use of multiple measures. Although decision-making models advocating the consideration of multiple factors in retention decisions have been in place for decades, placement decisions have too often been exclusively based on or disproportionately swayed by single test scores. Raforth (2002) indicates that the failure to master skills (especially in reading), coupled with low achievement test scores, is often enough to identify a child as a retention candidate after kindergarten or first grade. Expanding assessment data to include other sources helps to broaden the scope of what might be an effective intervention strategy.

Factors that can be reviewed in the decision-making process range from those that describe the abilities and behaviors of the child to those that assess the capacity of the school and the support of the child's family. Retention decision-making models can include such information as the physical size of the child, academic potential, the child's self-concept, parental support, chronological age, and administrative disposition toward retention, along with a host of other factors. All of these factors could play a part in the success or failure of a student. The intent of this text is to focus on those factors that are most closely related to classroom activities. As teachers become more knowledgeable about issues of assessment, rejecting single-score decisions should be the basis of their stance on retention. Accepting multiple sources of data demonstrates a recognition of the value of broader definitions of student success and helps to make invention plans more comprehensive.

As noted earlier, the use of multiple measures in the retention process has been advocated for years; however, teachers and other school professionals have failed to effectively use information to develop intervention plans for retention candidates. If students can be identified as retention candidates using multiple indicators, then the same indicators ought to frame any effective instructional intervention plan. Equally important to classroom teachers is to develop a means to systematically work with critical retention factors in order to coordinate and structure preretention decisions. The intent is to identify, along with members of a pupil personnel team, important retention indicators and to intervene to address those areas with children who are academically at risk. Retention is an action that school professionals should try to avoid. The coordination of a retention and intervention plan requires the selection of important personnel, the effective use of critical assessment data, and the development of a timetable for actions that are thoughtful and student centered.

Key Personnel in the Retention Decision-Making Process

First, let's discuss who should be involved in the retention decision-making process. Many school districts use an identified group (an instructional support team or a pupil personnel team) to discuss data, develop a plan, and ultimately render a final decision about the student's grade placement. The makeup of this group varies, but it may be composed of any combination of classroom teachers, parents or guardians, the principal, a school psychologist, an instructional support teacher, a reading specialist, itinerant teachers, and other resource personnel. It is critical to make the final decision using multiple perspectives, but initially it is more important for this group to act in a supportive way to focus efforts on assisting the child. In essence, much of the pupil personnel team's first actions can be viewed as preventive—that is, putting into effect intervention methods and measures that help the child to make sufficient progress toward the next grade. The most thoughtful initial approach to retention is a stance that the pupil personnel team will exhaust every effort to enable the child to continue to the next grade and that retention is exercised as a last resort.

Your role as a member of the pupil personnel team is important, because you are perhaps the only person able to provide evidence of the student's progress in daily classroom activities. Membership is an accepted responsibility of all classroom teachers because they are (a) closer to the teaching and learning environment than any other member of the pupil personnel team, (b) professionally trained to make accurate observations and sound assessments, and (c) knowledgeable about the students in their classrooms. Boyd-Batstone (2004) suggests that the person closest to the classroom experience is in a unique position to see and communicate a reliable and valid instructional perspective of the child. The next step in the development of an effective plan is to identify, collect, and evaluate existing and/or newly generated data to inform the retention and intervention decision.

Why should several people be consulted in the decision making for a retention and intervention candidate?

Student Histories of Achievement and Other Sources of Important Data

Most school districts maintain permanent record folders for students that contain a history of academic achievement as well as written documentation of efforts to gain placements or services for children. These records are important data sources for teachers who must make decisions about the functioning of students in their classrooms. Permanent records provide a window through which to view the performance of a single student in a progression of classrooms. Unfortunately, some teachers (or other school personnel) resist reviewing permanent records prior to meeting any of their students. Their justification is that the permanent-record information may cause them to prejudge the student and therefore bias their actions toward the student. They contend that they can be much more objective in their judgments by allowing the student to be part of their classroom and reacting to the student's performance.

This could be a reasonable position to take at the beginning of the school year, especially in the case of a teaching assignment that requires the teacher to meet several different classes of children each day. However, I am not in agreement with this stance for teachers who are experiencing immediate or severe academic difficulties during the year. Maintaining a degree of objectivity should not be more important than reviewing a child's prior performances and gaining an understanding of his or her academic needs. There is value in reviewing previous student work and learning as much as possible about the students who are struggling with assignments or who are generally unsuccessful in critical academic areas. Maintaining objectivity should be a professional disposition of teachers and school professionals throughout the year; it is no more important to making sound judgment at the beginning of the year than in the middle or at the end of the year. There is much to be learned from permanent records that can assist in developing a plan for a student who is experiencing academic difficulties. Knowing what information to look for and how to interpret it is an important assessment skill for teachers.

Following are six categories of information that can be found in a student's permanent record folder. The discussion of each category includes its importance and some suggestions about its utility and interpretation.

An Individualized Educational Plan (IEP)

A student who transfers into your school district might have an IEP in his or her permanent record that occasionally goes unnoticed by school personnel and unmentioned by parents. This occurs more often when the permanent record arrives at the receiving school months later than the student. If there is an IEP, indicating that the student has been identified as a student with special needs, the pupil personnel team might decide to progress no further with any retention and intervention decision. The modification and accommodation of instructional and assessment practices is required by law. There are few justifiable reasons to identify this student as a retention candidate. A careful review of a well-written IEP should indicate what the child ought to be experiencing in the classroom. If the instructional and social goals for the student are clearly stated in the IEP, the pupil personnel team should meet to coordinate efforts to ensure that the student's IEP is being met. Students who are supposed to receive special services have often been retained earlier in their schooling, and further retention simply increases the likelihood of social behavioral problems and dropping out of school.

A Previously Developed Intervention Plan

Retention candidates who are not retained in one school year might be considered for it again the following year. The primary justification for retention is low achievement, especially in reading. Students who struggle to learn in one grade seldom find it easy to learn in the next grade, especially without special services or appropriate interventions. Since most schools are organized similarly from one grade to the next, it is not difficult to predict that a student will be identified as a retention candidate in more than one year. It is important to analyze the nature of the suggestions from the last instructional or intervention plan and discuss its success with other members of last year's pupil personnel team. Determine, from the analysis and discussions, the success of the designed intervention practices, and reevaluate the actions that appeared to be ineffective. Similarly, intervention strategies that were successful or effective should be resumed and even expanded to other areas. The repetition of failed practices is not a thoughtful approach to providing for the needs of a struggling student.

The Grades of the Student in Previous Academic Years

The examination and interpretation of grades earned by a student in previous grades should always be completed with caution. The younger the child and the fewer the number of grade levels to be examined, the more caution that should be exercised. A student who is considered at risk in second grade has only two years (K and 1) of grades to examine. Chapter 6 described the subjectivity that can be associated with developing letter grades and completing report cards. For upper-grade retention decisions, there is more material to review and more people who have completed an evaluation of the student's achievement, effort, and progress. The increased number of grades offers a bit more validity to the decision making. Letter grades and summative report card information is consistently available in permanent record folders, but inferences should be cautiously drawn for them. As report card design shifts from letter grades to indicators of success in meeting state standards, interpretations from one state to the next will become increasingly difficult.

Student School Attendance Information

Attendance in school is a major consideration for the pupil personnel team in making a retention and intervention decision. There are myriad reasons for students to be justifiably absent from class, but a high absentee rate is universally problematic to student achievement. Absenteeism can appear in patterns or be relatively unpredictable. The following examples point out how different each case of absenteeism may be. On the one hand, a student might be experiencing an initial exposure to a communicable illness and, as a result, have a vulnerability to the illness that affects his or her ability to come to school. On the other hand, a child might be entirely responsible for getting himself or herself off to school and, consequently, make his or her own decision about coming to school. Although there are legal boundaries and parental responsibilities to deal with the latter, in each case the student will face the challenging dilemma of missed instruction. Despite intense efforts at home and school to keep the student at a level with his or her peers, missed participation in daily instructional activities usually results in the chronically absent student being at great risk of academic difficulty. In the event of little to no support at home, a high rate of absenteeism is highly predictable of student difficulty.

The importance of attendance is magnified in the early years because of the need to develop fundamental reading and math skills. In the upper grades, a pattern of absenteeism can be noted from the permanent record folder. For teachers who are new at gauging how much absenteeism is problematic, consider the amount of absenteeism in the framework of a typical instructional unit. In most states there are approximately 180 instructional days. If a student is absent 20 days during the school year, then he or she has missed instruction on the average of 1 day every 2 weeks. If the student has accumulated 40 absences, then he or she has averaged more than 1 day of absence per each week of school.

This breakdown makes it easy to see how students who are frequently absent from school would have difficulty maintaining continuity with material and would consistently have to work hard to catch up with their peers. Catching up can be a nearly impossible burden for a student who struggles to learn and/or lacks a caring support structure at home. Sandoval and Hughes (1981) found that the children who made academic and social gains after repeating first grade had shown signs of academic difficulty in school because of a lack of exposure to academic material. This lack of exposure was defined as high absenteeism, illness, or frequent family moves. This is not mentioned as a justification for retention but to show the importance of attendance as a factor in determining student success. Teachers should rely on members of the pupil personnel team to assist with efforts to get children to school.

Medical Information

Medical records may be included in the permanent record folder; however, school districts may keep them separate. Information contained in those records can be helpful in making decisions about students. Part of coming to school ready to learn hinges on the student being able to make complete use of his or her senses. If a teacher intentionally plans lessons designed to appeal to multiple modalities, children who have one or more unrecognized sensory disabilities will not experience the benefit of the teacher's efforts. This is especially true in the lower grades, when students are beginning to develop phonemic awareness and the alphabetic principle. The development of those skills are in part linked to the student's ability to imitate the sound the teacher is making during instruction. If the student is unable to clearly hear the sound, the likelihood of him or her making the correct sound or symbol connection is low. A hearing disability of any sort makes the challenge of unlocking sound and symbol relationships more difficult for beginning readers. Earlier in this chapter we discussed how the ability to read is a key variable in the success of students in elementary school. Hearing difficulties can place an otherwise very capable student at risk academically.

Following is an actual experience that took place while I was teaching fifth grade. A mother came to me during parent visitation night and thanked me for seating her son near my desk. She indicated that I was the first teacher to place him so that his "good" ear was facing the teacher. The child was, in fact, deaf in one ear, and the mother had had that information placed in the child's medical record in first grade. In the course of several family moves to different states, the mother had neglected to make sure that each new classroom teacher knew this information. When I later checked this fifth grader's medical record, there was a single entry from first grade recording a hearing problem. The frequent movements of the family had allowed this student to "fall through the cracks" of regular hearing tests, so I made sure that the medical record was changed to indicate that the child was deaf in his right ear, and I discussed with the parents the importance of each teacher knowing that information. How had I known that the student was deaf in one ear? The answer is that I didn't; I had placed him close to my desk simply because he talked incessantly when seated anywhere else in the classroom. I did not share this information with the parents.

Knowing information about a student's medical condition is important for the development of effective instructional practices throughout the school year. In the above case, developing an instructional plan to accommodate the student's hearing difficulties is fundamental. Each person on the pupil personnel team should be informed, and the persons who interact with the child instructionally need to make appropriate accommodations.

Standardized Test Information

Students in American schools are the most tested students in the world. The current emphasis on external testing measures ensures that permanent record folders are likely to contain standardized test scores of one type or another. Externally generated scores provide a way to view how the student compares with other students nationally and, in the case of local norms, other students in the school district. To make sure that you understand and are able to interpret the derived scores associated with standardized testing, see chapter 7. The information presented there provides a means for interpreting scores that have been generated for a single year. Remember the following about interpreting standardized test information from multiple years:

1. Try not to overinterpret grade equivalent scores. Score units are not the same at different grade levels. For example, a score in reading of 1.5 to 2.0 is much greater than the gain from 6.0 to 6.5 for a primary grade student.

2. Gaining a full year in grade equivalency (e.g., 4.5–5.5) is not the same in all tests and should not be an expectation for students. Besides the test differences, students with limitations in reading are unlikely to be able to achieve a full year of growth across the test battery.

3. The average range of student performance as reported using percentile ranks is from the 25th percentile rank to the 75th percentile rank. Should a student score at the 30th percentile rank on any subtest, he or she is actually scoring in the low average range. The score is not a great score, but some teachers and most parents unfortunately view the score as they would a 30% score, which is hardly "average" on a classroom test. A misinterpretation of this information can easily result in poor decision making about the student's instructional plan.

Another important aspect of interpreting standardized test results is not to detach the test results from what you have seen in the pupil's performance and behavior all year long. There is a tendency among school professionals to isolate the test results and interpret the national percentile ranks and stanine scores as though they were the scores of a child the teacher did not know. For example, if a fifth-grade student receives a score of 59 as a national percentile rank and scores in the fifth stanine, we can expect this student to have performed at an average ability during the school year in mathematics. Interpreting anything beyond that requires more information. Try to link that score to what you have observed. Has the student been more capable than average about certain concepts? Are there areas of the math curriculum that were challenging for the student? In other words, the student might excel in the area of decimal fractions but experience difficulty with problem solving. The breakdown of a student's correct and incorrect responses according to subskill areas of the test can be provided to the classroom teacher. This makes linking the test performance to what you have observed in the classroom a bit easier.

Around the country, value-added assessment is being used to assist principals and teachers in making decisions about students' placement and instruction needs (Sanders & Horn, 1994). Value-added assessment is a statistical analysis of achievement data that reveals academic growth over time for students and groups of students (such as grade levels) in a school. An additional benefit of this data is to provide educators with a probability score that predicts the student's degree of success in the next grade. By using this data, school personnel can recommend and employ more precise intervention plans for students. The use of this type of data is more likely to become more widespread in the future.

What about cases in which the test scores deviate greatly from what we expected from the student? There are several explanations of what might have occurred to result in this. The first is student effort. In the upper elementary grades, a student might believe that standardized tests are not important and decide to create a pattern in the bubbles on the answer sheet. This student clearly does not understand the ramifications of such a decision in these days of increased accountability. As standardized testing takes on increased importance within school districts, students should be strongly dissuaded from engaging in such harmful practices. However, it might be a possible explanation for a variant score.

Second, it is possible that your instructional practices failed to adequately review the knowledge and skills necessary for this child to achieve. One element to keep in mind is maintenance. There are times when a student learns material, then quickly forgets it because he or she has not used it enough to recall it at a later date. If you want students to remember critical information or specific skills, then you must work with them at different intervals to maintain the newly learned knowledge or skills. Perhaps the students mastered the skills in the short-term interval but could not recall the information at a later date for the test. If the skill is essential, repeat it in 1 week, recall it in 4 weeks, and practice it every month. The students will then be more likely to recall the skill when necessary.

Third, it's possible that the curriculum you are teaching is mismatched with the test. For example, if the standardized test in your district assesses several skills that your curriculum fails to include, those become items in which student success is determined by something other than your teaching. Some students will have an advantage because of the resources and opportunities available to them in their environment; others might be penalized by what they have not experienced outside the classroom. In this case the students have not failed; the school district has actually created a situation that has set up students for the increased likelihood of failure. In an age of increased reliance on test scores as a determinant of quality, it is important for districts to align their curricula with the material that is being tested on standardized measures of choice.

Making decisions about the identification of students at risk involves the review of existing materials that can be found in permanent record folders. Care should be given to use that information in meaningful ways to guide instructional practices and to inform future decisions that deal with placement, intervention, and services.

Reflection

You just read about six categories of data that should be considered in retention and intervention decisions. How would you order them from most important to least important in the decision-making process?

Developing a Timetable for the Effective Review of Information

Although it is important for the pupil personnel team to use multiple data sources, the reality is that all are not equally important or available at the same time. Therefore, identifying the important data and setting up a plan to review it is extremely important for sound decision making. The following plan is offered not as a "how to" manual but rather as a rough blueprint for teachers and other school professionals to adapt to their specific children and district policies. This blueprint operates with two main ideas. First, it is crucial to identify the most critical data in the retention decision-making process. Second, it is important to gather as much pertinent information as possible. This means that teachers need to be aware of data from previous years and the current year, and even anticipate when new data will become available. The following data should be considered in the intervention and retention process:

- Curriculum-based classroom assessments
- Attendance

- Social interactions and behaviors
- Standardized testing information

After determining the specific data to consider, you should also accumulate any historical data that is available so that a profile of the student can emerge. Patterns can be noted, and the decision making of the team will not be restricted to using only current data. If a pupil personnel meeting is convened in January, it is important to collect data about the aforementioned categories from previous years as well as from this year. The discussion below provides examples of each type of data required in considering retention and developing an intervention plan.

Curriculum-based assessment data includes summarized data as well as student samples of classroom performances in reading, math, and writing (including intervention strategies) completed from September to January. These include running records, miscue analyses, and tests. Student samples that provide insight into specific problem areas are important. A wide range of student samples is always helpful. For example, student-generated products could include those that were completed independently, those that were completed with minimal student or teacher assistance, those completed with intense teacher support, and homework samples. These provide information about the ability of the student to work and succeed independently. Other data could include teacher comments, grades, and reports from the last 2 academic years.

Attendance data includes the number of student absences in past years as well as up to the date of the conference. Any pattern of absence in the current school year is worth noting.

Social interaction and behavior data includes summaries of student behavior from previous years. This can be important information, but some states do not permit disciplinary data to be accumulated and applied to subsequent years. Data from classroom participation to date can take the form of anecdotal records that include student behaviors and their frequencies. Itinerant teachers can usually contribute valuable insights in this area.

Standardized testing data includes percentile ranks and stanine scores from major discipline areas for the last several years. Scaled scores from state tests administered in the last 2 years can provide additional information. Scores from intelligence or aptitude tests are important as well. It is essential to note whether the tests were group or individually administered. Any single-subject tests (e.g., Key Math, Gates-MacGinitie) that were administered during the student's academic history are helpful.

Table 13-1 shows a retention and invention data collection instrument.

The retention and intervention data collection instrument assists efforts to include key retention information and a data collection range. It also helps to construct a timetable for interventions that can assist the retention candidate. It is possible to emphasize different areas and develop alternative strategies for each student, but the major goal is to coordinate the efforts of the pupil personnel team with the best

Table 13-1.   Retention and Intervention Data Collection Instrument

	Previous Years and Beginning of This Year	January	Intervention
Data Sources			
Curriculum-Based Success			
a. Reading and Language Arts			
b. Math			
c. Other Subject Areas			
Attendance			
History of Testing			
Social Behaviors			
Support: Home and School			

interests of the student's achievement. The key idea here is "If we intend to retain a student based on a set of factors, how can we best assist the student in meeting those factors?" The next section gives several examples of curriculum-based data, indicating the types of interventions and the importance of their documentation for the team.

Examples of Curriculum-Based Interventions to Share at a Pupil Personnel Meeting

Students identified for retention consideration usually begin experiencing academic difficulties early in the school year. Difficulty in reading, especially in the lower grades, generally triggers a concern for retention. According to Christie (2005), Iowa schools are required to inform parents at least twice a year of their child's reading level in K–3 and inform them of any interventions deemed necessary. Schools must provide parents with strategies to enable them to improve their children's skills and must suggest district resources that parents can use to reinforce classroom reading instruction. Oklahoma and Utah have similar policies.

The data stream for this begins with the first days the student is in your classroom. It would be prudent to begin keeping samples of student work along with intervention and modification strategies used with the student. If you are finding that a third grader is having difficulty with text comprehension, you should list the success rates of the interventions, such as directed reading or thinking activities, modification of the reading level of material, or color coding of important text material. Your primary intention is to assist the student's comprehension of the text, but you also want to determine which strategies are most successful and which ones are ineffective. This information helps to build a more solidly based intervention strategy for the pupil personnel team.

Suppose you discovered that a second grader had difficulty completing addition problems. Modifying the instruction for that student might mean providing the student with concrete experiences, assigning shorter math tasks but more frequently throughout the day, or providing extended time to complete the assignments. Many intervention strategies can be used, but it is critical to document your adaptations and to take note of the student's success based on that change. Organization and good record keeping is essential to providing this information to the pupil personnel team.

Monitoring Student Progress From January to May

In this text, January was chosen as the month in which to initiate a retention and intervention process. School districts may move that forward and decide to identify candidates earlier in the school year in order to provide a longer intervention period. Regardless of what month is chosen to initially identify the retention candidate, monitoring his or her progress should be completed regularly and involve parents and teachers continually. The schedule that follows indicates the frequency of teacher-parent communication and pupil personnel team (PPT) meetings.

Initial retention and invention meeting (PPT)	January
Informal communication between teacher and parent	As necessary
Midpoint of third grading period	February
Informal communication between teacher and parent	As necessary
Completion of third grading period (PPT)	March
Informal communication between teacher and parent	As necessary
Final meeting of PPT to evaluate intervention	April
Final promotion and retention decision (PPT)	May

Summer Activities as an Intervention

The final decision to retain a student might be made during the last days of the school year or, in exceptional cases, later in the summer. The latter time is usually based on a school district's decision to have the retention candidates attend summer school as part of a continuing intervention. There is good reason to have students who are struggling enroll in a well-structured summer school program. Borman (2003) suggests that students lose more than a month's worth of skill in math and reading between June and September. Providing summer school programs is especially important in areas where low-income families cannot afford summer tutoring for children.

Guidelines for the expenditure of federal funds under No Child Left Behind have facilitated shifting allocations toward the development of summer remedial programs. In some school districts this has resulted in summer school becoming mandatory for students with identified weaknesses in math and reading. The expectations for student achievement under No Child Left Behind are constructed on an ambitious ascending scale that borders on the impossible. It has long been accepted that students learn at different rates and that they all possess different capacities for learning. This inherent characteristic of children will not change because of federal legislation. If the learning rates of children remain uneven, it is extremely important for school professionals to increase the opportunities for children to learn. Summer programs are a means by which to provide students with increased instructional activities and a longer school year. The key to the success of such programs is that they support, reinforce, and develop the critical skills that students will need to be successful in school and everyday life.

Summary

Retaining children in a grade is a controversial issue. Decades of research clearly indicate that it is unsuccessful in developing academic and social skills. Despite these findings, parents and school personnel continue to believe that retention is a reasonable option for students who fail to meet established standards. It is extremely unlikely that retention will disappear from American schools; therefore it is important that school systems use the key retention factors to develop thoughtful intervention plans.

January is when schools and districts typically begin to identify students who are not making sufficient academic progress. Effective intervention planning includes the formation of a pupil personnel team, examination of past and current data, and a timetable for the effective implementation of the plan. Teachers are key players in the retention process because they can collect important information, employ and record different instructional strategies, communicate to colleagues and parents, and provide ongoing encouragement to the student. The most effective retention plans are ones in which the pupil personnel team designs and executes interventions that are successful enough to avoid retaining students.

Teaching Activities

1. Interview an elementary school principal and inquire about the retention policy of the school or school district. If there are written guidelines, ask where you might obtain them. Ask what types of interventions are in place in the school for students who are experiencing difficulties.

2. If you are not teaching, volunteer to assist those who are teaching summer school. Ask to work with one student who is experiencing difficulty in math or reading. Work closely with the diagnosed needs of the student and develop several instructional activities that you think will assist the student's understanding or improve his or her skill levels. After each activity, evaluate how well it helped the student.

February and March: Welcoming New Students Into Your Classroom—Dealing With the Movement of Families

1. To recognize the challenges associated with students who change classrooms frequently

2. To understand the importance of assessing incoming students in order to assist their transitions

3. To identify important strategies that aid in the socialization of new students

Student Mobility

By this point in the school year, you have developed an excellent working knowledge of your students' strengths and weaknesses. Unfortunately, just as you begin to feel most comfortable about the composition of your classroom, it is likely to change. The movement of students in and out of elementary and middle school classrooms is a reality that faces all teachers. Your responsibilities when a student leaves your classroom include preparing materials to be sent to the student's new school and, if possible, communicating with the receiving classroom teacher. You have an even greater responsibility, however, when a child is added to your classroom. Knowing how to accommodate new students in your classroom is important because the increased levels of accountability make effective use of instructional time a critical factor in providing for students' instructional needs. It is equally important to make the student feel welcomed into the social climate of your classroom.

Whether you are teaching in a rural, suburban, or urban school, you can be sure that you will have students move into and leave your classroom at various times during the school year. Certain areas of our country, however, experience higher percentages of transient populations, leading to continuity of instruction problems for these school districts.

The challenges facing school professionals due to a high number of transient students include the following:

1. Stress on schools in making staffing and calendar decisions

2. Increased review of materials for individual students, resulting in slower curriculum pace and decreased opportunities for all students to learn

3. Expansion of the achievement gap between students who move frequently and those who do not

School professionals are constantly working on solutions to the problem of providing for the needs of highly mobile student populations. As a teacher, you should be prepared to address the movement of children and to recognize the importance of assessment in the process of accommodating new students.

The Effect of Student Mobility on Achievement

According to the U.S. Census Bureau (2001), 4.3 million Americans moved between March 1999 and March 2000. The reasons for these moves vary but include the need to find employment, job relocation, poor domestic relationships, and escape from high crime rates. Unfortunately, the fallout from this trend is an effect on children and their school performance. Student mobility is gaining credence as a major factor contributing to the academic achievement gaps that in the past have been attributed to race, ethnicity, gender, and socioeconomic status. According to Kerbow (1996), repeated school changes result in a cumulative academic lag; students who move more than 3 times in a 6-year period can end up being 1 full academic year behind stable students. A high level of student mobility clearly creates challenges not just for students but also for teachers and other school professionals who must report and accept responsibility for their test results.

Although the reasons for a high rate of movement by families and students are outside the control of school officials and the individual teacher, the responsibility for student learning nevertheless resides with the teacher. Frustration among school officials and teachers can develop when they are faced with the responsibility of teaching students who appear to be constantly moving in and out of schools. The pressures exerted from high-stakes testing can result in negative feelings toward students who frequently move. Nonetheless, classroom teachers are charged with the responsibility of caring for and educating all students regardless of the frequency of their moves. This challenge means that teachers need to be prepared to address the problems of transient students in an organized and thoughtful manner. A first step might be to organize an assessment strategy to address the variety of students moving into your classroom.

Types of Student Movement

The students who move into your classroom will vary greatly in their experiences and the environments from which they have come. Each child who moves into your classroom possesses unique academic, social, economic, and, perhaps language and cultural differences that will require your attention. Adequately addressing each of these important areas depends on specific and detailed accommodations that are beyond the scope of this text. General suggestions that utilize assessment practices are offered here as a means by which to address the needs of new students. Let's divide the students who move into your classroom into three groups.

Students Transferring in the Same School District

Most frequently you will receive a student who is transferring from a school in the same district in which you teach. Teachers receive complete permanent records as well as specific and familiar information concerning the student's academic history. Textbooks are often adopted on a districtwide basis, so there is a reasonable chance that the student has had experience with the textbook or program that you are using in your classroom. However, asking the transferring student to identify his or her current place in a text can be a dangerous practice. Children might forget or exaggerate their place in the textbook. You should seek more information from the permanent record before starting the student with a textbook or in a reading group. This can be accomplished by speaking directly with or e-mailing the former teacher.

Cumulative or permanent record folders contain information that is critical to a teacher's quick action. If the students have a history of referrals, these folders will have information that requires careful reading and thorough review. You might find, through reading the cumulative folder, that your new student has an IEP that requires external levels of support. If students have a history of referrals but do not have current IEPs, the referrals might provide useful information about the academic and social histories of the student. However, not all the information in a permanent record is of equal value in the process of accommodating a new student in your classroom.

Some of the information that you review from the permanent record is general in nature and not detailed enough to provide clarifying instructional information. For example, a report card might give a sense of general achievement, but there is not usually any accompanying explanation of how the letter grades were derived. Report cards seldom list the specific content covered within the grading period, and the factors that entered the teacher's calculation of the grade are not clearly expressed. When you understand the subjective decisions upon which grades are calculated, you also recognize the clear danger of basing placement decisions on report card grades (see chapter 6). Perhaps an e-mail or a telephone call to the previous teacher will help you to gain a sense of the student's specific strengths and weaknesses. As the receiving teacher, you will also want to have a sense of the student's attitudes and dispositions toward school, peers, and specific subject areas. This type of information will not be present on the permanent record and is best gathered from personal contact with the former teacher. Table 14-1 provides a checklist of activities for welcoming new students from within your district.

Table 14-1. Checklist for Welcoming New Students From Within Your School District

Date	Action	Comments
	Contact former teacher by telephone or e-mail. Verify textbook or materials used by the sending school. Inquire about reading level if the district is using leveled reading series and mathematics placement. Analyze and review student work that might be part of portfolios.	
	Review permanent record folder to get an idea of student performance over several years. Check attendance patterns. Check for IEP, second-language assistance, previous referrals.	
	Check health records for important information.	
	Send home welcoming letter or introductory material to parent or primary caregiver. Make a telephone contact. Plan to meet with the parents or caregivers if possible.	
	Introduce the new student to the class and use a welcoming activity that assists the student in becoming part of the classroom. Assign a student to "buddy up" with the new student for at least the first week. Walk the student through the building to provide an idea of where things are located.	
	Administer diagnostic curriculum-based assessments (especially in math and reading) to gain specific information about the student.	
	Prepare and administer an inventory of student interests for use in grouping and motivation.	

Students Transferring From Outside Your School District

Another type of transfer student will come from another district, state, or country. This student requires much more of an adjustment to your classroom because of greater displacement issues: distance, climate, language, as well as friends. The arrival of the permanent record may take weeks or months, depending on the organization and practices of the other school system. In school districts that have high levels of student mobility, cumulative folders can have a difficult time catching up to the student. Do not postpone your actions until you receive the permanent record. With students who have moved a considerable distance; it is important to take quick action in determining their instructional level in a variety of subjects. Having some informal means of assessing the background knowledge and skills of a new student will help to get both of you off to a more comfortable start.

Table 14-2 provides a checklist of activities for welcoming new students from outside your school district. As you can see, it is not very different from Table 14-1. The major difference in assessing new students from other school districts is that their supportive academic and health information might not be as quickly received and easily accessed. Parents or primary caregivers of new students from your own district are usually familiar with the policies and practices of the district. When students arrive from out of state or from other countries, the receipt of academic and health records might be late at best and nonexistent at worst.

Table 14-2. Checklist for Welcoming New Students From Outside Your School District

Date	Action	Comments
	Send home welcoming letter or introductory material to parent or primary caregiver. Make phone contact. Plan to meet with the parents or caregivers if possible.	
	Introduce the new student to the class and use a welcoming activity that assists the student in becoming part of the classroom. Assign a student to "buddy up" with the new student. Personally take the student on a walk through the school.	
	Administer diagnostic curriculum-based assessments (especially in math and reading) to gain specific information about the student.	
	Prepare and administer an inventory of student interests for use in grouping and motivation.	
	Review permanent record folder to get an idea of student performance over several years. Check attendance patterns. Check for IEP, second-language assistance, previous referrals. Review student materials that might be sent in a portfolio.	
	Check health records for important information.	

Students With Limited English Proficiency

Some new students, regardless of what school district they come from, might possess limited English proficiency (LEP). The number of students entering American schools with limited English skills is increasing. According to Lenski, Daniel, Ehlers-Zavala, and Alvayero (2004), an estimated 9.6% of the nation's school population is identified as English language learners (ELLs). It therefore makes sense that teachers possess skills in welcoming non-English-speaking students into their classrooms. Specifically recognizing non-English speakers as a group is not intended to single out LEP students but to suggest that the attention required of the teacher to make a comfortable placement for them is likely to be more intense than with other new students. An LEP student will often need help learning a new language and a new culture in addition to the content requirements. Since communication skills are at the very core of instruction, the language problems in and of themselves can constitute obvious discomfort and challenges for the student and the teacher.

Lenski et al. (2004) believe that the tests typically administered to ELL students in English fail to assess the degree of school literacy the students possess in their first language. They suggest that because second-language acquisition does not happen linearly and ELLs can be at varying levels of productive and receptive language, teachers should develop their own language proficiency tests. These assessments should measure language and content area knowledge without being totally language dependent. Specific assessment instruments might include portfolios, language assessment checklists, story retellings, and personal interviews with ELL students. Rollins (2001) offers the following list of indicators that can be used to evaluate the quality of assessments used with ELLs.

- Assessment activities should help teachers to make instructional decisions. If the data generated does not help with instructional decisions, the assessment instrument might be the problem.

- Assessment strategies should help teachers to find out what students know and can do instead of what students do not know. Your purpose is to assess content knowledge, not knowledge of the second language.

- The holistic context for learning should be considered and assessed for being sensitive to the cultural and affective filters of the ELL student.

- Assessment activities should grow out of authentic learning activities. These would include daily written and oral responses.

- The best assessments are longitudinal in nature. Multiple samples of work from different periods make for better decision making than individual written tests.

- Each assessment activity should possess a curriculum-based purpose and should permit the ELL to demonstrate mastery of the objective without being limited to articulating a concept in English.

Jimenez (2004) suggests that information derived from typical classroom assessments can be greatly enhanced with a language profile and an educational history. The profile generally includes the languages with which the child has had contact and where they were encountered. For example, the profile would include what languages are typically spoken when the child goes home, to the store, or to his or her house of worship. This profile provides information on the intensity of language immersion that the student experiences outside the classroom. The student might benefit from "more contact with native speakers of English, overt instruction on specific linguistic forms, or opportunities to use their native language to clarify misunderstandings" (p. 576).

Adapting instruction for LEP students is an important part of helping the student to experience success in your classroom. School districts must provide services to children who are non-English speaking; this is often a beginning step for teachers who are unfamiliar with teaching LEP students. Adapting instruction for LEP students is beyond the scope of this text, but accommodating their needs as part of sound assessment is fundamental.

General suggestions for the modification of instruction and assessment of ELLs include the following:

- Present content vocabulary and concepts using real objects, pictures, and hands-on activities whenever possible.

- Provide written and oral messages directly to students. The written messages can be housed in a vocabulary notebook or a day planner that you provide for the student.

- Build background knowledge and discuss key vocabulary. Second-language learners often have a difficult time understanding idiomatic expressions.

- Accept oral responses in place of written responses. This allows the student to display understanding in a more confident medium. Provide choices in the types of projects and assessments that are used. Care must be given to make sure that the content and tasks are equitable indicators of student understanding.

- Model thought processes. This helps all students, but especially LEP students, who need repetition of strategies to locate information, organize materials, or solve problems.

Two Major Goals in Welcoming a New Student

Regardless of whether the student moves into your classroom from within your school district or from halfway around the world, your goals are the same. From a practical standpoint you should address two major areas with each new student. First, try to make the student feel wanted and accepted by you and your students. Second, determine where the student functions academically in order to begin meaningful instruction as soon as possible.

One means for making the new student feel comfortable in his or her new placement is to develop a contact with the new parents or primary caregiver as soon as possible. This is comforting for any new student. There is a feeling of security when the new student knows that his or her parents have been to the school and met the teacher. One important benefit of this connection is that the parents can comfort the child's anxiety about the new situation. This is extremely important in the early grades, because young children are sometimes still adjusting even to the idea of going to school. Leaving a caring teacher and facing a completely different group of children can be a daunting experience for a 5- or 6-year-old. It is especially helpful if the new student, the parents, and the teacher can meet together for a relaxed conversation prior to the student's first day in the new school. This lets the child know that the parents and teacher have met and they are both working together.

If personal contacts are difficult to arrange, teachers can prepare new-student packets. These contain information that is usually disseminated to parents early in the school year and help to explain school policies and practices. It's a good idea to include a student handbook and a copy of the school schedule in the packet as well as other important policy information. When economically possible, a small welcoming gift goes a long way in making the student and caregivers feel welcome in the new school. The presence of a new-student packet indicates that the district understands it will have students who move into the district and that teachers and the school community will do all that they can to accommodate the new student.

If you worked in a school district that did not have a welcoming packet for new students, how could you begin one? What materials would you want to include in a welcoming packet for new students?

Another means of welcoming a new student is to complete an *interest inventory*. These can be part of several early assessments that a teacher uses to measure the capabilities, interests, and habits of his or her students. The inventories may be short and can be constructed around 15–20 questions, such as the following:

- Do you have a hobby?

- Do you have brothers or sisters?

- What kinds of things do you like to do after school?

- Which subject in school is your favorite? Which one is your least favorite?

From a series of questions like these, you can determine the student's interests and attitudes toward academic subjects and activities outside the classroom. This information becomes helpful if you plan to have students work together, because now you have the necessary knowledge to group students with similar interests, which can be beneficial. These peer arrangements can be used instructionally. For example, if an LEP student has difficulty taking notes because of language processing, the partner can either take notes or check for omissions or misunderstandings. Finding out the interests of new students is an effective may to shape instructional plans that are directly appealing to the students. Imagine the welcome feeling that students experience if their name and hobbies are used in a math problem that is required homework for every student. Small actions such as these go a long way in helping new students to adjust to their environment.

Another means by which to assist new students' adjustment is children's literature. The following books address the first day of school or the first days in a new school for elementary students:

- *Sumi's First Day of School Ever* by Soyung Pak. This is a thoughtful picture book about a young Korean girl trying to find her place in a new classroom on the first day of school.

- *The Brand New Kid* by Katie Couric. Lazlo Gasky doesn't look or speak quite like the other kids, and no one is sure what to make of him. This story is about tolerance and the need to give others a chance.

- *Wemberly Worried* by Kevin Henkes. Wemberly worried about the start of school more than anything she had ever worried about before. This story shows how much fear of the unknown vanishes after the first days of school.

- *Franklin Goes to School* by Paulette Bourgeois and Brenda Clark. Franklin experiences a "jumpy tummy" about going to school. Franklin's exciting, fun-filled day makes him forget his knotted stomach, and he is eager to return to school.

- *Froggy Goes to School* by Jonathan London. At school Froggy finds out it's hard to sit still long enough to learn. This book is a perfect choice for reading aloud.

The following books address the first days in a new school or the awkwardness of moving for upper elementary and middle school students:

- *Matthew Jackson Meets the Wall* by Patricia Giff. Matthew can't understand why his family had to leave New York and the Polk Street School for Deposit, Ohio, but he knows he hates it. Matthew leaves behind good friends and must deal with a neighbor boy so tough he was called "the Wall."

- *The Godmother Tree* by Ruth Wallace-Brodeur. Laura Cate's family has always moved around a lot, but this time it seems harder than ever. Once again, Laura has to face the loneliness of a new school. She makes connections with her new home and her new school.

- *Faith, Hope and Chicken Feathers* by Andrea Wyman. Three new students start sixth grade in Whispering Springs, West Virginia, and quickly bond. The novel contains likable, well-drawn characters and appropriate humor. Children find a new perspective with which to examine the world.

Providing for the comfort of a new student within your classroom does not necessarily make you a more assessment-literate teacher. It does, however, demonstrate how assessment issues are linked to contextual factors in elementary classrooms. Assessing and formulating placements for students should be based on data that is reliable and valid. If new students are uncomfortable and anxious about their new school, their teacher, and their classroom, the likelihood of getting accurate assessment data is diminished. Making a student feel comfortable in your classroom requires time, care, and patience and cannot be completed in one effort. Assisting the student in gaining comfort with his or her new setting leads to more accurate instructional decisions. Part of being an assessment-literate elementary and middle school teacher is knowing how to accommodate students in order to get a clear idea of their potential and their achievement.

Academic Placement Starts With Reading

In many lower elementary classrooms, most instructional time is spent on increasing reading competence. It makes sense, then, that the first and most important placement decision involves assigning the student to an appropriate reading level or group. Finding the proper reading level of a student is especially important in the lower grades, where the differences demand precise diagnosis. Informal reading inventories (IRIs) can be used to inform the teacher of a student's reading skills. IRIs were designed more than 50 years ago to assess multiple aspects of students' reading skills in authentic situations (Paris & Carpenter, 2003). In the past 5–7 years, several state assessment programs and commercial reading assessments have used leveled texts with running records or miscue analysis as formative and summative assessments of early reading (Paris & Hoffman, 2004). IRIs often include running records, miscue analyses, the assessment of prior knowledge, fluency checks, listening comprehension assessments, repeated reading checks, and silent reading exercises. The employment of these activities requires that the teacher devote a significant amount of attention to the student being assessed. The information is of such importance that you should administer the assessments as soon as the student has settled into your classroom. Although the IRI is a very acceptable means of gauging a student's skill levels, its use as a summative measure of a student's reading ability must be approached with caution.

In some school districts the teacher is not assigned the responsibility of leveling, or diagnosing, new student reading abilities. This important task is instead assigned to a building or district reading specialist. If you are a new teacher, it is important to find out who is responsible for completing the reading diagnostic assessment of the new student.

Making a Suitable Math Placement

For mathematics, you should develop a similar type of quick assessment that allows you to assess the student in areas that you have covered up to that point in the year. The key here is to create one or two problems in each of the major areas you have covered. This provides you with a rough estimate of the student's mathematical understanding. If you are grouping students in your classroom or school, this provides you with a reasonable means by which to determine the student's initial group placement. A practical rule is that in cases of indecision, assign students to a group in which they are likely to experience the most success. If a student has been placed in a group that is clearly working below his or her functioning level, it is easy to move the student to a higher functioning group placement. Placing a new student in a group that is functioning beyond his or her mathematical skill level is likely to result in problems for the student and the teacher, there are self-esteem issues involved in being moved to a lower achieving group.

Suppose you have given a student several problems to complete that assess each of the major areas you have covered in your third-grade class. If the student appears unable to accurately complete subtraction problems that require regrouping, you might want to work with the child on regrouping while you continue with your regular mathematics classroom instruction. More important, if you are working in a school that groups students for mathematics instruction, you will want to place the student with other students who need a similar level of instruction. The most important thing to remember is to get a quick snapshot of the student's ability. By using a short assessment you are able to place the student and begin instruction. As you collect more data from classroom assignments, tests, and observations, you will be able to make more informed decisions about the mathematical knowledge and skills of your new student.

When the permanent record arrives, it is always a good idea to review it closely to determine if conditions exist that require your immediate attention. Consider the following:

1. Does this student have an exceptionality that requires accommodations and modifications?

2. Was this student tested for a placement at an earlier date?

3. Do the parents have on record that they oppose participation in certain events for religious reasons? (This has little to do with assessment, but it is always a good idea to know this before it becomes problematic.)

4.   Does this student have any medical problems? Some medical problems can impact instructional needs and therefore affect assessment issues. Outside the assessment area, but of equal importance, you should check to see if the student has an allergy to peanuts, tomatoes, or another common food. Notify the appropriate staff members and keep this important medical issue in mind.

Summary

Family movement is a concern for educators in American schools regardless of geographical area, income level, or ethnic background. Keeping families stable and maintaining children in one school lies outside the control of educators, so they need to know how to use assessment information to help a student to adjust to a new setting. Teachers must be prepared to face the inevitability of new students moving into their classrooms during the school year. Addressing the academic needs of the student through the use of effective assessment methods is only one responsibility of elementary and middle school teachers. An additional responsibility lies in creating a welcoming and supportive environment in which new students can fully participate. This aspect of welcoming a new student can also be achieved through the use of effective assessment methods. As populations become more transient and achievement scores become more of a concern, the transition of students to new schools is likely to become an important aspect of effective teaching.

Teaching Activities

1.   If you are teaching or intend to teach in an elementary or a middle school, assemble a list of community services that would help new students and their families to acclimate to their new school. The following questions provide examples to assist your efforts in generating the list:

What houses of worship are in your area?

What sports are available for boys and girls?

Are there scouting organizations in the area?

Are there services available for the family of the new student?

2.   Secure several blank permanent records from a variety of school districts so that you can examine and compare the categories of information that are kept in each. What differences do you notice? Which areas would you, as the teacher, be directly responsible for, and which do think you would examine most often? Are you surprised by the presence or absence of any category of information?

3.   Contact the federal programs director of a school district and ask him or her to come to your class and discuss accommodating students with limited

English proficiency. The diverse ethnicity of students is more likely to increase in the future, so it will be important for teachers to be aware of language services and resources for students. Ask the federal programs director who might be able to provide discuss services for students moving into the district.

April: Preparing for Externally Developed Tests by Focused Instruction and Improved Feedback

Goals of the Chapter

1. To recognize the elements of effective feedback and their importance in raising achievement levels in elementary and middle school students

2. To be able to effectively develop lessons that prepare students for state-mandated assessments

3. To become familiar with the limitations of grades and rating scales as feedback mechanisms

4. To recognize patterns in feedback practices and understand how to adjust them to be more beneficial in facilitating student success

The Importance of Sustained Preparation

Most external assessments that are mandated by state or federal requirements are administered in the spring of the school year. Although there is usually a considerable flurry of preparation in the weeks leading up to the test, realistic designs for raising test scores must be sustained throughout the school year. In this chapter we will describe how we can effectively align our instructional practices with these exams. In short, we want to teach material and skills similar to those that will be tested on these important exams, and we want our students to have practice answering the types of test questions that appear on the exam. For example, if students are consistently tested throughout the year using objective written exams, it is fairly predictable that those same students will experience difficulty with performance assessment formats. Likewise, if they are not required to communicate in writing about how they solved a mathematics problem, they are unlikely to be able perform that skill with any degree of ease on a formal state examination.

We will also discuss the effective use of feedback for increased achievement in elementary and middle school students. Although most reform efforts involve the coordination and cooperation of a large number of faculty members, the improved use of feedback can be completed by an individual faculty member who wants to enhance his or her instructional and assessment practices. In that respect, improving feedback is attractive to reformers because it not only makes sense but is also economically sustainable. Understanding aspects of effective feedback and providing high-quality feedback to elementary and middle school students is part of being an assessment-literate teacher.

Examining the Required State Tests

Regardless of where you are teaching, there is probably a state test that you are required to administer that is designed for the purpose of gauging student achievement in two of the most respected disciplines in American schools: mathematics and reading. In order to develop instructional practices that are aligned with state-developed instruments, it is advisable to examine the state test that is currently used in your state. Your state may require that the tests be administered only in several grades. However, with the passage of the No Child Left Behind Act, there is a federal mandate requiring standardized testing in every grade from 3 through 8. Given the increased importance of state tests, it is essential that teachers are able to prepare students to be successful on them.

As with any instructional design process, we need to know the instructional targets. In this case, the Pennsylvania Department of Education has made that easily accessible by publishing the four major goals for reading in Pennsylvania. Students must be able to do the following:

- Understand and make sense of the text they read

- Make curriculum connections with the content they read

- Make personal connections with the text or parts of the story line

- Think critically and use information about what they have read in order to make decisions

The advantage we have now is that we know what major goals are emphasized on the Pennsylvania System of School Assessment reading exam. It is very likely that you can access the goals on which your state exam is based. To enhance our understanding, let's examine the types of items found on state reading exams. (Many states publish practice copies of tests that have gone out of use so that teachers and pupils can gain experience working with them.)

An examination of the practice tests might show two separate formats, one that utilizes multiple-choice test items and one that requires students to read a passage and comment on how they would react under the same circumstances as the person in the passage. We can see how the test formats accommodate the desired targets. Multiple-choice formats are used to assess the comprehension and recall skills, but the application skills (and written expression) are assessed using a supply item format. Now we know the beginning and the end—that is, we know the goals and we know the assessments. We must fill in the middle ground.

Teachers must design instructional activities throughout the year that address the goals and subskills within each goal and that utilize assessments similar to those used on the state assessment. For example, since we know that one state goal is for students to be able to make personal connections with literary characters, and since we have seen the types of questions that are asked, the following types of learning experiences would help to prepare students. Throughout the school year students should observe you making connections with characters in literature selections. They can be asked to write a different ending to a story from the perspective of a character, or they might develop a Venn diagram and compare themselves to a story character. These are a limited sample of a multitude of activities that can be completed to develop the ability to relate to story characters. For additional reading activities and assessments, see chapter 9. The same process of examining the goals of the state test, analyzing the test items, and developing instructional activities can be used to prepare students for the externally developed mathematics exams.

Why do you think that most state exams are constructed using two different types of test questions—usually multiple choice and essay?

Although we have discussed how knowledge of the instructional goals of the test allows us to prepare the students for taking the test, we have not discussed how to improve the student's current level of achievement. After all, it is entirely possible that a teacher's planned learning activities are on target with the standards and the externally developed test but nevertheless seem to be ineffective in improving the passing rates of students. The rest of this chapter is devoted to discussing how feedback can be used to improve student learning.

The Importance of Feedback to Increased Achievement

Given the current state and federal expectations for increased rates of student achievement under No Child Left Behind, teachers and other school professionals must seek ways to improve student learning. The challenges facing teachers and administrators include narrowing the achievement gap between specific subpopulations and ensuring that lower-achieving students learn at a better rate. School systems are creating new practices and expanding programs to increase opportunities for student learning. However, the methods designed to provide extra learning opportunities, such as special tutoring, summer programs, and reduced class size, are expensive. The increased use of effective feedback in classrooms will not resolve the above challenges, but it might provide incremental improvement in learning rates that is desirable, economically feasible, and sustainable.

Feedback and Its Presence in Classrooms

Understanding the genesis of the term *feedback* can be helpful to its use in classroom practices that effectively contribute to achievement gain. According to Black and Wiliam (1998), *feedback* was first used to describe the arrangement in an electrical circuit whereby information about the gap between the actual level and the desired level of output was fed back to the system. The purpose of the feedback was to reduce the gap between the actual and desired output. Applied in an instructional context, feedback is designed to assist the student in closing the gap between his or her performance and an acceptable or desired level. In short, we are describing the student effort or improvement required to progress from the basic level to the proficient level or from the proficient level to the advanced level.

The most logical means of affecting student achievement through the use of improved feedback lies in the area of formative classroom assessment. Formative assessments determine the rate and depth of student learning for the purpose of monitoring learning and informing instruction. According to Hanna and Dettmer (2004), formative assessment assists with learning while it is still in progress—that is, while it is being formed. Because formative assessments are such a large part of daily classroom practice, it is important for school professionals to understand feedback's relationship to classroom assessment. A more in-depth definition of formative assessment can be found in chapter 1.

Qualities of Effective Feedback

Marzano, Pickering, and Pollock (2001) indicate that the use of feedback should be guided by three qualities: Feedback should be corrective in nature, specific, and timely.

Corrective feedback means that students are provided with an explanation of what they are doing correctly and what they are doing incorrectly. The example that follows shows that there is considerable variance in the corrective quality of the feedback that students receive.

Bloom and Bourdon (1980) identified seven types of comments from the feedback practices of 180 elementary teachers. When asked to score a student math assignment (20 addition problems), teacher feedback patterns took these forms:

1. Right only (correct responses were identified by checks or circles)

2. Wrong only (incorrect responses were identified by checks or circles)

3. Right and wrong (both were identified by checks or circles)

4. Redo (incorrect responses were marked for the student to redo)

5. Corrective feedback (incorrect responses were marked and the teacher corrected the answers)

6. Teacher assistance (both were identified and the teacher met with the pupil)

7. Diagnostic and prescriptive (incorrect responses were identified, corrective steps were written on the paper, and the pupil had to redo the problems based on the teacher's suggestions)

The feedback in this research was clearly corrective but uneven in its ability to assist the learner. Each of the teacher responses differs in its ability to help the student close the gap between actual and desired performance. Because corrective feedback differed in form and intensity, it most likely generated uneven results in student learning. We can see the importance of corrective feedback and its possible effect on student success. We can also see how practice items that students engage in for state exams might lose their effectiveness if the practice fails to provide students with information about how to improve or advance to the next level of achievement.

Why can corrective feedback be so different among teachers? Should students be exposed to different types of corrective feedback?

The second quality, that feedback should be specific, is accomplished by directing comments about the knowledge or skills that are part of the student's process or product. This often takes place as students complete projects or supply formats that involve the development of a product. Examining teacher comments might help to clarify the types of feedback teachers use to inform students of their efforts. Below is a list of statements generated from teachers who were using written comments to improve student writing. The differences in the specificity of the remarks concerning the focus of the writing sample are easily noted. Students who were writing in response to an informational prompt about animals received the following written feedback from their teacher:

Student A: "You really know a lot about dolphins."

Student B: "You stayed focused during the writing."

Student C: "The focus of this paper is good, but shouldn't the reader want to know more about . . . ?"

Student D: "The topic sentence provided a great focus for the beginning of this piece of writing."

Student E: "Your paper has good focus, but your topic sentence is weak. Rewrite the topic sentence so that it starts the reader thinking about your point."

An examination of the comment to student A shows that it is flattering to the student but does not give a specific comment about the focus of the student writing. The comment, though praising the student's knowledge, would be better if it were directed at the content of the paper. The comment made to student B is a statement about the actions of the student and has no direct link to the actual focus of the paper. The likelihood of these two comments positively affecting the quality of the students' work on this assignment is minimal.

The suggestion to student C is initially affirming but trails off. Perhaps the teacher's intent was to stimulate thinking on the part of the student. This is well-intended, but the ambiguous ending might result in confusion. Completing the sentence in this case would help to clarify the idea to the student. The statement to student D is affirming and helpful if it is followed by additional comments about the focus of the student's writing. The comment to student E is affirming and corrective. It is specific about the weakness of the paper and leads the student to an action that could improve the quality of the assignment. From these examples, it is clear that what teachers write on student papers has a different degree of impact on closing the gap. The differences in the quality of teacher feedback could be a determining factor in the student's rate of learning or improvement.

The most difficult part of developing specific feedback (especially as it pertains to written expression) is crafting comments that are precise enough to be corrective without giving away the necessary action to the student. In this example, the teacher must be careful not to rewrite the paper but instead to lead the student by providing specific comments on the development of a more focused paper.

The statements about the focus of the students' writing differ in their detail, and several are more geared to praising students than providing specific feedback on the focus of their papers. Unfortunately, praise, like other cues that draw attention to self-esteem and away from an academic task, generally has a negative effect (Tunstall & Gipps, 1996). The quality of feedback seems to be undermined by comments that are less specific about the student product and more praising to the student. This does not mean that teachers should avoid praising students; rather, teachers must be aware that not all students react to praise in the same manner. Burnett (2001) polled students ages 8–12 about their preferences for teacher praise and feedback. The results were that 91% preferred to be praised often or sometimes, and only 9% reported that they never wanted praise. It was also found that most students (84%) preferred to be praised for trying hard or putting forth effort rather than for having good ability. In addition, 69% of the students preferred not to have public praise, whereas only 13% wanted public praise. The findings suggest that if teachers meet students' preferences for praise, they will usually give private feedback directed at student efforts.

The literature is straightforward about the third quality, the need for feedback to be timely. In general, the more delay that occurs in providing feedback, the less improvement there is in student achievement. The organizational structure of schooling might not facilitate the immediate return of student work; teachers whose workload requires them to meet large numbers of students on a daily basis frequently encounter this challenge. One suggestion, offered by Marzano et al. (2001), is that teachers move away from the idea that feedback must be provided exclusively by the teacher. Countryman & Schroeder (1996) endorse having students provide feedback to their peers. The recognized danger in this case is that students are not skilled at addressing the appropriate comments necessary for corrective action. Although students are not skilled at providing corrective feedback, they can be taught to improve the quality and type of their responses to their peers. Providing timely feedback to large numbers of students will always remain a challenge for conscientious teachers.

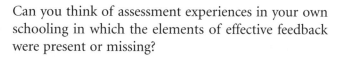

Reflection   Can you think of assessment experiences in your own schooling in which the elements of effective feedback were present or missing?

Common Forms of Teacher Feedback

Although most feedback in classrooms is embedded in formative assessment, the ways in which teachers communicate feedback to students can vary. Feedback can be supplied to students as grades, written comments, oral comments, rubrics, nonverbal actions, and checklists. This chapter will address three forms of teacher feedback that are frequently used in classrooms: grades, rubrics, and written comments. Each will be evaluated for its ability to provide effective feedback that might contribute to the achievement gain of students.

Grades as Feedback

Despite wide recognition and general acceptance of their reporting capabilities, letter grades or scores provide minimal corrective feedback to students. This is especially true if grades are derived from norm-referenced comparisons, indicate a student's standing in relation to other students and do not address the student's mastery of knowledge and skills. It could be argued that if schools were designed with learning as their core concern, corrective and precise feedback would be required and norm-referenced grading of student efforts would be optional. (For additional information on the disadvantages of norm referenced grading, see chapter 6.)

There are other reasons that grades do not provide adequate feedback to students. Brookhart (2004) explains that grading is a descriptive exercise and, as such, fails to provide adequate detail that is corrective in nature. Grades are not specific, and because teachers use grades to accomplish a variety of purposes, misinterpretations by students are a possible result. Students can, however, be motivated by grades, so teachers should understand how grades can be used to accomplish that purpose.

Grades motivate students differently. Cronbach (1977) notes that grades serve as goals that some students seek to attain but that some students are not motivated when they believe that high grades are out of reach. Black, Harrison, Lee, Marshall, and Wiliam (2004) report that grades on students' products often result in students' ignoring the teacher's corrective comments. Cronbach (1977) summarizes grades as they relate to feedback: "Grades tend to be holistic judgments rather than descriptions of strengths and weaknesses and thus do not tell students what they need to do better so that their current performance more closely resembles the desired final performance" (p.153). The use of a single grade (whether represented by a letter, raw score, check, or minus) constitutes feedback, but its corrective value is limited. Shifting the focus of teacher evaluation and student motivation to corrective feedback in a grading environment requires time, effort, and support. Nevertheless, if school systems are going to enhance the achievement levels of students, consideration must be given to the purpose and importance of grades. In short, assessment-literate teachers should realize that grades are an inadequate feedback mechanism and that student achievement is generally not enhanced by the feedback that grades provide.

Rubrics as Feedback

The emergence of performance assessment as an acceptable and valued means of gauging student achievement has resulted in the increased presence of rubrics in today's classrooms. Scoring rubrics are especially useful assessment instruments because they provide qualitative descriptions of performance criteria that work well with the process of formative evaluation. For additional information on the development of scoring rubrics, see chapter 4.

Tierney & Simon (2004) suggest that rubrics vary in the ability to provide feedback to students. They point out that the most accessible rubrics, particularly those available on the Internet, contain design flaws that affect validity and instructional usefulness. Criteria statements, a key element in the design of rubrics, are most helpful to students when they describe levels of quality and don't merely judge them. Central to the rubric's value as a feedback mechanism is an agreement between the student and the teacher on the precise meaning of the criteria statements. Developing rubrics with input from students diminishes the potential miscommunication that can result from the use of rubrics that are commercially or entirely teacher developed.

Criteria statements are static descriptions of important features or elements of a student product or process. They serve the purpose of scoring a person's effort or product, but they generally do not offer sufficient feedback that closes the gap for students. For example, if a student scores at the second level of mastery on a rubric, the criteria describe what is expected at the third level but do not indicate how the student might achieve those skills or knowledge. Rubrics might be described as a form of leveling with an accompanying description that serves an explanatory function to the teacher and the student. This is not meant to dismiss the essential contribution that rubrics provide to the assessment process, but merely to caution against the use of rubrics without some accompanying corrective feedback. Rubrics help to focus student efforts and report the comparison of student actions to a desirable level defined by quality, quantity, or intensity. Corrective teacher feedback, used in support of clear criteria statements, is more likely to move children from one level to the next on scoring rubrics.

Figure 15-1 shows a rubric that was developed using parts of a checklist as well as a comments section. The design of this rubric enhances the teacher's opportunity to make suggestions on how the student's performance could be improved on a take-home project that was checked by the parent before being returned to school.

Reflection

How do you personally respond to grades and rubrics? Are they effective in communicating corrective information to you?

Student: _____   **Date:** _____

Category	4	3	2	1
Identifies Important Information	The student shows complete understanding of the reading by detailed written answers.	The student shows an adequate understanding of the reading with a logical progression of thought.	The student has limited understanding of the material.	The student does not understand the important information with accuracy.
Corrective Comments:				
Takes Pride in Work	Responses show exceptional evidence of neatness, and it's apparent that the student took time to complete his or her best work.	Responses show evidence of neatness and that the student took time to complete his or her best work.	Responses show little evidence of neatness and that the student took time to complete his or her best work.	Responses are brief and careless as completed and show no evidence that the student took time to complete his or her best work.
Corrective Comments:				
Conventions (capitalization, punctuation, word usage, and spelling)	The student has no convention errors.	The student has 1 or 2 convention errors.	The student has 3–5 convention errors.	The student has more than 5 convention errors.
Corrective Comments:				

Student Followed Directions

Completed and turned in on time   Yes   No   Comment

Signed by both parent and student   Yes   No   Comment

Answers are in complete sentences   Yes   No   Comment

Figure 15-1. Take-Home Comprehension Activity
(Courtesy Liz Auer and Janelle Proctor)

Written Comments as Feedback

The familiarity of written comments can result in their being taken for granted, but they are a powerful tool for creating learning in students. First, all written comments have the potential to be corrective, specific, and timely. It is helpful to think of the assessment as a student opening a discussion with the teacher, and the corrective responses of the teacher as a continuing dialogue with the student about his or her answers. From this perspective, corrective and specific feedback is dependent on the teacher's use of clear writing and precise terminology. The proper use of written comments might require an examination of traditional practices. The use of a single word, like *good* or *vague,* or the placement of a question mark in the margin of the student's paper fails to be adequately specific or corrective. A first step in evaluating one's feedback is to closely examine the comments and degree of detail that is supplied to students' efforts or products.

Higgins, Hardley, and Skelton (2002) conducted a study on feedback that was provided to college students, and even though the age-appropriateness of these findings is not directly generalizable to elementary or middle school, the basic premise is nonetheless enlightening. The study found that "Often, feedback comments employ the academic language used to express assessment criteria, but only 33% of the respondents claimed to understand the comments" (p. 56). This can be true in elementary and middle school classrooms, as shown in the following example. As teachers develop the qualities of focus and style in student writing, care should be given to comments about "distinct focus" or "relational" organization. Written comments that are not understood by the students are a waste of both teacher and student time.

Providing feedback with written comments has been a long-standing practice in the teaching of language arts and English. Strickland, Bodino, Buchan, Jones, and Rosen (2001) note that the wave of standard-based reform is focusing increased attention on the importance of writing instruction in other academic areas. Many state exams now require written responses in reading, science, and mathematics. Employing corrective and specific feedback to student writing skills thus has the ability to affect achievement in areas other than writing. Although the purpose of writing can change with content area, corrective feedback can always be employed to address the quality of content, organization, and conventions. There is value in meeting with individual students to discuss whether they truly understand the nature of your comments.

Grades, rubrics, and written comments remain the most common forms of feedback to students in elementary and middle schools. School professionals need to be able to apply the most appropriate feedback practices to assist students in closing the gap between actual and desired levels of achievement.

Suggestions for Improving Feedback Practices

Following are a brief set of guidelines for teachers to improve their use of feedback with students:

- Recognize that feedback differs greatly in its ability to affect learning among students.

- Employ feedback that is timely, corrective, and specific as often as possible.

- Be clear with written comments, making sure that students understand the suggestions, recommendations, or editorial comments.

- Be careful with praise; respond in order to encourage the effort of students.

- Avoid being so corrective as to give away the answer to the student.

- Understand that providing excellent feedback to students requires thoughtfulness and a commitment of time.

Summary

Mandated testing is likely to remain an area of intense teacher responsibility over the next decade. Assessment-literate teachers possess the skills and knowledge to be able to examine the goals of the state exams, analyze the types of assessment used in the state exams, and provide students with opportunities to learn in meaningful ways. The element of congruency is important in raising student achievement. If teachers can develop learning experiences that are congruent and supportive of the goals and assessments of the state, student achievement is likely to be positively affected.

Increasing student learning is central to the purpose of all teaching. All learning theories list feedback to the learner as an important aspect of student achievement. Feedback differs according to the contextual factors of the classroom, the teacher, and the students. Elements of effective feedback, however, have been identified in the research on formative assessment. Feedback is most effective when it is timely, specific, and corrective. Teachers must understand how to employ the elements of effective feedback in order to close the gap between actual student performance and desirable student performance. By understanding the limitations of existing feedback methods, teachers can improve their ability to communicate specific information that will facilitate student learning.

Teaching Activities

1. Access released state tests in math and reading. Examine the types of questions that students will be asked in your particular area of teaching. Also examine a test from a higher or lower grade level. What do you notice about the similarities or differences in the types of questions on both tests?

2. Download several rubrics from Web sites. Review the criteria statements and check the quality of their feedback. Discuss how the rubric statements will help students progress to the next level of achievement. Are there ways in which the rubric statements can be improved?

3. Examine the papers or tests that have recently been returned to you. Evaluate the effectiveness or ineffectiveness of the feedback. Determine whether the feedback was timely, corrective, and specific. How could it have been improved?

Chapter 16

May: Challenging Assessment Issues and Professional Development

Goals of the Chapter

1. To recognize the need for ongoing professional development in the area of assessment as it relates to contemporary elementary and middle school classrooms

2. To become exposed to opportunities for professional development activities that promote assessment literacy

3. To be able to utilize selected readings, journals, and Web sites that promote the acquisition of assessment literacy

The Need for Assessment Literacy

Significant change has occurred in the nature of classroom assessment and teaching over the last two decades. The need to become assessment literate and apply that important knowledge and skill in classrooms is more critical now than at any point in the history of American education. Although this might sound like hyperbole, the influence of standards-driven education and the impact of the No Child Left Behind Act puts the teacher squarely in the center of efforts to reform education. Student assessment and, particularly, attention to test results currently drive the quality assumptions of reform advocates. It would be difficult to function in this time of increased accountability without a well-grounded understanding of classroom assessment. As Popham (2004) says:

> In education, the linchpin of the accountability system is our students' test performance. Astonishingly, however, when it comes to this key indicator of education quality, the vast majority of educators reside in blissful ignorance. Such assessment illiteracy is surely a prescription for professional suicide. (p. 82)

The need for an increased degree of assessment literacy among teachers and other school personnel is critical. As more teachers and school professionals are able to understand assessment issues and practices, they can speak more forcefully about how assessment affects their livelihood. More important, they will be able to address the effects of assessment policy changes and suggested practices on the performances and dispositions of their students. In short, they will become more accomplished and articulate professionals. For some teachers, becoming assessment literate will mean beginning their careers by being mindful and professionally oriented to addressing assessment issues. For others, it will mean professional development in an area that to this point was guided primarily by past practice and a lack of systematic and meaningful training.

Addressing Your Own Assessment Literacy

For elementary and middle school teachers who have recently begun their careers, the formal study of measurement and assessment literacy most likely began with a course that was part of the curriculum at their teacher preparation institutions. However, Stiggins (1999) found that only 25 states required specific assessment competencies for a teacher credential, and prior to the 1990s, assessment training was virtually nonexistent. The assessment preparation of elementary and middle school teachers remains uneven across the country.

Regardless of your teacher preparation program's emphasis on the development of assessment literacy, there remains an unavoidable need to continue to build on your assessment knowledge and skills. If you are sincere about expanding what you know about assessment, you might want to begin by referring the "Standards for Teacher Competence in the Educational Assessment of Students" (AFT et al., 1990). These standards have effectively served as a framework for addressing content offerings in teacher preparation programs and teacher induction models.

Each of the standards is listed below, along with a brief discussion of what I believe future elementary and middle school educators will need to know and be able to do as part of their ongoing professional development in the area of assessment literacy. This text has been designed to provide entry-level skills and knowledge, but the development of assessment literacy should be viewed as a continual and dynamic goal of all teachers, regardless of their levels of experience.

Standard 1: Teachers Should Be Skilled in Choosing Assessment Methods Appropriate for Instructional Decisions

After reading this text you should be familiar with the importance of choosing correct assessment tools based on contextual, temporal, and curriculum issues. You will recall that the choice of the correct assessment is linked to the determination of the desired targets of knowledge, skills, and dispositions as well as the developmental levels of children. Despite the existence of clearly written standards for all grades, it can sometimes be difficult to establish performance levels for the skills and knowledge that are prescribed within each standard. Identifying the essential learning targets and the appropriate levels of performance will continue to be challenging for teachers and other education professionals.

Ongoing professional development that addresses the choice of appropriate assessments also includes addressing the instructional and assessment needs of students with exceptionalities. More attention and emphasis will undoubtedly be placed on modifying and accommodating classroom assessments and external measures. The need to stay abreast of federal, state, and local mandates as they affect classroom practices is, and will remain, part of your professional responsibility. More attention is being placed on the achievement levels of subpopulations, including poor, minority, special needs, and ESL students. No amount of undergraduate assessment preparation will enable you to deal with the changes and subsequent knowledge and skills you will need to address the diversity and assessment challenges of future classrooms.

As technology continues to impact instructional processes, changes in the manner and substance of assessments will require clear thinking and an increased technical expertise on the part of the classroom teacher. Some of our future classrooms will contain children who will be the most technically capable students in the history of American education. Recognizing how technology can assist instruction, management, and administration will be part of selecting and using sound assessment practices. Choosing the correct assessment will remain a fundamental skill of teachers, but future challenges will include attention to standards-driven teaching, assisting students with special needs, and the effective uses of appropriate technology.

Standard 2: Teachers Should Be Skilled in Developing Assessment Methods Appropriate for Instructional Decisions

Assessment-literate teachers will not only have to be able to select appropriate assessment material, they will also have to develop and adapt measures to fit the needs of the students in their classrooms. On many occasions teachers have indicated to me that most of the assessment materials they use are commercially developed or are provided from workshops in which they have participated. I fully understand the need to be able to access and use material that does not require hours of personal work by the teacher. For that reason, being able to adapt instructional materials and commercially developed assessment measures to the needs of your students requires ongoing skill development. Most commercially developed assessment instruments provide a solid beginning for the assessment of children. However, the ability to recognize the flaws and inadequacies of assessment materials will make for more accurate assessment. The development of these types of skills requires time, interest, and the ability to work with others. Some of my most effective and professionally rewarding experiences as a consultant have been in the development of assessment materials with peers and colleagues in elementary and middle school. The need to possess skills that enable you to properly gauge the potential effectiveness of assessment-related material will be of importance throughout your professional career.

Another important challenge that teachers will face in the future is gaining a clear understanding of how to use assessment data to inform instruction. The age of data-driven decision making is upon us, and it is likely to remain part of the teaching responsibilities of all future teachers. Teachers and administrators will have to be able to differentiate data that is important to the instructional process from data that is not. The addition of data to the decision-making process will not improve teacher decisions unless teachers are well prepared to analyze the validity and interpret the meaning of the information. The challenge of analyzing, interpreting, and using data will become more difficult as it increases in volume and level of sophistication. The need to stay in tune with understanding assessment-driven data will be a professional development challenge for teachers, principals, and other school professionals.

Standard 3: Teachers Should Be Skilled in Administering, Scoring, and Interpreting the Results of Both Externally Produced and Teacher-Produced Assessment Methods

This standard is so broad and contains such a variety of knowledge and skills linked to professional development that it is difficult to adequately address it within the limits here. From reading this text you should gain a sufficient background that permits you to feel confident in your abilities to administer, score, and interpret the results of teacher-produced assessments. Your future challenges will most likely be in the area of interpreting the results. As shifts take place in instructional philosophies and practices, the accompanying assessments will require a different set of skills and knowledge for interpreting the results. For example, as reading instruction incorporates the use of increased differentiation for individual readers, process-oriented work, and subjective assessments, elementary teachers will need to acquire adequate and appropriate assessment skills. These types of shifts in reading and mathematics are reasonably predictable over the course of one's teaching career. Once you realize the essential link of assessment to instruction, it would be foolhardy to believe that assessment will not be an essential part of each forthcoming instructional shift in elementary and middle school teaching. Policy makers and reformers should recognize that successful and sustained curriculum change is impossible without well-planned assessment strategies.

This standard also addresses administering, scoring, and interpreting externally produced assessments. With the accountability issues facing states and school districts, teachers are given little latitude in the administering and scoring of external measures. This is largely because federal and state guidelines make deliberate efforts to maintain test security and rigid attention to detail in the administration of the tests. As more states develop tests that are aligned with their standards, however, teachers will have to become more aware of the interpretation of those results. Interpretation of externally produced test results has significant value for two reasons. First, the results must be understood so that they inform the teacher of his or her students' success or lack of success. Second, interpreting results is important to assist students and parents in understanding the levels of achievement in student performance. This will require additional professional development because states are moving to improve the formats and elements of standards-based assessment.

For example, several years ago one state changed from a 5-point rubric to a 4-point rubric to assess the writing skills of its students. Another change in the writing assessment required the inclusion of objective test items to assess the conventions, or mechanics, areas of student writing. These types of changes required teachers to adjust to the scaling differences in rubric use and recognize the instructional implications of the shifted emphasis toward grammar, punctuation, and spelling. Much difficulty with interpretation surrounded the decision to shift to a 4-point rubric, because the original 5-point scale had coincided with the traditional letter-grade (A, B, C, D, F) system. Teachers also began to address the assessment of writing conventions in the form of "Locate the error among the following four sentences" formats. In summary, the changes that occur in state testing are likely to continue to impact the instructional and assessment practices of elementary and middle school teachers.

Standard 4: Teachers Should Be Skilled in Using Assessment Results When Making Decisions About Individual Students, Planning Teaching, Developing Curriculum, and Improving School

So far there has been an emphasis on the interpretation of student work for a variety of purposes. This standard is devoted to the use of the results to make important educative decisions. Using information differs greatly from recognizing the credibility and quality of results. Each of the targeted areas—students, teaching, curriculum development, and school improvement—requires skills and knowledge for effective use.

Using information to inform decisions about students and teaching requires a different pace from the use of data for curriculum development and school improvement. The pace of change in student skill development within elementary classrooms is extraordinary. Young children develop expressive communication skills at rates that require frequent and ongoing interpretative skills. In order to accommodate that rapid growth, teachers should be skilled in recognizing and validating inferences about student progress. This often requires a sophisticated combination of the knowledge of literacy development, content, child development, and assessment practices. This inference making is important at all levels of instruction, but the pace of develop-ment in younger students makes the challenge all the more daunting. Dylan Wiliam, Educational Testing Services director, supports this notion by suggesting that "for-mative assessment is not assessment that takes place every five to six weeks, but as-sessment that takes place every ten seconds" (Sausner, 2005). In short, the use of classroom data has an immediacy that distinguishes it from using data to enhance curriculum and school reform.

The use of assessment results to develop curriculum and enhance school reform requires the teachers to be reflective and understand how their students' performances fit into the larger picture of their district and regional schooling. Using results to inform these types of decisions requires that teachers be able to articulate the value and meaning of the results to peers and administrators. Teachers need to develop skills and understanding that will provide them with the confidence to share their results and inferences based on the data collected in their classrooms. It is also im-portant for teachers to advocate for assessments and data that are instructionally sensitive. This requires the skill to be able to recognize data that can be used in mean-ingful ways to improve curriculum offerings. It should be clearly understood that school reform is best accomplished when teachers alter or change practices with chil-dren, not when philosophical or programmatic changes are made to documents and policy statements.

Standard 5: Teachers Should Be Skilled in Developing Valid Pupil Grading Procedures That Use Pupil Assessments

With the impact of improved communication opportunities, grading and report cards are likely to be the focus of some of the most dramatic future changes for teachers. The possibility that report cards in hard copy will one day be replaced with an en-tirely electronic communication does not appear to be far off. Currently, increased numbers of school districts are requiring teachers to post grades so that parents can access their child's grades at any time on the Internet. Opening up a teacher's grade book to parents constitutes a substantial shift in the teacher-parent relationship—one that may initially generate some consternation. This real-time snapshot of how students are doing requires teachers to pay close attention to their grading practices, communication skills, and the success of all students.

More important than the change in the mode of communication, however, is the possible change in the substance of the report card. Report cards went virtually un-changed for decades prior to the 1990s. Since that time, elementary report cards have gone through numerous changes in format and content. The changes most likely to influence report card composition are the use of new developmental continuums and the modification of current state standards. The use of developmental continuums has gained a foothold in the reporting of progress in lower grades and is likely to gain more universal acceptance as a means for reporting student success. Middle schools do not seem to have experienced the frequency or amount of change that has been characteristic of elementary schools. The grading shifts that exert the most pressure on middle school teachers are the use of standards as achievement targets in place of, or concurrent with, the use of traditional letter grades.

Historically, American schools have resisted many attempts to eliminate the five-letter grading system, but the standards movement that employs four levels of student achievement might constitute the most formidable threat to date. Teachers will be faced with the challenge of understanding how to report the progress of students within the changed format of standards and scaling differences associated with the terms *advanced, proficient, basic,* and *below basic.* This will involve philosophical questions, communication skills, and the ability to work with parents and other school professionals.

Standard 6: Teachers Should Be Skilled in Communicating Assessment Results to Students, Parents, Other Lay Audiences, and Other Educators

Changes in the communication of assessment results will require teachers to enhance their understanding of assessment results to include classroom, district, state, and standardized measures. Although this book offers entry-level explanations of assessments, the range and depth of understanding that will be required of teachers is likely to expand. With increasing frequency, school districts are expending resources to develop assessments that can be used to prepare students to take state-mandated tests. There are practice sessions so all students can take a test that approximates the state exam. The results help to identify students who demonstrate difficulty with the test format or material. Developing effective interventions for students who are experiencing problems involves communicating results and suggestions for instructional strategies with other school professionals and parents. Much of the knowledge and skill discussed in the other standards also applies in this standard.

Standard 7: Teachers Should Be Skilled at Recognizing Unethical, Illegal, and Otherwise Inappropriate Assessment Methods and Uses of Assessment Information

The nature of unethical and illegal assessment has changed because the stakes of the testing has increased. The change can be attributed to the emphasis of high-stakes evaluation based on a single measure in No Child Left Behind. The emphasis on increased accountability measures calls into question the practices and procedures that school districts and teachers employ to focus the learning experiences of children.

While the stakes have grown higher, the guidelines for ethical practices have remained consistent. Teachers and other school professionals should be familiar with the *Code of Fair Testing Practices in Education* (APA, 1988). The code presents standards for educational test developers and users in four areas: developing and selecting tests, interpreting scores, striving for fairness, and informing test takers. It is directed primarily at professionally developed tests such as those sold by commercial test publishers or used in formally administered testing programs. The standards are not intended to cover tests made by individual teachers for use in their own classrooms.

Becoming a More Complete Professional

The challenge for teachers seeking to be consummate professionals is that they must assume the responsibility to develop into caring and competent teachers in all aspects of their jobs and in the lives of their students. This requires their development to be focused on expanding their knowledge and maintaining and enhancing their skills. In a perfect world, the burden of professional development would be shared by the individual teacher, administrative personnel, and the district in which the teacher is employed. There is no more important resource to a school district than the professionalism of its teachers. Unfortunately, the resource capacity of school districts is uneven, and the ability of school systems to support rigorous and sustained professional development can be limited. Given the reality of less than complete support, the responsibility of ongoing and purposeful professional development rests, for the most part, with the individual teacher. Below are suggestions for professional development aimed at increasing the assessment literacy of preservice or inservice teachers.

Conferences

One way to develop assessment literacy is to participate in conferences that provide opportunities for professional growth, generally across a variety of subjects, assessment practices, skills, and dispositions. Conferences that are helpful to the professional development of teachers can be local, state, or national. The relevance and importance of the conference to the development of the teacher lies fundamentally in the professional needs of the teacher, but proximity can be very important. Local conferences appeal to most teachers because they are more likely to address themes or areas of study that are important within that state or district. They also tend to be less of a strain on professional development resources. Local conferences reduce travel expenses and generally require smaller conference registration fees.

State conferences—which might be considered as local, depending on proximity—can also facilitate assessment literacy. They are frequently organized by state chapters of educational organizations or learned societies. For example, the Association for Supervision and Curriculum Development (ASCD), the International Reading

Association (IRA), and the American Educational Research Association (AERA) maintain active chapters in many states. Generally, the state chapter sponsors a conference that is open to its membership and the public. One advantage of state conferences is that they are more likely than local conferences to attract persons who are involved in larger professional development projects. The downside is that their registration fees are usually more expensive than locally sponsored conferences. Departments of education also sponsor statewide meetings to inform teachers and school professionals. For example, teachers might be asked to participate in state curriculum review and development, to score writing samples using a state-adopted assessment instrument, or to participate in training sessions that promote deeper understanding of state standards for regular education students. Participation in these types of activities is an important part of professional development.

Conferences are often sponsored by learned groups, who have as one of their major functions the dissemination of information to their constituencies as well as to the general public. The following is a brief list of some of the learned societies that might sponsor state or regional conferences that can enhance assessment literacy within a certain subject area:

- National Council of Teachers of Mathematics (NCTM)
- National Council for Social Studies (NCSS)
- National Council of Teachers of English (NCTE)
- National Council on Measurement in Education (NCME)
- National Science Teachers Association (NSTA)

Larger organizations, such as ASCD, AERA and IRA, might hold national assemblies at major conference sites. National conferences shift yearly to different areas of the country in order to provide members with equitable travel requirements. Conferences typically rotate from the East to the Midwest to the West. The speakers at these conferences have often gained national recognition in their particular area of study. The travel and registration fees associated with national conferences can make them cost prohibitive in the absence of financial support. There is a significant benefit to viewing the teaching profession as a membership organization that includes colleagues from not only your immediate area but also the state and the nation.

Web Sites and Other Internet Resources

The Internet has increased access to information that can assist in the professional development of teachers. Many colleges and universities offer online courses at advanced levels that permit teachers to participate in post-baccalaureate study without the burden of travel and without strict schedules of face-to-face attendance. This flexibility eliminates some of the logistical obstacles that previously faced teachers who were seeking enrollment in graduate study. With the proliferation of these courses and entire degree programs, the ability to enhance one's professional development has been made more convenient and accessible. As with the pursuit of any degree program, caution should be exercised to ensure the quality of the individual course offerings or degree.

The Internet also offers less structured means to acquire enhanced knowledge and skills in the area of assessment literacy. The following Web sites afford teachers and school district personnel the opportunity to investigate assessment issues and practices:

www.assessmentinst.com

www.nwrel.org

www.mcrel.org

www.ets.org

www.makingstandardswork.com

www.nagb.org

www.ccsso.org

www.enc.org

www.tcrecord.org

Periodicals and Journals

Teachers who are seeking to develop professionally must read in their chosen field in order to stay current and to develop skills that ultimately contribute to the ability to reflect on their practice. Journals are generally included as part of a membership fee in a learned society. For example, a membership in the Association for Supervision and Curriculum Development (ASCD) entitles one to receive the periodical *Educational Leadership*, among other benefits. Other journals provide online memberships. *Teachers College Record*, for example, offers an online membership that permits the viewing of articles that are unavailable to nonsubscribers. The following journals afford teachers the opportunity to develop professionally:

Phi Delta Kappan

Educational Leadership

Education Week

Educational Researcher

Teaching and Learning K–8

Educational Measurement: Issues and Practices

Reading Research Quarterly

The Reading Teacher

The development of an assessment-literate teacher follows a parallel path to over-all professionalism. Understanding the importance of assessment within the context of curriculum and instruction is a necessity for all elementary and middle school teachers. This chapter has provided some suggestions for beginning the pursuit of assessment literacy and the greater goal of enhanced professional development.

Summary

Accepting the challenge of becoming assessment literate is a necessary career goal for those teachers who want to be well rounded and informed professionals. The education community accepts that assessment is required for effective teaching and learning and that a return to an era when assessment was the primary responsibility of testing companies is unthinkable. With that awakening comes the responsibility to accept classroom assessment as a legitimate area of study that involves specific knowledge and skills appropriate to contextual factors as well as external influences. The pursuit of assessment literacy should be ongoing.

Issues and practices that influence future assessment literacy will be dynamic and perhaps somewhat contentious. Assessment-literate teachers will have to be able to ground their understanding in an informed position of accepted research and psychometric principles. They will also need to be able to apply their knowledge and skills in practical ways to affect the success rates of all students. Swift shifts in federal and state accountability standards will create practical dilemmas that are sometimes left unaddressed by the assessment community. The need to make sound assessment decisions amid a changing landscape of standards, varying student demographics, and shifting instructional strategies faces all teachers. Assessment-literate teachers will be the more distinguished elementary and middle school professionals.

Teaching Activities

1. Investigate one of the learned societies by examining its Web site. Find out as much as you can from the Web site about the benefits of membership, state chapters, annual conferences, and journals. Check to see if student memberships are available.

2. Examine the *Code of Fair Testing Practices in Education*. Find an area in which you believe you have experienced or observed an unfair or unethical practice during your school career. Does that practice continue in schools today? Discuss how you might help to keep the unfair practice from recurring in future classrooms.

Essential Components of a Lesson Plan and Their Importance to Assessment

1. To understand the assessment role of each of the essential elements of a lesson plan
2. To be able to plan lessons with assessment as a guiding focus

Essential Components of a Lesson Plan Format

One of the most enduring questions in undergraduate teacher preparation is "Which lesson plan format is the right one?" or "Why does one professor require guided practice in her lesson plan format, but another professor does not?"

Lesson plan formats are templates (blueprints) for designing a lesson. They provide a design from which one can build a quality lesson. Just as a blueprint for the construction of a house changes according to the design of the house, a lesson plan format changes with the design of the lesson. Fortunately, despite differences in house designs, there are features that are common to all blueprints for houses. So it is too with lesson plan formats.

Although there might be differences in what is required regionally or philosophically, six basic lesson plan components can be found in most classrooms throughout the country. Each of these is described below.

Objectives

State in clear language what you would like the learner to be able to do after instruction.

Think about what you want to have happen in children's brains and how their success will be noted in their behaviors. (What will they learn as a result of participating in your lesson, and how will that learning be clearly noted by you?) Try not to make it so specific that your teaching is full of a large number of isolated skills; if so, your objectives will quickly lose importance to you.

Example: After instruction and completing several practice problems, students will be able to correctly solve four of the five word problems independently.

The activity that is taking place in the student's brain is the ability to solve word problems, and completing four out of five correctly shows the teacher the degree of success that is taking place in the student's work.

Make sure the objectives you construct make sense. Avoid sentence construction like the following, offered by a student in my Teaching of Science course: "In this introductory lesson students will be exposed to the harmful effects of radiation." Besides the unfortunate double meaning, the objective contains no clear idea of the mental process that is going to take place and no evidence of the students' success. This objective is more of a description of what the teacher will do to the students than of the task required of the students.

Refer to suggested lists of behavioral verbs to use when constructing objectives, then make sure that what you have planned will develop that mental behavior in students. For example, avoid using the verb *compare* if all students are going to do is list the characteristics or properties of two different items.

Procedures

Detail the instructional activities that are to occur. What are you going to do that encourages or facilitates the mental activity you want to develop in your students?

Procedures are the set of activities that you have designed to engage the students in the learning process. The degree of detail necessary for the procedures has a great deal to do with your experience in teaching. Experienced teachers tend to develop routines and do not have to be specific in the procedures of a lesson plan. (It's best to err on the side of too much detail rather than too little.) Plan an activity that will allow the students to meet the target objective. If your objective calls for students to do an analysis, and your procedures are limited to reading from the text, it's likely that your teaching will not permit the students to complete the analysis. The brightest students may be successful, and that might deceive you into believing that your methods were successful. You might then assume that the students who failed weren't paying attention or aren't capable. Instead, your instruction might have failed to stimulate the necessary mental activity in your students' minds. If the objective indicates analysis, then the procedures should outline activities that promote the development or use of analysis by students.

Materials

List all materials (for both students and teacher) that are necessary to execute the lesson.

This component is easily understood and should be treated in a practical way. Listing the materials that are necessary for the lesson helps you to avoid interruptions and a loss of pace in your teaching. Including the items that every student has available is generally not necessary in a lesson plan. For example, listing pencils and crayons for a lesson is not necessary, however, securing a certain type of paper prior to a particular art lesson might be a helpful reminder to you. What you are trying to do here is remind yourself of all the materials that are required for the lesson so that you can concentrate on delivering instruction without interruption and confusion. The lesson plan gives a means by which to anticipate your needs and assemble the necessary teaching materials prior to your lesson.

Student Assessment

You should be able to determine what the students were able to achieve as a result of the planned teaching activities.

This is sometimes referred to as evaluation, but if you recall the definitions of the two terms, *assessment* is the means by which we collect data about students, and *evaluation* is a process that requires a judgment on the part of the teacher. Evaluation of the lesson's effectiveness is clearly a teacher decision. The basis for the judgment of success of the lesson should be tied closely to the degree of demonstrated student success. Any post-instructional evaluation ought to begin with or include this important question: "Did you achieve the instructional objective designed for this lesson?" Linking the objective to the assessment of student success brings focus to the achievement of students and importance to the need for thoughtful and precise planning.

It is equally important in the planning stage to consider the first principle of sound assessment. Of all the possible assessment formats available to you as a teacher, which assessment tool will generate the most valid data indicating that the students have met or failed to meet the objective?

Accommodations

Intentionally adapt instructional strategies, content, and materials to facilitate the instruction of individuals or small groups of children.

Providing quality learning experiences for all children requires planning. Changes in the composition of classrooms based on the presence of students with disabilities and/or cultural and linguistic differences require the thoughtful attention of teachers. It is beyond the scope of this text to discuss all the different adaptations that are necessary in the development of responsive lesson plans, but it is nonetheless critical to recognize that accommodations are a daily part of teaching.

Evaluation

Render a judgment on the success of the lesson and the effectiveness of the teaching. The evaluation of the success of the lesson is directly linked to student performance. In the past, methods of evaluating teacher quality focused on acceptable and desirable teacher behaviors. In this increased age of accountability, the central focus is the achievement of the students. Consider the following example.

Mary, a student teacher, teaches a lesson on homophones to a small group of first graders. The students participate in activities that help to define and show the different meanings of several homophones. After much practice, the students complete a work sheet asking them to use the correct homophone in a sentence. Mary stands in front of the class as the students correct their own papers. After the lesson is over, she asks the students, "How many of you got them all correct?" All hands are raised. As they prepare for lunch, Mary walks around to informally check the papers and finds that every student in the group missed the sentences using *bear* and *bare*. Mary now understands that she must base her evaluations on verifiable evidence of her students' success. The students were very willing to celebrate their successes and ignore the question that had posed a problem.

Gaining a Framework of Thinking

1. To gain an understanding of the different levels of cognition and affect
2. To be able to make effective connections between the levels of cognition and affective and classroom applications

Levels of Thinking

If you polled a group of people about what content was most important for children to master in American schools, teachers, parents, and people from different walks of life are likely to create an exhaustive list ranging from good manners to the solution of complex problems. This is why we must always be attuned to the needs of our students when we make decisions about what to teach and, just as important, what not to teach. Our job is to prepare students to function and contribute to a democratic society. In order to do that effectively, students must know essential content that prepares them to understand and be successful in our culture. However, it is no longer acceptable to merely know the content; it is equally important to possess the skills to be able to do something with that content.

The ability to process information and use it in meaningful ways requires thinking. As a teacher or a teacher candidate in an upper level education course, it should be easy for you to understand the fundamental importance of thinking or cognition. The ability to think might be the most important skill we can develop in our students. It follows, then, that if it is worth teaching, we must understand thinking, at least to a usable degree.

One of the starting points for understanding thinking is to be able to recognize the difference between lower level thought processes and what we call higher level, or higher order, thinking. A useful tool in doing that is Bloom's taxonomy of the cognitive domain. Benjamin Bloom (1956) and a group of colleagues were concerned that the development of thinking in students seemed to be lacking from the American curriculum and hoped to assist the teaching of thinking by the development of a taxonomy that facilitates the differentiation of higher level thinking from lower level thinking processes. Taxonomies are structures that classify items into a hierarchy, one of the most common being the order of species.

Bloom's Taxonomy of the Cognitive Domain

Bloom's taxonomy lists six different levels of thinking. We will discuss them in order from the lowest level of thinking to the highest.

Knowledge Level

The knowledge level is usually associated with memorization. Students might be called upon to remember facts, concepts, generalizations, or procedures. Examples would be students memorizing state capitals, definitions, important historical documents, or arithmetic facts. It is important for children to engage in the memorization of some material. Higher order thinking requires a knowledge of content; we cannot operate efficiently by constantly requiring students to rediscover or retrieve material. Because memorization makes the recall of information automatic, it is sometimes dangerously confused with understanding. Consider this example. A third grader who was asked to write the Pledge of Allegiance wrote, "and to the republic of Richard Stance, one nation under God." For an indeterminable number of days, the student had been reciting this at the knowledge level, devoid of any association with the meaning. Memorization cannot be trusted as the sole means by which students attain understanding. In short, although we can readily acknowledge the need for higher order thinking, we have to remember that students will need to learn some basic information. The key is to avoid turning your classroom into a training area for Trivial Pursuit participants.

Key words associated with the knowledge thought process are *define, list, name, recall, recite, describe, state,* and *tell.*

Questions that are written at a knowledge level include: (a) Which of the 50 states is the largest in square miles? (b) Who is the current president of the United States? (c) Four plus four equals what?

Comprehension Level

The comprehension level is usually associated with explaining the meaning of a word, story, or concept. Students are required to restate or to describe information or procedures in their own words. Although there is a slight difference from memorization because the student is putting something in his or her own words, this too is not to be confused with deep understanding. The key here is that students have internalized some of the understanding of what was previously memorized, read, or encountered in other ways.

Key phrases associated with the comprehension thought process are *tell in your own words, retell the story, explain* (*why, how,* or *when*) or *predict.*

Questions that are written at a comprehension level include: (a) What did the author mean by this statement? (b) From this graph, can you tell which animal is the class favorite? (c) What do you think the picture is intended to remind us to do? (d) Give me an example of . . .

The comprehension level of thought is only one level higher than rote memorization. It has a place in our classrooms much like the knowledge level does—that is, in the acquisition of facts, concepts, and directions. We must, however, be careful not to overuse this level of thought processes with students.

Application Level

At the application level students utilize prior knowledge or skills to solve a problem. An example is the use of math story problems, which require students to use (apply) prior skills to solve problems. Suppose you intend to purchase a new automobile in the next few weeks, and you are a wise consumer (not an impulsive, money-is-no-object spender). Consider the skills that you would need in order to arrive at your decision. You would have to calculate your present income, factor in the down payment from your present car, and calculate the loan you will need. The math skills that you learned in school are applied here to solve your problem. (The social skills you used in negotiating a lower interest rate for your loan might be an equally impressive application!)

Application occurs in other areas of the curriculum as well. For example, process writing asks students to use a sequential step delivery process to develop effective written communication. In social studies, students might be required to use an interview process to gain valuable information. The scientific method of inquiry is a respected application of skills that students can be called upon to use in many situations.

Key words associated with the application thought process are *calculate, diagram, demonstrate,* and *solve.*

Instructions that are written at an application level include: (a) Create a graph from this data. (b) Construct a closed circuit from the materials I have provided for you. (c) Develop a travel brochure for a city of your choice that closely resembles the one we prepared in class.

Analysis Level

The analysis level is considered to be a higher order mental process. The term *analysis* means to break down for the purpose of inspecting an isolated part of a whole. Employing analysis skills asks students to seek dimensions of a certain event, concept, or conclusion. This level requires that students seek relationships between events or ideas that extend beyond simple cause and effect. A common classroom activity that is associated with this level of thinking is comparing and contrasting (or, in the early grades, identifying same and different). Sorting different types of assessments—objective versus subjective, selection versus supply, and so forth—requires analysis.

Key phrases associated with the analysis thought process are *Identify the reasons for, uncover evidence, diagram, break into component parts,* and *prioritize.*

Instructions that are written at an analysis level include: (a) Identify the component organs in the dissected animal. (b) Recognize several possible reasons why the character behaved the way she did. (c) Sort these items by their different properties. (d) In what ways was Columbus's voyage like that of space travel today?

Synthesis Level

The synthesis level of thought requires the development of a product from separate pieces of information or different data sources. The instructional target for students is to have them formulate a new thought, pattern, structure, or procedure. Synthesis answers are usually not confined to a single correct answer. (Thus we probably should not think of using the true/false format to test synthesis.) Caution must be used, however, so that teachers do not accept creative answers that are not plausible. We are seeking creative designs, but, student products must be grounded in reality. Fiction writing is a desirable skill to be developed in children, but the need for believability is more important in this case. For example, if our students are to develop a plan to reduce the poverty level of the local community, the answer isn't simply to give each family a million dollars or develop plant life that produces money in large denominations.

Key words associated with the synthesis thought process are *design, develop, brainstorm, propose, discover, reorganize,* and *create.*

Instructions that are written at a synthesis level include: (a) Brainstorm a solution for a lunchtime dilemma in the upper grades. (b) Create a healthy diet that stays within the budget limitations. (c) What would have happened if Japan had not attacked Pearl Harbor? (d) Propose a solution to the unequal funding of schools.

Evaluation Level

Thought processes at the evaluation level involve the ability to judge the value of material based on a set of criteria. Students might be asked to judge the quality or completeness of a process, the historical influence of a person, or the deep meaning of some democratic principle. We are not asking students for their opinion. This is not "Who do you think will win the Super Bowl?" We can ask that question, but it is considered evaluation only if the student provides detailed reasons and statistical support that would argue for his choice. The student may be asked to develop criteria, the class might collaborate on the development of the criteria, or the criteria can be imposed from an external source.

Key words and phrases associated with evaluation thought process are *argue the merit of, convince, evaluate, judge,* and *assess the value of.*

Instructions that are written at an evaluation level include: (a) Prepare a letter to the editor that clarifies your position on . . . (b) Take the opposition's side and argue on its behalf. (c) Support the selection of your best piece of writing this year.

All the levels of Bloom's taxonomy of the cognitive domain are supportive of the highest level, evaluation. Beginning with the recall of facts and continuing with their comprehension, application, analysis, and synthesis is a progression that culminates in evaluation. There is a place in American classrooms for all the levels of thinking. There certainly is a need for the understanding and recall of facts; these levels provide an opportunity for teachers to change how we use what we teach (content and skills). The dedication to teaching children to think requires that we take the content and skills that children possess and stretch them to apply higher levels of thinking. To use higher order thinking to find solutions and encourage good decision making is the essence of teaching. Nevertheless, knowledge attainment, skill development, and cognition are not the sole determiners of success. In academic performance, the attitudes of students are also important.

Bloom's Taxonomy of the Affective Domain

Student success is also influenced and shaped by feelings and emotions. Acknowledging and appealing to children's emotions can lead to increased student motivation and understanding. Krathwohl, Bloom, and Masia (1964) developed a hierarchical set of objectives that describe the levels of acceptance of other's ideas, customs, beliefs. Given the egocentric tendencies of children and the increased levels of diversity in today's classrooms, the importance of affect in teacher understanding is indisputable. From an assessment perspective, the desired targets for instruction—knowledge, skills, and attitudes or dispositions—includes affect.

Each of the levels is described below, and a classroom connection is provided.

Attending Level

After the student recognizes or is aware of an issue, a practice, or information, the first level of the affective domain is to attend to various aspects that make up the subject in question. For example, for the development of responsible environmental behaviors, we would determine if students have an awareness of an environmental issue, such as the importance of recycling trash.

Responding Level

At the responding level the student demonstrates a willingness to acknowledge and participate to some degree. In our example, the student would acknowledge the environmental problem and participate in brainstorming solutions or overtly demonstrate responsible actions.

Valuing Level

Students at the valuing level might internalize an idea but have difficulty overtly demonstrating it in public. At an upper level of valuing, the student is convinced of the importance of an idea and will actively pursue the goal. This might be demonstrated by students transferring the idea of environmental responsibility to their home or personal life outside the classroom.

Organization Level

Conceptualizing characterizes the organization level of affect. Students have progressed in their acceptance of an idea so that they see it as part of a larger personal belief system. Students at this stage might want to expand the idea of recycling to include greater areas of environmental responsibility, such as dealing with ground water problems or air pollution.

Characterization by Value, or Value Complex Level

The value complex level might be considered purist—responding to issues with a firm conviction about the ideas that have been developed. Students at this level would regard recycling as a smaller issue within the broader area of environmental responsibility. Students at this level are guided in their actions more by their greater sense of environmental responsibility than by deliberation over a single action. Students' actions demonstrate a strong conviction about their beliefs.

Understanding affect is an important part of our first principle of sound assessment. If we aspire to use multiple measures to increase student opportunities for success, we must consider the important area of emotions and dispositions. It is impossible to design our instruction around value-neutral content, and the beliefs of students help to determine their levels of interest, persistence, and commitment. Teachers who understand the importance of affect and consistently pursue topics that are engaging and meaningful increase motivation and enthusiasm in their students.

References

American Educational Research Association, American Psychological Association, & National Council on Measurement in Education. (1999). *Standards for educational and psychological testing.* Washington, DC: American Educational Research Association.

American Federation of Teachers (AFT), National Council on Measurement in Education, and National Education Association. (1990). Standards for teacher competence in the educational assessment of students. *Educational Measurement, 9* (4), 30–32.

American Psychological Association (APA). (1998). *Code of fair testing practices in education.* Washington, DC: APA Joint Committee on Testing Practices.

Andrade, H. G. (2000). Using rubrics to promote thinking and learning. *Educational Leadership, 57* (5), 13–18.

Armbruster, B., Lehr, F., & Osborn, J. (2001). *Put reading first: The research blocks for teaching children to read.* Washington, DC: National Institute for Literacy.

Arter, J. (1999). Teaching about performance assessment. *Educational Measurement, 18* (2), 30–44.

Arter, J., & Spandel, V. (1992). Using portfolios of student work in instruction and assessment. *Educational Measurement, 11* (1), 36–44.

Association for childhood education international (ACEI). (n.d.). *Standards.* Available online at www.acei.org/prepel.htm.

Benson, B., & Barnett, S. (1999). *Student-led conferencing using showcase portfolios.* Thousand Oaks, CA: Corwin Press.

Black, P., Harrison, C., Lee, C., Marshall, B., & Wiliam, D. (2004). Working inside the black box: Assessment for learning in the classroom. *Phi Delta Kappan, 86* (1), 9–21.

Black, P., & Wiliam, D. (1998). Assessment and classroom learning. *Assessment in Education, 5* (1), 7–68.

Bloom, B. S. (Ed.). (1956). *Taxonomy of educational objectives:* Vol. 1. *Cognitive domain.* New York: McKay.

Bloom, R. B., & Bourdon L. (1980). Types and frequencies of teachers' written instructional feedback. *Journal of Educational Research, 74* (1), 13–15.

Borman, G. D. (2003). How can Title I improve achievement? *Educational Leadership, 60* (4), 49–54.

Bourgeois, P., & Clark, B. (1995). *Franklin goes to school.* New York: Scholastic.

Boyd-Batstone, P. (2004). Focused anecdotal records assessment: A tool for standards-based, authentic assessment. *The Reading Teacher, 58* (3), 230–239.

Brookhart, S. (1991). Letter grading practices and validity. *Educational Measurement, 10* (1), 35–36.

Brookhart, S. M. (2003). Developing measurement theory for classroom assessment purposes and uses. *Educational Measurement, 22* (4) 5–12.

Brookhart, S. M. (2004). *Grading.* Columbus, OH: Merrill Prentice Hall.

Buck Institute for Education (BIE). (n.d.). *Project-based learning handbook.* Available online at http://www.bie.org/pbl/pblhandbook/intro.php.

Burnett, P. C. (2001). Teacher praise and feedback and students' perceptions of the classroom environment. *Educational Psychology, 22* (1), 5–16.

Canady, J. (1989). It's a good score, it's just a bad grade. *Phi Delta Kappan, 7* (1), 68–71.

Christie, K. (2005). Changing the nature of parent involvement. *Phi Delta Kappan, 86* (9), 645–646.

Clay, M. (1993). *An observation survey of early literacy achievement.* Auckland, New Zealand: Heineman.

Countryman, L., & Schroeder, M. (1996). When students lead parent-teacher conferences. *Educational Leadership, 53* (7), 64–68.

Couric, K. (2000). *The brand new kid.* New York: Doubleday.

Criswell, J. R. (2005). Improving feedback as a means to increase learning in elementary and middle school classrooms. *Pennsylvania Educational Leadership, 24* (2) 23–30.

Criswell, J. R., & Criswell, S. J. (2004). Asking essay questions: Answering contemporary needs. *Education, 124* (3), 510–517.

Crocker, L. (2003). Teaching for the test: Validity, fairness, and moral action. *Educational Measurement, 22* (3) 5–11.

Cronbach, L. (1977). *Educational psychology.* New York: Harcourt Brace Jovanovich.

Danielson, C. (1996). *Enhancing professional practice: A framework for teaching.* Alexandria, VA: Association for Supervision and Curriculum Development.

Ferrara, S., & McTighe, J. (1992a). Assessment: A thoughtful process. In A. L. Costa, J. Bellanca, & R. Fogarty (Eds.), *If minds mattered: A foreword to the future* (Vol. 2, pp. 337–348). Palatine, IL: Skylight.

Ferrara, S., & McTighe, J. (1992b). In K. Burke (Ed.), *Authentic assessment: A collection.* Palatine, IL: Skylight.

Frisbie, D. A., & Waltman, K. K. (1992). Developing a personal grading plan. *Educational Measurements, 11* (3), 35–42.

Giff, P. K. (1990). *Matthew Jackson meets the wall.* New York: Bantam Doubleday Dell.

Good, R. H., & Kaminski, R. A. (Eds.). (2001). *Dynamic indicators of basic early literacy skills* (5th ed.). Eugene, OR: Institute for the Development of Educational Achievement.

Goodman, Y. (1978). Kidwatching: Observing children in the classroom. In A. Jagger & M. T. Smith-Burke (Eds.), *Observing the language learner* (pp. 9–18). Newark, DE: International Reading Association.

Guskey, T. R. (1994). Making the grade: What benefits students? *Educational Leadership, 52* (2), 14–19.

Guskey, T. R. (1996). Reporting on student learning: Lessons from the past—prescriptions for the future. In *Communicating student learning* (ASCD Yearbook 1996). Alexandria, VA: Association for Supervision and Curriculum Development.

Guskey, T. R. (2002). Computerized gradebooks and the myth of objectivity. *Phi Delta Kappan, 83* (10), 775–780.

Guskey, T. (2003). How classroom assessments improve learning. *Educational Leadership, 60* (5) 6–11.

Hall, B. (2004, Winter). Taking a look at grade reporting changes. *Elizabeth Forward Forum,* pp. 8–9.

Hanna, G. S., & Dettmer, P. A. (2004). *Assessment for effective teaching.* Boston: Pearson.

Harlen, W., Gipps, C., Broadfoot, P., & Nuttall, D. (1992). Assessment and the improvement of education. *Curriculum Journal, 3,* 215–230.

Henderson-Montero, D., Julian, M. W., & Yen, W. M. (2003). Multiple measures: Alternative design and analysis models. *Educational Measurement, 22* (2), 7–12.

Henkes, K. (2000). *Wemberly worried.* New York: Scholastic.

Higgins, R., Hartley, P., & Skelton, A. (2002). The conscientious consumer: Reconsidering the role of assessment feedback in student learning. *Studies in Higher Education, 27* (1), 53–64.

Individuals With Disabilities Education Act, Amendments of 1997. 20 U.S. Code. Sec. 101.

Interstate New Teacher Assessment Support Consortium (INTASC). (1992). *Model standards for beginning teachers' licensure and development: A resource for state dialogue.* Washington, DC: Council of Chief State School Officers.

Jackson, P. W. (1967). *Life in classrooms.* Austin, TX: Holt, Rinehart & Winston.

Jimenez, R. T. (2004). More equitable literacy assessments for Latino students. *The Reading Teacher, 57* (6), 576–578.

Jimerson, S. R. (2001). Meta-analysis of grade retention research: Implications for practice in the 21st century. *School Psychology Review, 30* (3), 420–438.

Kellough, R. D., & Roberts, P. L. (2002). *A resource guide for elementary school teaching.* Columbus, OH: Merrill Prentice Hall.

Kerbow, D. (1996). Patterns of urban mobility and local school reform. *Journal of Education for Students Placed at Risk, 1* (2), 24–29.

Kober, N. (2002). What tests can and cannot tell us. *Test Talk, 2* (1), 8–9.

Krathwahl, D. R., Bloom, B. S., & Masia, B. B. (1964). *Taxonomy of educational objectives:* Handbook II. *Affective domain.* New York: McKay.

Kubiszyn T., & Borich, G. (2003). *Educational testing and measurement: Classroom application and practice.* New York: Wiley.

Lemlech, J. K. (2006). *Curriculum and instructional methods for the elementary and middle school* (6th ed.). Upper Saddle River, NJ: Pearson.

Lenski, S. D., Daniel, M., Ehlers-Zavala, F., & Alvayero, M. (2004). Assessing struggling English language learners. *Illinois Reading Council Journal, 5* (4), 12–14.

London, J. (1996). *Froggy goes to school.* New York: Penguin.

Mabry, L. (1999). Writing to the rubric: Lingering effects of traditional standardized testing on direct writing assessment. *Phi Delta Kappan, 80* (9), 673–679.

Marzano, R. J., Pickering, D. P., & Pollock, J. E. (2001). *Classroom instruction that works: Research-based strategies for increasing student achievement.* Alexandria, VA: Association for Supervision and Curriculum Development.

McTighe, J., & Ferrara, S. (1992). Assessment: A thoughtful process. In K. Burke (Ed.) *Authentic assessment: A collection.* Palantine, IL. IRI/Skylight.

McTighe, J., & Ferrara, S. (1996). Performance-based assessment in the classroom: A planning framework. In R. Blum & J. Arter (Eds.), *Student performance assessment in an era of restructuring.* Alexandria, VA: Association for Supervision and Curriculum Development.

McTighe, J., & Thomas, R. (2003). Backward design for forward action. *Educational Leadership, 60* (5), 52–55.

Meisels, S. J., & Piker, R. A. (2000). *An analysis of early literacy assessments used for instruction* (Tech. Rep. No. 3-002). Ann Arbor: University of Michigan Center for the Improvement of Early Reading Achievement.

Monk, D. D., & Bursuck, W. D. (2003). Grading students with disabilities. *Educational Leadership, 61* (2), 38–43.

Mosston, M., & Ashworth, S. (1990). *The spectrum of teaching styles.* New York: Longman.

National Board for Professional Teaching Standards. Generalist Middle Level (NBPTS). (n.d.). Available online at www.ets.org/nbpts/.

National Council of Teachers of Mathematics (NCTM). (2000). *Principles and standards for school mathematics.* Reston, VA: Key Curriculum Press.

Nitko, A. J. (2001). *Educational assessment of students.* Upper Saddle River, NJ: Prentice Hall.

No Child Left Behind Act of 2001, Pub L. No.107-100, 115 Stat. 1425. (2002). Available online at www.ed.gov/policy/elsec/leg/esea02/107.pdf.

O'Connor, K. (2002). *How to grade for learning: Linking grades to standards* (2nd ed.). Glenview, IL: Pearson Skylight.

Owings, W. A., & Magliaro, S. (1998). Grade retention: A history of failure. *Educational Leadership, 56* (1), 86–88.

Pak, S. (2003). *Sumi's first day of school ever.* New York: Viking Press.

Paris, S. G., & Carpenter, R. D. (2003). FAQs about IRIs. *The Reading Teacher, 56* (1), 578–580.

Paris, S. G., & Hoffman, J. V. (2004). Reading assessments in kindergarten through third grade: Findings for the center for the improvement of early reading achievement. *Elementary School Journal, 105* (2), 199–217.

Pennsylvania Department of Education (2006). *Writing Assessment Handbook.* Available online at www.pde.state.pa.us/a_and_t/lib/a_and_t/2005-2006WritingAssessmentHandbook.pdf.

Pennsylvania System of School Assessment. (2003–2004). *Testing Accommodations.* Harrisburg, PA.

Pitoniak, M. J., & Royer, J. M. (2001). Testing accommodations for examinees with disabilities: A review of psychometric, legal, and social policy issues. *Review of Educational Research, 71* (1), 53–104.

Popham, W. J. (2002). *Classroom assessment: What teachers should know.* Boston: Allyn & Bacon.

Popham, W. J. (2004). Why assessment illiteracy is professional suicide. *Educational Leadership, 62* (1), 82–83.

Raforth, M. A. (2002). Best practices in preventing academic failure and promoting alternatives to retention. In A. Thomas & J. Grimes (Eds.), *Best Practices in School Psychology* (Vol. 4). Bethesda, MD: National Association of School Psychologists.

Reynolds, C. R., Livingston, R. B., & Willson, V. (2006). *Measurement and assessment in education*. Boston: Allyn & Bacon.

Rollins, S. (2001). Assessment in the content areas for students acquiring English. *National Clearinghouse for Bilingual Education, 1* (4), 1–12.

Rowe, M. B. (1972). *Wait-time and rewards as instructional variables: Their influence on language and logic and fate control.* Paper presented at the annual meeting of the National Association for Research in Science Teaching, Chicago.

Sager, M. (2005). Stung by session defeat, Bush predicts teacher crisis. *The Tampa Tribune,* May 8, p. 6.

Sanders, W. L., & Horn, S. P. (1994). The Tennessee value-added assessment system (TVAAS): Mixed-model methodology in educational assessment. *Journal of Personnel Evaluation in Education, 8,* 299–311.

Sandoval, J., & Hughes, P. G. (1981). Success in non-promoted first grade children. Davis, CA: University of California. (ERIC Document Reproduction Service ED 212 317)

Sausner, R. (2005, August). Making assessments work. *District Administration,* pp. 31–34. Available online at www.districtadministration.com/page.cfm?p=1188.

Schurr, S., Lewis, S., LaMore, K., & Shewey, K. (1996). *Signaling student success.* Columbus, OH: National Middle School Association.

Shavelson, R. J. (1987). What is the basic teaching skill? *Journal of Teacher Education, 48,* 148–151.

Shepard, L. (1995). Using assessment to improve learning. *Educational Leadership, 52* (5), 38–43.

Siskind, T. G. (1993). Teachers' knowledge about test modifications for students with disabilities. *Diagnostique: Professional Bulletin of the Council for Educational Diagnostic Services, 18* (2), 145–157.

Stiggins, R. J. (1997). *Student-centered assessment* (2nd ed.). Columbus, OH: Merrill.

Stiggins, R. J. (1999). Evaluating classroom assessment training in teacher education programs. *Educational Measurement, 18* (1) 23–27.

Stiggins R. J. (2001). *Student-involved assessment.* Upper Saddle River, NJ: Prentice Hall.

Strickland, D. S., Bodino, A., Buchan, K., Jones, K. M., & Rosen, M. (2001). Teaching writing in a time of reform. *Elementary School Journal, 101* (4), 385–397.

Tierney, R. J., Carter, M. A., & Desai, L. E. (1991). *Portfolio assessment in the reading-writing classroom.* Norwood, MA: Christopher-Gordon.

Tierney R. J., Crumpler, T. P., Bertelsen, C. D., & Bond, E. L. (2003). *Interactive assessment: Teachers, parents, and students as partners.* Norwood, MA: Christopher-Gordon.

Tierney, R. J., & Simon, M. (2004). What's still wrong with rubrics: Focusing on the consistency of performance criteria across scale levels. *Practical Assessment: Research and Evaluation, 9* (2). Available online at www.paneonline.net/getvn.asp?v=9&n=2.

Tunstall, P., & Gipps, C. (1996). How does your teacher help you to make your work better? Children's understanding of formative assessment. *Curriculum Journal, 7,* 185–203.

U.S. Census Bureau. (2001). *Geographic mobility: March 1999–March 2000.* Available online at http://www.census.gov.population/www/socdem/migrate.html.

Wallace-Brodeur, R. (1988). *The godmother tree.* New York: HarperCollins.

Wells, D., & Miller, M. (1993). Teacher extent of training to deal with student retention problems. *Education, 113* (3), 451–455.

Wiggins, G. (1993). *Assessing student performance.* San Francisco: Jossey-Bass.

Wiggins, G., & McTighe, J. (1998). *Understanding by design.* Alexandria, VA: Association for Supervision and Curriculum Development.

Wilkerson, J. R., & Lang, W. S. (2003). Portfolios, the pied piper of teacher certification assessments: Legal and psychometric issues. *Education Policy Analysis Archives, 11* (45). Available online at http://epaa.asu.edu/epaa/v11n4s/.

Wright, R. G. (1994). Success for all: The median is the key. *Phi Delta Kappan, 75* (9), 723–725.

Wyman, A. (1998). *Faith, hope and chicken feathers.* New York: Avon Books.

John R. Criswell, Ed. D., is a professor in the Elementary Education Department at Edinboro University of Pennsylvania. He spent the first 14 years of his career as an elementary classroom teacher and principal. In addition to his university teaching responsibilities, he has served as an assistant department chairman, an NCATE coordinator, and an acting dean of education. He has published articles and presented at regional, state, and national conferences on classroom assessment-related issues.

Index

accommodations, 187–188, 279
achievement tests, 121, 129
alignment, 7, 8, 9 10, 23, 254
in performance assessment, 60
American Association for the Advancement of Science (AAAS), xx
American Association of Colleges for Teacher Education (AACTE), 224
American Educational Research Association (AERA), 5, 273
American Federation of Teachers (AFT), xix
American Psychological Association, 5
anchor papers, 81
anecdotal records, 64, 72–74, 165
ask, pause, and call (APC), 34–35
assessment
    alternative, 58
    authentic, 59
    communication of results of (*see* feedback)
    vs. evaluation, 3–4
    examples of, 4
    formative, 10, 13–14
    linked to instruction, 7–10
    literacy, need for, 265
    objective, 12–13, 50, 51, 52, 58, 185–186, 189 (*see also* questions)
    peer, 219
    performance (*see* performance assessment)
    quality of, 14–19
    selection, 13
    standardized (*see* standardized tests)
    standards for teacher competence in, 266–272
    subjective, 12–13
    summative, 11, 13–14, 179–180
    supply, 13
    terminology of, 3
    three principles of sound, 4–11, 137–138
    types of, 12–14, 59–60
    use of multiple measures in, 5–7
Association for Childhood Education International, xix
Association for Supervision and Curriculum Development (ASCD), 272, 273, 274
attendance, 229–230
attitudes, 27

Bloom's taxonomy of the affective domain, 285–286
Bloom's taxonomy of the cognitive domain, 38, 217, 282–286
Buck Institute for Education, 213

Center for the Improvement of Early Reading Achievement, 156
checklists, 61–66, 73
classroom
    management plan, 149–152
    physical arrangement of, 150–151
    rules and consequences, 151–153
Code of Fair Testing Practices in Education, 272
conferences, professional development, 272–273
congruency, 7, 8, 9, 10, 23, 169
constructs, 76–78
continuum, 78–79
cooperative learning, 217–218

criteria statements, 79–80, 148, 261
curriculum specialists, 131

decision making
    teachers and, 21–31
discipline, 152
dispositions. *See* attitudes
Dynamic Indicators oof Basic Early Lit-
    eracy Skills (DIBELS), 157, 158

Educational Testing Services, 270
Elementary and Secondary Education Act
    (ESEA), xix, 130
evaluation, 3, 4, 280
    peer, 219
every pupil response technique (EPRT),
    36–37, 39

feedback, 10–12
    in classrooms, 256
    common forms of, 259–263
    and grading, 98, 260
    improvement of, 263–264
    to parents, 11, 122, 138–145
    qualities of effective, 257–259
    rubrics as, 260–261
    to school personnel, 11
    and scoring, 53
    and standardized tests, 254
    to students, 10
    in writing portfolios, 92–94
    written comments as, 262–263
fluency, 158–162

grade book, use of, 146–148
grade equivalent scores, 125–127, 231
grading
    and American school system, 100–101
    and averages (mean vs. median), 111–
        112
    calculations involved in, 106–108, 109–
        112
    comparisons in, 101–105, 119–120
    on a "curve," 103–104
    and extra credit, 108
    and feedback, 100, 260
    guidelines, 99–100

impact on learning of, 101
policies, 143–144
of projects, 216
and report cards, 105–106
and retention, 229
and students with exceptionalities,
    108–109

higher level thinking, 37–38, 49, 51, 281–
    282

individualized education plan (IEP), 228
Individuals With Disabilities Education
    Act (IDEA), 190
inference making, 16, 18, 119–120
informal reading inventory (IRI), 248
instructional planning. *See* lesson plans
intelligence tests, 129, 130
International Reading Association (IRA),
    272–273
Internet, use of, 142, 210, 273–274
Interstate New Teacher Assessment Sup-
    port Consortium (INTASC), xix, 22

knowledge, 27
K-W-L chart, 212

learning centers
    assessing student use of, 212–213
    diagnostic, 211–212
    to explore different topics, 210–211
    opportunities of, 208
    to reinforce material or skills, 209–210
lesson plans, 7
    children's developmental levels and,
        26–27
    components of, 277–280
    constants and context in, 23–24
    content of, 27–29
    daily, 22–23
    quality of, 29–30
    time and, 24–26
literacy development, 155–156, 169

mathematics, 170–177
    new students and, 249–250
modifications, 187

of essay item format, 190–191
of objective item formats, 189
for students with special needs, 188

National Association for the Education of
Young Children, 27
National Association of School Psychologists, 224
National Board for Professional Teaching
Standards (NBPTS), xx
National Council for Social Studies
(NCSS), 273
National Council on Measurement in
Education (NCME), xix, 5, 273
National Council of Teachers of English
(NCTE), 273
National Council of Teachers of Mathematics (NCTM), xx, 170, 273
National Education Association, xix
national percentile rank, 124, 231
National Science Teachers Association
(NSTA), 273
No Child Left Behind Act, xix, 119, 130,
132, 166, 224, 225, 237, 254, 256, 265, 271

parent-teacher conferences
discussion of student performance in,
198–203
frequency of, 204–205
importance of, 195–196
logistical arrangements and atmosphere of, 197–198
reasons for, 196–197
role of student in, 203–204
parents
communication with, 11, 122, 138–145
use of standardized test data by, 132
Pennsylvania Department of Education,
254
Pennsylvania System of School Assessment, 254
performance assessment
definition of, 58–59
ethical issues in, 80–81
four steps in planning and designing of,
61–75
implementation of, 60–61

purpose of, 61–62
testing and redesign, 75
use of, 57–58
periodicals, professional development,
274–275
phonemic awareness, 157
phonics instruction, 157–158
portfolios
arranging contents of, 95–96
implementation of, 83–86
obstacles in use of, 84
purposes of, 87–90
recommendations about, 90–91
writing, 91–95
preteaching activities, 137–138
principals, 131
project-based learning, 213
challenges in assessment of, 216–220
compared to other activities, 214–215
interdisciplinary nature of, 219–220
psychologists, school, 131–132
pupil personnel team (PPT), 226–227, 236

questions. *See also* tests
completion, 47–48, 189
development of, 185–186
distribution of, 35–36
essay, 49–54, 190–191
importance of, 33
levels of, 37–38
matching, 12, 13, 38, 44–46, 48, 163,
190
multiple-choice, 12, 13, 38, 41–44, 48,
163, 189
oral, 33–38
true/false, 12, 13, 38, 39–41, 189
written, 38–39

reading, 155–169
comprehension, 163–165
importance of, 155–156
new students and, 248–249
state tests in, 165–169
strategies, 164
reflection, 218–219
reliability, 14, 17–19
alternate form, 17

internal consistency, 17
    stability, 17
report cards, 12
    behavioral portion of, 151
    grading and, 105–106
    format of, 112–115, 146, 270
    of Millcreed Township School District,
      113–114, 147–148
    of Union City, 115, 148, 149, 150, 152,
      212
retention, 223
    of elementary school children, 224–226
    interventions for, 235–237
    key personnel in the decision of, 226–
      227
    timetable for review of information for,
      233–235
    use of student records in, 227–233
rubrics, 64, 66–72, 73, 76–80
    as feedback, 260–261
    fluency, 159
    for learning centers, 211, 213
running records, 160–161

scores, raw vs. derived, 123
scoring
    essay questions, 52–54
    performance assessments, 64–75
    rubrics (see rubrics)
skills, 27
spelling, teaching of, 7–9
standardized tests
    administration of, 121–122
    error of measurement in, 130, 133
    examination of, 254–255
    feedback and, 256
    interpreting the results of, 123–128
    limitations of, 132–133
    names of, 117–118
    preparation for, 253–254
    purpose of, 117–120
    in reading, 165–169
    retention and, 224, 231–233
    selection of, 120–121
    two types of, 129
    use of data from, 130–132
standards, 62–64

grading by, 102–103
stanines, 124–125
student records, 227–233, 241–242
    medical, 230–231
students, new, 239
    academic placement of, 248–250
    effect of mobility on achievement of,
      240
    from another school district, 242–243
    from same school district, 241–242
    ways to welcome, 245–248
    with limited English proficiency, 244–
      245
summer school, 237
superintendents, 130–131

teachers
    roles of, 106–107
    use of standardized test data by, 132
tests. See also questions
    accommodating and modifying, 187–
      192
    answer key for, 186
    blueprint of, 180–183
    length of, 183–184
    standardized (see standardized tests)
    weighting of items on, 184

validity, 14, 15–16, 18–19
    construct, 15
    content, 15
    criteria, 15
vocabulary, 162–163

wait time, 35